Lecture Notes in Computer Science   12961

More information about this subseries at http://www.springer.com/series/7411

Leszek Gąsieniec · Ralf Klasing ·
Tomasz Radzik (Eds.)

Algorithms
for Sensor Systems

17th International Symposium on Algorithms and Experiments
for Wireless Sensor Networks, ALGOSENSORS 2021
Lisbon, Portugal, September 9–10, 2021
Proceedings

Springer

Editors
Leszek Gąsieniec 🆔
University of Liverpool
Liverpool, UK

Ralf Klasing
CNRS and University of Bordeaux
Talence, France

Tomasz Radzik
King's College London
London, UK

ISSN 0302-9743   ISSN 1611-3349   (electronic)
Lecture Notes in Computer Science
ISBN 978-3-030-89239-5   ISBN 978-3-030-89240-1   (eBook)
https://doi.org/10.1007/978-3-030-89240-1

LNCS Sublibrary: SL5 – Computer Communication Networks and Telecommunications

This Springer imprint is published by the registered company Springer Nature Switzerland AG
The registered company address is: Gewerbestrasse 11, 6330 Cham, Switzerland

Preface

The 17th International Symposium on Algorithms and Experiments for Wireless Sensor Networks (ALGOSENSORS 2021) was originally scheduled to take place during September 9–10, 2021, in Lisbon, Portugal. Due to the COVID-19 pandemic, those original arrangements had to be changed. The symposium was run online on the originally set dates of September 9–10, 2021, as part of the ALGO 2021 event, organized and coordinated from Lisbon by the ALGO 2021 Organizing Committee.

ALGOSENSORS is an international symposium dedicated to the algorithmic aspects of wireless networks. Originally focused on sensor networks, it now covers algorithmic issues arising in wireless networks of all types of computational entities, static or mobile, including sensor networks, sensor-actuator networks, and systems of autonomous robots. The focus is on the design and analysis of algorithms, models of computation, and experimental analysis.

The Program Committee of ALGOSENSORS 2021 received 28 submissions. Each submission was reviewed by at least three Program Committee members and some trusted external referees, and evaluated on its quality, originality, and relevance to the symposium. The Committee selected 10 papers for presentation at the symposium and inclusion in the proceedings.

One invited talk was given at ALGOSENSORS 2021, by Bernhard Haeupler (CMU, USA, and ETHZ, Switzerland). The invited talk was integrated in the global ALGO 2021 program, as a joint keynote. This volume includes the abstract of the invited talk.

The Program Committee selected the same contribution for the Best Paper Award and the Best Student Paper Award, both sponsored by Springer:

- Jannik Castenow, Jonas Harbig, Daniel Jung, Till Knollmann, and Friedhelm Meyer auf der Heide for their paper "Gathering a Euclidean Closed Chain of Robots in Linear Time".

We thank the Steering Committee for giving us the opportunity to serve as Program Chairs of ALGOSENSORS 2021, and for the responsibilities of selecting the Program Committee, the conference program, and publications.

We would like to thank all the authors who responded to the call for papers, the invited speaker for enriching the program of the ALGO 2021 event, and the Program Committee members, as well as the external reviewers, for their fundamental contribution in selecting the best papers resulting in a strong program. We would also like to warmly thank the ALGO 2021 organizers for kindly accepting to co-locate ALGOSENSORS with some of the leading events on algorithms in Europe. Furthermore, we would like to thank the local ALGO 2021 Organizing Committee, especially Arlindo Oliveira (chair), as well as the Steering Committee chair, Sotiris Nikoletseas, for their help in ensuring a successful ALGOSENSORS 2021.

We would like to thank Springer for publishing the proceedings of ALGO-SENSORS 2021 in their LNCS series and for their support.

Finally, we acknowledge the use of the EasyChair system for handling the submission of papers, managing the review process, and generating these proceedings.

September 2021

Leszek Gąsieniec
Ralf Klasing
Tomasz Radzik

Organization

Program Committee

Eleni C. Akrida	Durham University, UK
Petra Berenbrink	University of Hamburg, Germany
Christelle Caillouet	University of Côte d'Azur, France
Arnaud Casteigts	University of Bordeaux, France
Dibyayan Chakraborty	Indian Institute of Science, Bengaluru, India
Marek Chrobak	University of California, Riverside, USA
Giuseppe Antonio Di Luna	Sapienza University of Rome, Italy
Romaric Duvignau	Chalmers University of Technology, Sweden
Thomas Erlebach	University of Leicester, UK
Sándor Fekete	TU Braunschweig, Germany
Florent Foucaud	Clermont Auvergne University, France
Pierre Fraigniaud	CNRS and Paris Diderot University, France
Luisa Gargano	University of Salerno, Italy
Leszek Gąsieniec (Co-chair)	University of Liverpool, UK
Sun-Yuan Hsieh	National Cheng Kung University, Taiwan
Ling-Ju Hung	National Taipei University of Business, Taiwan
Ralf Klasing (Co-chair)	CNRS and University of Bordeaux, France
Irina Kostitsyna	Eindhoven University of Technology, The Netherlands
Dariusz R. Kowalski	Augusta University, USA
Kitty Meeks	University of Glasgow, UK
Nathalie Mitton	Inria Lille-Nord Europe, France
Tobias Mömke	Augsburg University, Germany
Oscar Morales-Ponce	California State University, Long Beach, USA
Rolf Niedermeier	Technical University of Berlin, Germany
Aris Pagourtzis	National Technical University of Athens, Greece
Tomasz Radzik (Co-chair)	King's College London, UK
Peter Rossmanith	RWTH Aachen University, Germany
Olga Saukh	Graz University of Technology and CSH Vienna, Austria
Grzegorz Stachowiak	University of Wrocław, Poland
Walter Unger	RWTH Aachen University, Germany
Yukiko Yamauchi	Kyushu University, Japan

Steering Committee

Josep Díaz	Universitat Politècnica de Catalunya, Spain
Magnús M. Halldórsson	Reykjavik University, Iceland
Bhaskar Krishnamachari	University of Southern California, Los Angeles, USA
Panganamala R. Kumar	Texas A&M University, USA
Sotiris Nikoletseas (Chair)	University of Patras and CTI, Greece
José Rolim	University of Geneva, Switzerland
Paul Spirakis	University of Liverpool, UK, and University of Patras, Greece
Adam Wolisz	Technical University of Berlin, Germany

External Reviewers

Bampas, Evangelos
Bentert, Matthias
Bhagat, Subhash
Bilò, Davide
Bärtschi, Andreas
Chen, Yen Hung
Das, Arun Kumar
Das, Shantanu
Di Stefano, Gabriele
Feuilloley, Laurent
Fischer, Dennis
Fuchs, Janosch
Gajjar, Kshitij
Hartmann, Tim A.
Jeż, Łukasz
Johnen, Colette
Kamei, Sayaka
Kao, Shih-Shun
Keldenich, Phillip

Krupke, Dominik
Kuhn, Fabian
Lee, Chuan-Min
Leonardos, Nikos
Lin, Chuang-Chieh
Moses Jr., William K.
Nisse, Nicolas
Papaioannou, Ioannis
Pattanayak, Debasish
Rieck, Christian
Schoeters, Jason
Sharma, Gokarna
Silvestri, Simone
Sudo, Yuichi
Swami, Ananthram
van Renssen, André
Yang, Jinn-Shyong
Yeh, Hao-Ping

Universally-Optimal Distributed Algorithms, (Congestion+Dilation)-Competitive Oblivious Routing, and Hop-Constrained Network Design

(Abstract of Invited Talk)

Bernhard Haeupler

CMU, USA & ETHZ, Switzerland
haeupler@cs.cmu.edu

Many tasks on graphs/networks are optimizing either

- ℓ_1 parameters like distances (e.g., computing short paths for low-delay communications),
- ℓ_∞ parameters like congestion (e.g., computing maximum flows for high-rate communications), or
- both parameter types jointly (e.g., asking for short & low-congestion paths for minimizing the completion time of a communication task)

While ubiquitous, tasks of this joint type tend to be much harder and are less well understood. This talk presents new tools to address this. These tools were developed during a 6-year-long freshly-completed effort to obtain the first universally-optimal distributed graph algorithms (e.g., for MST, min-cut, SSSP, etc.). A universally-optimal algorithm is (approximately) as fast as the fastest algorithm for every graph topology.

Other important results include:

- The first Oblivious Routings that give short & low-congestion routes.
- Fast distributed constructions of compact routing tables for such oblivious routings.
- The first approximation and online algorithms for many diameter-constrained versions of classical network design problems (e.g., (group) Steiner Tree/Forest).
- The first upper and lower bounds for how much (network) coding can speed up completion times of point-to-point network communications.

(joint work with M. Ghaffari, G. Zuzic, D. E. Hershkowitz, D. Wajc, J. Li, H. Raecke, T. Izumi)

Contents

Distributed Transformations of Hamiltonian Shapes Based on Line Moves

Abdullah Almethen$^{(\boxtimes)}$, Othon Michail, and Igor Potapov

Department of Computer Science, University of Liverpool, Liverpool, UK
{A.Almethen,Othon.Michail,Potapov}@liverpool.ac.uk

Abstract. We consider a discrete system of n simple indistinguishable devices, called *agents*, forming a *connected* shape S_I on a two-dimensional square grid. Agents are equipped with a linear-strength mechanism, called a *line move*, by which an agent can push a whole line of consecutive agents in one of the four directions in a single time-step. We study the problem of transforming an initial shape S_I into a given target shape S_F via a finite sequence of line moves in a distributed model, where each agent can observe the states of nearby agents in a Moore neighbourhood. Our main contribution is the first distributed connectivity-preserving transformation that exploits line moves within a total of $O(n \log_2 n)$ moves, which is asymptotically equivalent to that of the best-known centralised transformations. The algorithm solves the *line formation problem* that allows agents to form a final straight line S_L, starting from any shape S_I, whose *associated graph* contains a Hamiltonian path.

Keywords: Line movement · Discrete transformations · Shape formation · Reconfigurable robotics · Programmable matter · Distributed algorithms

1 Introduction

The explosive growth of advanced technology over the last few decades has contributed significantly towards the development of a wide variety of distributed systems consisting of large collections of tiny robotic-units, known as *monads*. These monads are able to move and communicate with each other by being equipped with microcontrollers, actuators and sensors. However, each monad is severely restricted and has limited computational capabilities, such as a constant memory and lack of global knowledge. Further, monads are typically homogeneous, anonymous and indistinguishable from each other. Through a simple set of rules and local actions, they collectively act as a single unit and carry out several complex tasks, such as transformations and explorations.

The full version of the paper with all omitted details is available on arXiv at: http://arxiv.org/abs/2108.08953.

© Springer Nature Switzerland AG 2021
L. Gąsieniec et al. (Eds.): ALGOSENSORS 2021, LNCS 12961, pp. 1–16, 2021.
https://doi.org/10.1007/978-3-030-89240-1_1

In this context, scientists from different disciplines have made great efforts towards developing innovative, scalable and adaptive collective robotic systems. This vision has recently given rise to the area of programmable matter, first proposed by Toffoli and Margolus [35] in 1991, referring to any kind of materials that can algorithmically change their physical properties, such as shape, colour, density and conductivity through transformations executed by an underlying program. This newborn area has been of growing interest lately both from a theoretical and a practical viewpoint.

One can categorise programmable matter systems into *active* and *passive*. Entities in the passive systems have no control over their movements. Instead, they move via interactions with the environment based on their own structural characteristics. Prominent examples of research on passive systems appear in the areas of population protocols [7,28,29], DNA computing [1,8] and tile self-assembly [15,33,37]. On the other hand, the active systems allow computational entities to act and control their movements in order to accomplish a given task, which is our primary focus in this work. The most popular examples of active systems include metamorphic systems [19,30,36], swarm/mobile robotics [10,21, 31,34,39], modular self-reconfigurable robotics [5,22,40] and recent research on programmable matter [12,13]. Moreover, those robotic systems have received an increasing attention from the the engineering research community, and hence many solutions and frameworks have been produced for milli/micro-scale [9,23, 26] down to nanoscale systems [16,32].

Shape transformations (sometimes called *pattern formation*) can be seen as one of the most essential goals for almost every system among the vast variety of robotic systems including programmable matter and swarm robotic systems. In this work, we focus on a system of a two-dimensional square grid containing a collection of entities typically connected to each other and forming an initial connected shape S_I. Each entity is equipped with a linear-strength mechanism that can push an entire line of consecutive entities one position in a single time-step in a given direction of a grid. The goal is to design an algorithm that can transform an initial shape S_I into a given target shape S_F through a chain of permissible moves and without losing the connectivity. That is, in each intermediate configuration we always want to guarantee that the graphs induced by the nodes occupied by the entities are connected. The connectivity-preservation is an important assumption for many practical applications, which usually require energy for data exchange as well as the implementation of various locomotion mechanisms.

1.1 Related Work

Many models of centralised or distributed coordination have been studied in the context of shape transformation problems. The assumed mechanisms in those models can significantly influence the efficiency and feasibility of shape transformations. For example, the authors of [2,17–19,27] consider mechanisms called sliding and rotation by which an agent can move and turn over neighbours through empty space. Under these models of individual movements, Dumitrescu and Pach [17] and Michail *et al.* [27] present universal transformations for any pair of connected shapes (S_I, S_F) of the same size to each other. By restricting to rotation only, the authors in [27] proved that the decision problem of transformability is in **P**; however, with a constant number of extra seed nodes connectivity preserving transformation can be completed with $\Omega(n^2)$ moves [27].

The alternative less costly reconfiguration solutions can be designed by employing some parallelism, where multiple movements can occur at the same time, see theoretical studies in [11,14] and more practical implementation in [34]. Moreover, it has been shown that there exists a universal transformation with rotation and sliding that converts any pair of connected shapes to each other within $O(n)$ parallel moves in the worst case [27]. Also fast reconfiguration might be achieved by exploiting actuation mechanisms, where a single agent is now equipped with more strength to move many entities in parallel in a single time-step. A prominent example is the linear-strength model of Aloupis *et al.* [5,6], where an entity is equipped with arms giving it the ability to extend/extract a neighbour, a set of individuals or the whole configuration in a single operation. Another elegant approach by Woods *et al.* [38] studied another linear-strength mechanism by which an entity can drag a chain of entities parallel to one of the axes directions.

A more recent study along this direction is shown in [4], and introduces the *line-pushing* model. In this model, an individual entity can push the whole line of consecutive entities one position in a given direction in a single time-step. As we shall explain, this model generalises some existing constant-strength models with a special focus on exploiting its parallel power for fast and more general transformations. Apart from the purely theoretical benefit of exploring fast reconfigurations, this model also provides a practical framework for more efficient reconfigurations in real systems. For example, self-organising robots could be reconfiguring into multiple shapes in order to pass through canals, bridges or corridors in a mine. In another domain, individual robots could be containers equipped with motors that can push an entire row to manage space in large warehouses. Another future application could be a system of very tiny particles injected into a human body and transforming into several shapes in order to efficiently traverse through the veins and capillaries and treat infected cells.

This model is capable of simulating some constant-strength models. For example, it can simulate the sliding and rotation model [17,27] with an increase in the worst-case running time only by a factor of 2. This implies that all universality and reversibility properties of individual-move transformations still hold true in this model. Also, the model allows the diagonal connections on the grid. Several sub-quadratic time centralised transformations have been proposed, including an $O(n\sqrt{n})$-time universal transformation that preserves the connectivity of the shape during its course [3]. By allowing transformations to disconnect the shape during their course, there exists a centralised universal transformation that completes within $O(n \log n)$ time.

Another recent related set of models studied in [10,20,24] consider a single robot which moves over a static shape consisting of tiles and the goal is for the robot to transform the shape by carrying one tile at a time. In those systems, the single robot which controls and carries out the transformation is typically modelled as a finite automaton. Those models can be viewed as partially centralised as on one hand they have a unique controller but on the other hand that controller is operating locally and suffering from a lack of global information.

1.2   Our Contribution

In this work, our main objective is to give the first distributed transformations for programmable matter systems implementing the linear-strength mechanism of the model of line moves. All existing transformations for this model are centralised, thus, even though they reveal the underlying transformation complexities, they are not directly applicable to real programmable matter systems. Our goal is to develop distributed transformations that, if possible, will preserve all the good properties of the corresponding centralised solutions. These include the *move complexity* (i.e., the total number of line moves) of the transformations and their ability to preserve the connectivity of the shape throughout their course.

However, there are considerable technical challenges that one must deal with in order to develop such a distributed solution. As will become evident, the lack of global knowledge of the individual entities and the condition of preserving connectivity greatly complicate the transformation, even when restricted to special families of shapes. Timing is an essential issue as the line needs to know when to start and stop pushing. When moving or turning, all agents of the line must follow the same route, ensuring that no one is being pushed off. There is an additional difficulty due to the fact that agents do not automatically know whether they have been pushed (but it might be possible to infer this through communication and/or local observation).

Consider a discrete system of n simple indistinguishable devices, called *agents*, forming a connected shape S_I on a two-dimensional square grid. Agents act as finite-state automata (i.e., they have constant memory) that can observe the states of nearby agents in a Moore neighbourhood (i.e., the eight cells surrounding an agent on the square gird). They operate in synchronised Look-Compute-Move (LCM) cycles on the grid. All communication is local, and actuation is based on this local information as well as the agent's internal state.

Let us consider a very simple distributed transformation of a diagonal line shape S_D into a straight line S_L, $|S_D| = |S_L| = n$, in which all agents execute the same procedure in parallel synchronous rounds. In general, the diagonal appears to be a hard instance because any parallelism related to line moves that might potentially be exploited does not come for free. Initially, all agents are occupying the consecutive diagonal cells on the grid $(x_1, y_1), (x_1 + 1, y_1 + 1), \ldots, (x_1 + n - 1, y_1 + n - 1)$. In each round, an agent $p_i = (x, y)$ moves one step down if $(x - 1, y - 1)$ is occupied, otherwise it stays still in its current cell. After $O(n)$ rounds, all agents form S_L within a total number of $1 + 2 + \ldots + n = O(n^2)$ moves, while preserving connectivity during the transformation (throughout, connectivity includes horizontal, vertical, and diagonal adjacency). See Fig. 1.

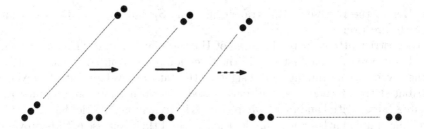

Fig. 1. A simulation of the simple procedure. From left to right, rounds $0, 1, 2, \ldots, n$.

The above transformation, even though time-optimal has a move complexity asymptotically equal to the worst-case single-move distance between S_I and S_F. This is because it always moves individual agents, thus not exploiting the inherent parallelism of line moves. Our goal, is to trade time for number of line moves in order to develop alternative distributed transformations which will complete within a sub-quadratic number of moves. Given that actuation is a major source of energy consumption in real programmable matter and robotic systems, moves minimisation is expected to contribute in the deployment and implementation of energy-efficient systems.

We already know that there is a centralised $O(n \log n)$-move connectivity-preserving transformation, working for a large family of connected shapes [3]. That centralised strategy transforms a pair of connected shapes (S_I, S_F) of the same order (i.e., the number of agents) to each other, when the associated graphs of both shapes contain a Hamiltonian path (see also Itai *et al.* [25] for rectilinear Hamiltonian paths), while preserving connectivity during the transformation. This approach initially forms a line from one endpoint of the Hamiltonian path, then flattens all agents along the path gradually via line moves, while successively doubling the line length in each round. After $O(n \log n)$ moves, it arrives at the final straight line S_L of length n, which can be then transformed into S_F by reversing the transformation of S_F into S_L, within the same asymptotic number of moves.

In this work, we introduce the first distributed transformation exploiting the linear-strength mechanism of the *line-pushing* model. It provides a solution to the line formation problem, that is, for any initial Hamiltonian shape S_I, form a final straight line S_L of the same order. It is essentially a distributed implementation of the centralised Hamiltonian transformation of [3]. We show that it preserves the asymptotic bound of $O(n \log n)$ line moves (which is still the best-known centralised bound), while keeping the whole shape connected throughout its course. This is the first step towards distributed transformations between any pair of Hamiltonian shapes. The inverse of this transformation (S_L into S_I) appears to be a much more complicated problem to solve as the agents need to somehow know an encoding of the shape to be constructed and that in contrast to the centralised case, reversibility does not apply in a straightforward way. Hence, the reverse of this transformation (S_L into S_I) is left as a future research direction.

We restrict attention to the class of Hamiltonian shapes. This class, apart from being a reasonable first step in the direction of distributed transformations in the given setting, might give insight to the future development of universal distributed transformations, i.e., distributed transformations working for any possible pair of initial and target shapes. This is because geometric shapes tend to have long simple paths. For example, the length of their longest path is provably at least $\sqrt{n}$. We here focus on developing efficient distributed transformations for the extreme case in which the longest path is a Hamiltonian path. However, one might be able to apply our Hamiltonian transformation to any pair of shapes, by, for example, running a different or similar transformation along branches of the longest path and then running our transformation on the longest path. We leave how to exploit the longest path in the general case (i.e., when initial and target shapes are not necessarily Hamiltonian) as an interesting open problem.

We assume that a pre-processing phase provides the Hamiltonian path, i.e., a global sense of direction is made available to the agents through a labelling of their local ports (e.g., each agent maintains two local ports incident to its predecessor and successor on the path). Similar assumptions exist in the literature of systems of complex shapes that contain a vast number of self-organising and limited entities. A prominent example is [34] in which the transformation relies on an initial central phase to gain some information about the number of entities in the system.

Now, we are ready to sketch a high-level description of the transformation. A Hamiltonian path P in the initial shape S_I starts with a head on one endpoint labelled l_h, which is leading the process and coordinating all the sub-procedures during the transformation. The transformation proceeds in $\log n$ phases, each consisting of six sub-phases (or sub-routines) and every sub-phase running for one or more synchronous rounds. Figure 2 gives an illustration of a phase of this transformation when applied on the diagonal line shape. Initially, the head l_h forms a trivial line of length 1. By the beginning of each phase i, $0 \leq i \leq \log n - 1$, there exists a line L_i starting from the head l_h and ending at a tail l_t with $2^i - 2$ internal agents labelled l in between. By the end of phase i, L_i will have doubled its length as follows.

First, it identifies the next 2^i agents on P. These agents are forming a segment S_i which can be in any configuration. To do that, the head emits a signal which is then forwarded by the agents along the line. Once the signal arrives at S_i, it will be used to re-label S_i so that it starts from a head in state s_h, has $2^i - 2$ internal agents in state s, and ends at a tail s_t; this completes the DefineSeg sub-phase. Then, l_h calls CheckSeg in order to check whether the line defined by S_i is in line or perpendicular to L_i. This can be easily achieved through a moving state initiated at L_i and checking for each agent of S_i its local directions relative to its neighbours. If the check returns true, then l_h starts a new round $i + 1$ and calls Merge to combine L_i and S_i into a new line L_{i+1} of length 2^{i+1}. Otherwise, l_h proceeds with the next sub-phase, DrawMap.

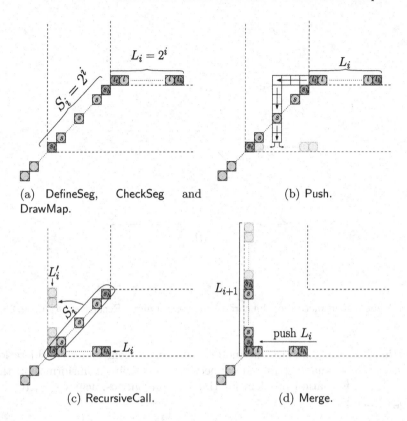

Fig. 2. From [3], a snapshot of phase i of the Hamiltonian transformation on the shape of a diagonal line. Each occupied cell shows the current label state of an agent. Light grey cells show ending cells of the corresponding moves.

In DrawMap, l_h designates a route on the grid through which L_i pushes itself towards the tail s_t of S_i. It consists of two primitives: ComputeDistance and CollectArrows. In ComputeDistance, the line agents act as a distributed counter to compute the Manhattan distance between the tails of L_i and S_i. In CollectArrows, the local directions are gathered from S_i's agents and distributed into L_i's agents, which collectively draw the route map. Once this is done, L_i becomes ready to move and l_h can start the Push sub-phase. During pushing, l_h and l_t synchronise the movements of L_i's agents as follows: (1) l_h pushes while l_t is guiding the other line agents through the computed route and (2) both are coordinating any required swapping of states with agents that are not part of L_i but reside in L_i's trajectory. Once L_i has traversed the route completely, l_h calls RecursiveCall to apply the general procedure recursively on S_i in order to transform it into a line L_i'. Figure 3 shows a graphical illustration of the core recursion on the special case of a diagonal line shape. Finally, the agents of L_i and L_i' combine into a new straight line L_{i+1} of 2^{i+1} agents through the Merge sub-procedure. Then, the head l_h of L_{i+1} begins a new phase $i + 1$.

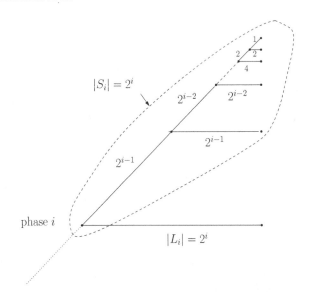

Fig. 3. A zoomed-in picture of the core recursive technique RecursiveCall in Fig. 2(c).

Section 2 formally defines the model and the problem under consideration. Section 3 presents our distributed connectivity-preserving transformation that solves the line formation problem for Hamiltonian shapes, achieving a total of $O(n \log n)$ line moves.

2   Model

We consider a system consisting of n agents forming a connected shape S on a two-dimensional square grid in which each agent $p \in S$ occupies a unique cell $cell(p) = (x, y)$, where x indicates columns and y represents rows. Throughout, an agent shall also be referred to by its coordinates. Each cell (x, y) is surrounded by eight adjacent cells in each cardinal and ordinal direction, (N, E, S, W, NE, NW, SE, SW). At any time, a cell (x, y) can be in one of two states, either empty or occupied. An agent $p \in S$ is a *neighbour* of (or *adjacent* to) another agent $p' \in S$, if p' occupies one of the eight adjacent cells surrounding p, that is their coordinates satisfy $p'_x - 1 \leq p_x \leq p'_x + 1$ and $p'_y - 1 \leq p_y \leq p'_y + 1$. For any shape S, we associate a graph $G(S) = (V, E)$ defined as follows, where V represents agents of S and E contains all pairs of adjacent neighbours, i.e., $(p, p') \in E$ iff p and p' are neighbours in S. We say that a shape S is connected iff $G(S)$ is a connected graph. The *distance* between agents $p \in S$ and $p' \in S$ is defined as the Manhattan distance between their cells, $\Delta(p, p') = |p_x - p'_x| + |p_y - p'_y|$. A shape S is called *Hamiltonian shape* iff $G(S)$ contains a Hamiltonian path, i.e., a path starting from some $p \in S$, visiting every agent in S and ending at some $p' \in S$, where $p \neq p'$.

In this work, each agent is equipped with the linear-strength mechanism introduced in [4], called the *line pushing mechanism*. A line L consists of a sequence of k agents occupying consecutive cells on the grid, say w.l.o.g, $L = (x, y), (x+1, y), \ldots, (x+k-1, y)$, where $1 \le k \le n$. The agent $p \in L$ occupying (x, y) is capable of performing an operation of a **line move** by which it can push all agents of L one position rightwards to positions $(x+1, y), (x+2, y), \ldots, (x+k, y)$ in a single time-step. The *line moves* towards the "down", "left" and "up" directions are defined symmetrically by rotating the system $90°$, $180°$ and $270°$ clockwise, respectively. From now on, this operation may be referred to as *move*, *movement* or *step*. We call the number of agents in S the *size* or *order* of the shape, and throughout this work all logarithms are to the base 2.

We assume that the agents share a sense of orientation through a consistent labelling of their local ports. Agents do not know the size of S in advance neither they have any other knowledge about S. Each agent has a constant memory (of size independent of n) and a local visibility mechanism by which it observes the states of its eight neighbouring cells simultaneously. The agents act as finite automata operating in synchronous rounds consisting of LCM steps. Thus, in every discrete round, an agent observes its own state and for each of its eight adjacent cells, checks whether it is occupied or not. For each of those occupied, it also observes the state of the agent occupying that cell. Then, the agent updates its state or leaves it unchanged and performs a *line move* in one direction $d \in \{up, down, right, left\}$ or stays still. A *configuration* C of the system is a mapping from $\mathbb{Z}_{\ge 0}^2$ to $\{0\} \cup Q$, where Q is the state space of agents. We define $S(C)$ as the shape of configuration C, i.e., the set of coordinates of the cells occupied in S. Given a configuration C, the LCM steps performed by all agents in the given round, yield a new configuration C' and the next round begins. If at least one move was performed, then we say that this round has transformed $S(C)$ to $S(C')$.

Throughout this work, we assume that the initial shape S_I is Hamiltonian and the final shape is a straight line S_L, where both S_I and S_L have the same order. We also assume that a pre-elected leader is provided at one endpoint of the Hamiltonian path of S_I. It is made available to the agents in the distributed way that each agent p_i knows the local port leading to its predecessor p_{i-1} and its successor p_{i+1}, for all $1 \le i \le n$.

An agent $p \in S$ is defined as a 5-tuple (X, M, Q, δ, O), where Q is a finite set of states, X is the input alphabet representing the states of the eight cells that surround an agent p on the square grid, so $|X| = |Q|^8$, $M = \{\uparrow, \downarrow, \rightarrow, \leftarrow, none\}$ is the output alphabet corresponding to the set of moves, a transition function $\delta : Q \times X \to Q \times M$ and the output function $O : \delta \times X \to M$.

We now formally define the problem considered in this work.

HAMILTONIANLINE. Given any initial Hamiltonian shape S_I, the agents must form a final straight line S_L of the same order from S_I via line moves while preserving connectivity throughout the transformation.

3   The Distributed Hamiltonian Transformation

In this section, we develop a distributed algorithm exploiting line moves to form a straight line S_L from an initial connected shape S_I which is associated to a graph that contains a Hamiltonian path. As we will argue, this strategy performs $O(n \log n)$ moves, i.e., it is as efficient w.r.t. moves as the best-known centralised transformation [3], and completes within $O(n^2 \log n)$ rounds, while keeping the whole shape connected during its course.

We assume that through some pre-processing the Hamiltonian path P of the initial shape S_I has been made available to the n agents in a distributed way. P starts and ends at two agents, called the head p_1 and the tail p_n, respectively. The head p_1 is leading the process (as it can be used as a pre-elected unique leader) and is responsible for coordinating and initiating all procedures of this transformation. In order to simplify the exposition, we assume that n is a power of 2; this can be easily dropped later. The transformation proceeds in $\log n$ phases, each of which consists of six sub-phases (or sub-routines). Every sub-phase consist of one or more synchronous rounds. The transformation starts with a trivial line of length 1 at the head's endpoint, then it gradually flattens all agents along P gradually while successively doubling its length, until arriving at the final straight line S_L of length n.

A state $q \in Q$ of an agent p will be represented by a vector with seven components $(c_1, c_2, c_3, c_4, c_5, c_6, c_7)$. The first component c_1 contains a label λ of the agent from a finite set of labels Λ, c_2 is the transmission state that holds a string of length at most three, where each symbol of the string can either be a special mark w from a finite set of marks W or an arrow direction $a \in A = \{\rightarrow , \leftarrow, \downarrow, \uparrow, \nwarrow, \nearrow, \swarrow, \searrow\}$ and c_3 will store a symbol from c_2's string, i.e., a special mark or an arrow. The local Hamiltonian direction $a \in A$ of an agent p indicating predecessor and successor is recorded in c_4, the counter state c_5 holds a bit from $\{0, 1\}$, c_6 stores an arrow $a \in A$ for map drawing (as will be explained later) and finally c_7 is holding a pushing direction $d \in M$. The "·" mark indicates an empty component; a non-empty component is always denoted by its state. An agent p may be referred to by its label $\lambda \in \Lambda$ (i.e., by the state of its c_1 component) whenever clear from context.

By the beginning of phase i, $0 \le i \le \log n - 1$, there exists a terminal straight line L_i of 2^i active agents occupying a single row or column on the grid, starting with a head labelled l_h and ending at a tail labelled l_t, while internal agents have label l. All agents in the rest of the configuration are inactive and labelled k. During phase i, the head l_h leads the execution of six sub-phases, DefineSeg, CheckSeg, DrawMap, Push, RecursiveCall and Merge. For simplicity and due to space restrictions, we shall only mention the affected components of the state of the agents. The high-level idea of this strategy has already been provided in Sect. 1.2 and illustrated in Fig. 2, therefore we can now immediately proceed with the detailed description of each sub-phase.

DefineSeg. The line head l_h transmits a special mark "Ⓗ" to go through all active agents in the Hamiltonian path P. It updates its transmission component

c_2 as follows: $\delta(l_h, \cdot, \cdot, a \in A, \cdot, \cdot, \cdot) = (l_h, \text{\textcircled{H}}, \cdot, a \in A, \cdot, \cdot, \cdot)$. This is propagated by active agents by always moving from a predecessor p_i to a successor p_{i+1}, until it arrives at the first inactive agent with label k, which then becomes active and the head of its segment by updating its label as $\delta(k, \text{\textcircled{H}}, \cdot, a \in A, \cdot, \cdot, \cdot) = (s_h, \cdot, \cdot, a \in A, \cdot, \cdot, \cdot)$. Similarly, once a line agent p_i passes "\text{\textcircled{H}}" to p_{i+1}, it also initiates and propagates its own mark "\text{\textcircled{1}}" to activate a corresponding segment agent s. The line tail l_t emits "\text{\textcircled{T}}" to activate the segment tail s_t, which in turn bounces off a special end mark "$\otimes$" announcing the end of DefineSeg. By that time, the next segment S_i consisting of 2^i agents, starting from a head labelled s_h, ending at a tail s_t and having $2^i - 2$ internal agents with label s, has been defined. The "$\otimes$" mark is propagated back to the head l_h along the active agents, by always moving from p_{i+1} to p_i.

Lemma 1. *DefineSeg correctly activates all agents of S_i in $O(n)$ rounds.*

CheckSeg. Once l_h observes "$\otimes$", it propagates its own local direction stored in component $c_4 = a \in A$ by updating $c_2 \leftarrow c_4$. Then, all active agents on the path forward a from p_i to p_{i+1} via their transmission components. Whenever a p_i having a local direction $c_4 = a' \in A$ observes $a' \neq a$, it combines a with its local direction a' and changes its transmission component to $c_2 \leftarrow aa'$. After that, if a p_i' having $c_4 = a'' \in A$ observes $a'' \neq a'$, it updates its transmission component into a negative mark, $c_2 \leftarrow \neg$. All signals are to be reflected by the segment tail s_t back to l_h, which acts accordingly as follows: (1) starts the next sub-phase DrawMap if it observes "$\neg$", (2) calls Merge to combine the two perpendicular lines if it observes aa' or (3) begins a new phase $i+1$ if it receives back its local direction a.

Lemma 2. *CheckSeg correctly checks the configuration of S_i in $O(n)$ rounds.*

DrawMap. This sub-phase computes the Manhattan distance $\Delta(l_t, s_t)$ between the line tail l_t and the segment tail s_t, by exploiting ComputeDistance in which the line agents implement a distributed binary counter. First, the head l_h broadcasts "\text{\textcircled{C}}" to all active agents, asking them to commence the calculation of the distance. Once a segment agent p_i observes "\text{\textcircled{C}}", it emits one increment mark "$\oplus$" if its local direction is cardinal or two sequential increment marks if it is diagonal. The "$\oplus$" mark is forwarded from p_i to p_{i-1} back to the head l_h. Correspondingly, the line agents are arranged to collectively act as a distributed binary counter, which increases by 1 bit per increment mark, starting from the least significant at l_t. When a line agent observes the last "$\oplus$" mark, it sends a special mark "\text{\textcircled{1}}" if $\Delta(l_t, s_t) \leq |L_i|$ or "\text{\textcircled{2}}" if $\Delta(l_t, s_t) > |L_i|$ back to l_h. As soon as l_h receives "\text{\textcircled{1}}" or "\text{\textcircled{2}}", it calls CollectArrows to draw a route that can be either heading directly to s_t or passing through the middle of S_i towards s_t. In CollectArrows, l_h emits " $\leftrightarrows$" to announce the collection of local directions (arrows) from S_i. When " $\leftrightarrows$" arrives at a segment agent, it then propagates its local direction stored in c_4 back towards l_h. Then, the line agents distribute and rearrange S_i's local directions via several primitives, such as cancelling out pairs of opposite directions, priority collection and pipelined transmission. Finally, the remaining arrows cooperatively draw a route map for L_i, see a demonstration in Fig. 4. The following lemma shows that this procedure calculates $\Delta(l_t, s_t)$ in linear time.

Lemma 3. *ComputeDistance requires $O(|L_i|)$ rounds to compute $\Delta(l_t, s_t)$.*

Lemma 4. *CollectArrows completes within $O(|L_i|)$ rounds.*

By Lemmas 3 and 4, we conclude that:

Lemma 5. *DrawMap draws a map within $O(|L_i|)$ rounds.*

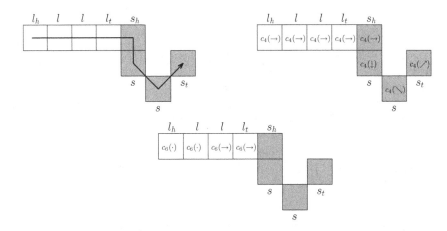

Fig. 4. Drawing a map: from top-left a path across occupied cells and corresponding local arrows stored on state c_4 in top-tight, where the diagonal directions, "$\searrow$" and "$\nearrow$", are interpreted locally as, "$\downarrow\rightarrow$" and "$\uparrow\rightarrow$". The bottom shows a route map drawn locally on state c_6 of each line agent.

Push. After some communication, l_h observes that L_i is ready to move and can start Push now. It synchronises with l_t to guide line agents during pushing. To achieve this, it propagates fast "(p1)" and slow "(p2)" marks along the line, "(p1)" is transmitted every round and "(p2)" is three rounds slower. The "(p1)" mark reflects at l_t and meets "(p2)" at a middle agent p_i, which in turn propagates two pushing signals "(p)" in either directions, one towards l_h and the other heading to l_t. This synchronisation liaises l_h with l_t throughout the pushing process, which starts immediately after "(p)" reaches both ends of the line at the same time. Recall the route map has been drawn starting from l_t, and hence, l_t moves simultaneously with l_h according to a local map direction $\hat{a} \in A$ stored in its map component c_6. Through this synchronisation, l_t checks the next cell (x, y) that L_i pushes towards and tells l_h, whether it is empty or occupied by an agent $p \notin L_i$ in the rest of the configuration. If (x, y) is empty, then l_h pushes L_i one step towards (x, y), and all line agents shift their map arrows in c_6 forwardly towards l_t. If (x, y) is occupied by $p \notin L_i$, then l_t swaps states with p and tells l_h to push one step. Similarly, in each round of pushing a line agent p_i swaps states with p until the line completely traverses the drawn route map and restores it to its original state. Figure 5 shows an example of pushing L_i through a route of empty and occupied cells. In this way, the line agents can transparently push through a route of any configuration and leave it unchanged. Once L_i has traversed completely through the route and lined up with s_t, then RecursiveCall begins. Below, we show that under this model there is a way to sync a Hamiltonian path of n agents in which all can preform concurrent actions in linear time.

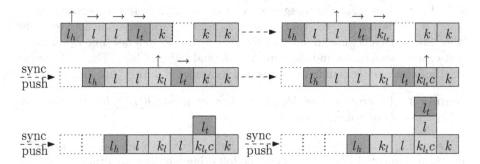

Fig. 5. A line L_i of agents inside grey cells (of labels l_t, l, and l_t), with map directions above, pushing and turning through empty and non-empty cells in blue (of label k). (Color figure online)

Lemma 6 (Agents synchronisation). *Let P denote a a Hamiltonian path of n agents on the square grid, starting from a head p_1 and ending at a tail p_n, where $p_1 \neq p_n$. Then, all agents of P can be synchronised in at most $O(n)$ rounds.*

Let R denote a rectangular path consisting of a set of cells $R = [c_1, \ldots, c_{|R|}]$ on $\mathbb{Z}^2$, where c_i and c_{i+1} are two cells adjacent vertically or horizontally, for all $1 \leq i \leq |R| - 1$. Let C be a system configuration, C_R denotes the configuration of R where $C_R \subset C$ defined by $[c_1, \ldots, c_{|R|}]$. Then, we give the following lemma:

Lemma 7. *Let L_i denote a terminal straight line and R be a rectangular path of any configuration C_R, starting from a cell adjacent to the tail of L_i, where $R \leq 2|L_i| - 1$. Then, there exists a distributed way to push L_i along R without breaking connectivity.*

In the following lemma, we provide the complexity of Push on the number of line moves and the communication rounds.

Lemma 8. *A straight line L_i traverses a route R of any configuration C_R, taking at most $O(|L_i|)$ line moves in $O(|L_i| \cdot |R|)$ rounds.*

RecursiveCall. When a segment tail s_t swaps states with l_h, it accordingly acts as follows: (1) propagates a special mark transmitted along all segment agents towards the head s_h, (2) deactivates itself by updating label to $c_1 \leftarrow k$, (3) resets all of its components, except local direction in c_4. Similarly, once a segment agent p_i observes this special mark, it propagates it to its successor p_{i+1}, deactivates itself, and keeps its local direction in c_4 while resetting all other components. When the segment head s_h notices this special mark, it changes to a line head state $(c_1 \leftarrow l_h)$ and then recursively repeats the whole transformation from round 1 to $i - 1$. Figure 3 presents a graphical illustration of RecursiveCall applied on a diagonal line shape.

Merge. This sub-phase begins once RecursiveCall has transformed S_i into a straight line L'_i, with the tail of L'_i occupying a cell adjacent to the head l_h of L_i. First, Merge calls CheckSeg to check whether L'_i is in line or perpendicular to L_i. If the latter is true (that is both L_i and L'_i are perpendicular to each other), then l_h calls Push to move L_i towards L'_i and form a new line L_{i+1}. Otherwise, they swap states and elect one head l_h and tail l_t of L_{i+1}. Thus, all agents require linear cost of communications and movements during this sub-phase:

Lemma 9. *An execution of Merge requires at most $O(|L_i|)$ line moves and $O(|L_i|)$ rounds of communication.*

Overall, given a Hamiltonian path of individuals with limited knowledge in an initial connected shape S_I. Then, the following lemma states that S_I can be transformed into a straight line S_L through a series of line moves that match the optimal centralised transformation and satisfy the connectivity-preserving condition.

Lemma 10. *Given an initial Hamiltonian shape S_I of n agents, this strategy transforms S_I into a straight line S_L of the same order in $O(n \log_2 n)$ moves and $O(n^2 \log_2 n)$ rounds, while preserving connectivity during transformation.*

Thus, we can finally provide the following theorem:

Theorem 1. *The above distributed transformation solves* HAMILTONIANLINE *within $O(n \log_2 n)$ line moves and $O(n^2 \log_2 n)$ rounds.*

References

1. Adleman, L.M.: Molecular computation of solutions to combinatorial problems. Science **266**(11), 1021–1024 (1994)
2. Akitaya, H.A., et al.: Universal reconfiguration of facet-connected modular robots by pivots: the o (1) musketeers. Algorithmica **83**(5), 1316–1351 (2021)
3. Almethen, A., Michail, O., Potapov, I.: On efficient connectivity-preserving transformations in a grid. In: Pinotti, C.M., Navarra, A., Bagchi, A. (eds.) ALGOSENSORS 2020. LNCS, vol. 12503, pp. 76–91. Springer, Cham (2020). https://doi.org/10.1007/978-3-030-62401-9_6

4. Almethen, A., Michail, O., Potapov, I.: Pushing lines helps: efficient universal centralised transformations for programmable matter. Theoret. Comput. Sci. **830–831**, 43–59 (2020)
5. Aloupis, G., et al.: Efficient reconfiguration of lattice-based modular robots. Comput. Geom. **46**(8), 917–928 (2013)
6. Aloupis, G., Collette, S., Demaine, E.D., Langerman, S., Sacristán, V., Wuhrer, S.: Reconfiguration of cube-style modular robots using O(logn) parallel moves. In: Hong, S.-H., Nagamochi, H., Fukunaga, T. (eds.) ISAAC 2008. LNCS, vol. 5369, pp. 342–353. Springer, Heidelberg (2008). https://doi.org/10.1007/978-3-540-92182-0_32
7. Angluin, D., Aspnes, J., Diamadi, Z., Fischer, M., Peralta, R.: Computation in networks of passively mobile finite-state sensors. Distrib. Comput. **18**(4), 235–253 (2006)
8. Boneh, D., Dunworth, C., Lipton, R.J., Sgall, J.: On the computational power of DNA. Discret. Appl. Math. **71**(1–3), 79–94 (1996)
9. Bourgeois, J., Goldstein, S.: Distributed intelligent MEMS: progresses and perspective. IEEE Syst. J. **9**(3), 1057–1068 (2015)
10. Czyzowicz, J., Dereniowski, D., Pelc, A.: Building a nest by an automaton. Algorithmica **83**(1), 144–176 (2021)
11. Daymude, J., et al.: On the runtime of universal coating for programmable matter. Nat. Comput. **17**(1), 81–96 (2018)
12. Derakhshandeh, Z., Gmyr, R., Porter, A., Richa, A.W., Scheideler, C., Strothmann, T.: On the runtime of universal coating for programmable matter. In: Rondelez, Y., Woods, D. (eds.) DNA 2016. LNCS, vol. 9818, pp. 148–164. Springer, Cham (2016). https://doi.org/10.1007/978-3-319-43994-5_10
13. Derakhshandeh, Z., Gmyr, R., Richa, A., Scheideler, C., Strothmann, T.: Universal shape formation for programmable matter. In: Proceedings of the 28th ACM Symposium on Parallelism in Algorithms and Architectures, pp. 289–299. ACM (2016)
14. Di Luna, G.A., Flocchini, P., Santoro, N., Viglietta, G., Yamauchi, Y.: Shape formation by programmable particles. Distrib. Comput. **33**, 69–101 (2019)
15. Doty, D.: Theory of algorithmic self-assembly. Commun. ACM **55**, 78–88 (2012)
16. Douglas, S., Dietz, H., Liedl, T., Högberg, B., Graf, F., Shih, W.: Self-assembly of DNA into nanoscale three-dimensional shapes. Nature **459**(7245), 414 (2009)
17. Dumitrescu, A., Pach, J.: Pushing squares around. In: Proceedings of the Twentieth Annual Symposium on Computational Geometry, pp. 116–123. ACM (2004)
18. Dumitrescu, A., Suzuki, I., Yamashita, M.: Formations for fast locomotion of metamorphic robotic systems. Int. J. Robot. Res. **23**(6), 583–593 (2004)
19. Dumitrescu, A., Suzuki, I., Yamashita, M.: Motion planning for metamorphic systems: feasibility, decidability, and distributed reconfiguration. IEEE Trans. Robot. Autom. **20**(3), 409–418 (2004)
20. Fekete, S.P., Gmyr, R., Hugo, S., Keldenich, P., Scheffer, C., Schmidt, A.: CADbots: algorithmic aspects of manipulating programmable matter with finite automata. Algorithmica **83**(1), 387–412 (2021)
21. Flocchini, P., Prencipe, G., Santoro, N.: Distributed computing by oblivious mobile robots. Synthesis Lect. Distrib. Comput. Theory **3**(2), 1–185 (2012)
22. Fukuda, T.: Self organizing robots based on cell structures-CEBot. In: Proceedings of IEEE International Workshop on Intelligent Robots and Systems (IROS 1988), pp. 145–150 (1988)

23. Gilpin, K., Knaian, A., Rus, D.: Robot pebbles: one centimeter modules for programmable matter through self-disassembly. In: 2010 IEEE International Conference on Robotics and Automation (ICRA), pp. 2485–2492. IEEE (2010)
24. Gmyr, R., et al.: Forming tile shapes with simple robots. Natural Comput. **19**(2) 375–390 (2020)
25. Itai, A., Papadimitriou, C., Szwarcfiter, J.: Hamilton paths in grid graphs. SIAM J. Comput. **11**(4), 676–686 (1982)
26. Knaian, A., Cheung, K., Lobovsky, M., Oines, A., Schmidt-Neilsen, P., Gershenfeld, N.: The milli-motein: a self-folding chain of programmable matter with a one centimeter module pitch. In: 2012 IEEE/RSJ International Conference on Intelligent Robots and Systems, pp. 1447–1453. IEEE (2012)
27. Michail, O., Skretas, G., Spirakis, P.: On the transformation capability of feasible mechanisms for programmable matter. J. Comput. Syst. Sci. **102**, 18–39 (2019)
28. Michail, O., Spirakis, P.: Simple and efficient local codes for distributed stable network construction. Distrib. Comput. **29**(3), 207–237 (2016)
29. Michail, O., Spirakis, P.: Elements of the theory of dynamic networks. Commun. ACM **61**(2), 72–81 (2018)
30. Nguyen, A., Guibas, L., Yim, M.: Controlled module density helps reconfiguration planning. In: Proceedings of 4th International Workshop on Algorithmic Foundations of Robotics, pp. 23–36 (2000)
31. Prakash, V.P., Patvardhan, C., Srivastav, A.: Effective heuristics for the bi-objective euclidean bounded diameter minimum spanning tree problem. In: Bhattacharyya, P., Sastry, H., Marriboyina, V., Sharma, R. (eds.) NGCT 2017. CCIS, vol. 827, pp. 580–589. Springer, Singapore (2017). https://doi.org/10.1007/978-981-10-8657-1_44
32. Rothemund, P.: Folding DNA to create nanoscale shapes and patterns. Nature **440**(7082), 297–302 (2006)
33. Rothemund, P., Winfree, E.: The program-size complexity of self-assembled squares. In: Proceedings of the 32nd Annual ACM Symposium on Theory of Computing (STOC), pp. 459–468. ACM (2000)
34. Rubenstein, M., Cornejo, A., Nagpal, R.: Programmable self-assembly in a thousand-robot swarm. Science **345**(6198), 795–799 (2014)
35. Toffoli, T., Margolus, N.: Programmable matter: concepts and realization. Phys. D Nonlinear Phenomena **47**(1–2), 263–272 (1991)
36. Walter, J., Welch, J., Amato, N.: Distributed reconfiguration of metamorphic robot chains. Distrib. Comput. **17**(2), 171–189 (2004)
37. Winfree, E.: Algorithmic self-assembly of DNA. Ph.D. thesis, California Institute of Technology (1998)
38. Woods, D., Chen, H., Goodfriend, S., Dabby, N., Winfree, E., Yin, P.: Active self-assembly of algorithmic shapes and patterns in polylogarithmic time. In: Proceedings of the 4th Conference on Innovations in Theoretical Computer Science, pp. 353–354. ACM (2013)
39. Yamashita, M., Suzuki, I.: Characterizing geometric patterns formable by oblivious anonymous mobile robots. Theoret. Comput. Sci. **411**(26–28), 2433–2453 (2010)
40. Yim, M., et al.: Modular self-reconfigurable robot systems [grand challenges of robotics]. IEEE Robot. Autom. Mag. **14**(1), 43–52 (2007)

Stand up Indulgent Gathering

Quentin Bramas[1]([✉]), Anissa Lamani[1], and Sébastien Tixeuil[2]

[1] ICUBE, Strasbourg University, CNRS, Strasbourg, France
`bramas@unistra.fr`
[2] Sorbonne University, CNRS, LIP6, Paris, France

Abstract. We consider a swarm of mobile robots evolving in a bidimensional Euclidean space. We study the stronger variant of crash-tolerant gathering: if no robot crashes, robots have to meet at the same arbitrary location, not known beforehand, in finite time; if one or several robots crash at the same location, the remaining correct robots gather at the crash location to rescue them. Motivated by impossibility results in the semi-synchronous setting, we present the first solution to the problem for the fully synchronous setting that operates in the vanilla Look-Compute-Move model with no additional hypotheses: robots are oblivious, disoriented, have no multiplicity detection capacity, and may start from arbitrary positions (including those with multiplicity points). We furthermore show that robots gather in a time that is proportional to the initial maximum distance between robots.

1 Introduction

The study of swarms of mobile robots from an algorithmic perspective was initiated by Suzuki and Yamashita [14], and the simplicity of their model fostered many research results from the Distributed Computing community [12]. Such research focused in particular on the computational power of a set of autonomous robots evolving in a bidimensional Euclidean space. More precisely, the purpose is to determine which tasks can be achieved by the robots, and at what cost.

Typically, robots are modeled as points in the two dimensional plane, and are assumed to have their own coordinate system and unit distance. In addition, they are *(i)* anonymous (they can not be distinguished), *(ii)* uniform (they execute the same algorithm) and, *(iii)* oblivious (they cannot remember their past actions). Robots cannot interact directly but are endowed with visibility sensors allowing them to sense their environment and see the positions of the other robots. Robots operate in cycles that comprise three phases: Look, Compute and Move (LCM). During the first phase (Look), robots take a snapshot to see the positions of the other robots. During the second phase (Compute), they either compute a destination or decide to stay idle. In the last phase (Move), they move towards the computed destination (if any). Three execution models have been considered in the literature to represent the amount of synchrony between robots.

This work was partially funded by the ANR project SAPPORO, ref. 2019-CE25-0005-1.

L. Gąsieniec et al. (Eds.): ALGOSENSORS 2021, LNCS 12961, pp. 17–28, 2021.
https://doi.org/10.1007/978-3-030-89240-1_2

The fully synchronous model (FSYNC) assumes all robots are activated simultaneously and execute their LCM cycle synchronously. The semi-synchronous model (SSYNC) allows that only a subset of robots are activated simultaneously. The asynchronous model (ASYNC) makes no assumption besides bounding the duration of each phase of the LCM cycle.

Although a number of problems have been considered in this setting (*e.g.*, pattern formation, scattering, gathering, exploration, patrolling, etc.), the gathering problem remains one of the most fundamental tasks one can ask mobile robots to perform, *e.g.* to collect acquired data or to update the robots' algorithm. To solve gathering, robots are requested to reach the same geographic location, not known beforehand, in finite time. Despite its simplicity, the gathering problem yielded a number of impossibility results due to initial symmetry and/or adversarial scheduling. The special case of two robots gathering is called rendezvous in the literature.

When the number of robots in a swarm increases, the possibility of having one robot crash unpredictably becomes important to tackle. Previous work on fault-tolerant gathering considered two variants of the problem. In the weak variant, only correct (that is, non failed) robots are requested to gather, while in the strong variant, all robots (failed and correct) must gather at the same point. Obviously, the strong variant is only feasible when all faulty robots crash at the same location. In this paper, we consider the strong version of the crash-tolerant gathering problem, that we call *stand up indulgent gathering* (SUIG). In more details, an algorithm solves the SUIG problem if the two following conditions are satisfied: *(i)* if no robot crashes, all robots gather at the same location, not known beforehand, in finite time, and *(ii)* if one or more robots crash at some location l, all robots gather at l in finite time. The SUIG problem can be seen as a more stringent version of gathering, where correct robots are requested to rescue failed ones should any unforeseen event occur. Of course, robots are unaware of the crashed status of any robot as they have no means to communicate directly.

Related Works. A fundamental result [14] shows that when robots operate in a fully synchronous manner, the rendezvous can be solved deterministically, while if some robots are allowed to wait for a while (this is the case *e.g.* in the SSYNC model), the problem becomes impossible without additional assumptions. The impossibility result for SSYNC rendezvous extends to SSYNC gathering whenever bivalent initial configurations[1] are allowed [8], or when robots have no multiplicity detection capabilities [13]. On the positive side, FSYNC gathering is feasible [7], even when robots have no access to multiplicity detection [2].

Early solutions to weak crash-tolerant gathering in SSYNC for groups of at least three robots make use of extra hypotheses: *(i)* starting from a distinct configuration (that is, a configuration where at most one robot occupies a particular position), at most one robot may crash [1], *(ii)* robots are activated one at a time [9], *(iii)* robots may exhibit probabilistic behavior [10], *(iv)* robots share a common chirality (that is, the same notion of handedness) [4], *(v)* robots agree

---

[1] A configuration is *bivalent* if all robots are evenly spread on exactly two distinct locations.

on a common direction [3]. It turns out that these hypotheses are *not* necessary to solve deterministic weak crash-tolerant gathering in SSYNC, when up to $n-1$ robots may crash [6].

The case of SUIG mostly yielded impossibility results: with at most a single crash, strong crash-tolerant gathering $n \geq 3$ robots deterministically in SSYNC is impossible even if robots are executed one at a time [9,10], and probabilistic strong crash-tolerant gathering $n \geq 3$ robots in SSYNC is impossible with a fair scheduler [9,10]. However, probabilistic strong crash-tolerant gathering $n \geq 3$ robots becomes possible in SSYNC if the relative speed of the robots is upper bounded by a constant [9,10]. The special case of $n = 2$ robots is also impossible to solve in SSYNC [5]. The only positive result so far [5] is for the special case of two robots, also called the SUIR (Stand-Up Indulgent Rendezvous) problem: starting from arbitrary initial positions, two robots eventually gather in FSYNC, without additional assumptions (such as multiplicity detection).

This raises the following open question: in FSYNC, for $n \geq 3$ robots, is it possible to deterministically gather all robots (if none of them crashes) at the same position, not known beforehand, or to deterministically gather at the position of the crashed robots, if some of them crash unexpectedly at the same location? Are additional hypotheses (such as multiplicity detection capability, or starting from a non-bivalent or even distinct configuration) necessary to solve the problem?

Our Contribution. We answer positively to the feasibility of SUIG in mobile robotic swarms. Our approach is constructive, as we give an explicit algorithm to solve the SUIG problem in the FSYNC execution model, using only oblivious robots with arbitrary local coordinate systems (there is no agreement on any direction, chirality, or unit distance), without relying on multiplicity detection (robots are unaware of the number of robots, or approximation of it, on any occupied location). Furthermore, a nice property of our algorithm is that no assumptions are made about the initial positions of the robots (in particular, we allow to start from a configuration with multiplicity points, and even from a bivalent configuration), so the algorithm is self-stabilizing [11]. The time complexity of our SUIG algorithm is $O\left(\frac{D}{\delta} + \log\left(\frac{\delta}{u_{min}}\right) + \log^2\left(\frac{u_{max}}{u_{min}}\right)\right)$ rounds, where u_{max}, resp. u_{min}, denotes the maximum, resp. minimum, unit distance among robots, D is the maximum distance between two robots in the initial configuration, and δ is the minimum distance a robot is assured to travel each round.

To achieve this result, we introduce a new *level-slicing* technique, that permits to partition robots that execute specific steps of the algorithm within a class of configurations, according to a level. This level permits to coordinate robots even when they do *not* agree on a common unit distance. We believe that this technique could be useful for other problems related to mobile robotic swarms.

Outline. The rest of the paper is organized as follows. Section 2 presents the execution model. Section 3 describes our solution to the SUIG problem, while Sect. 4 provides some concluding remarks.

2   Model

Let $\mathcal{R} = \{r_1, r_2, \ldots r_k\}$ be the set of $k \geq 2$ robots modeled as points in the Euclidean two-dimensional space. Robots are assumed to be anonymous (they are indistinguishable), uniform (they all execute the same algorithm) and oblivious (they cannot remember past actions).

Let Z be a global coordinate system. Let $p_i(t) \in \mathbb{R}^2$ be the coordinate of either a robot or a set of collocated robots at time t with respect to Z. Given a time t, a *configuration* at time t is defined as a set $\mathcal{C}_t = \{p_1(t), p_2(t), \ldots p_m(t)\}$ ($m \leq k$) where m is the number of occupied points in the plane and $p_i(t) \neq p_j(t)$ for any $i, j \in \{1, \ldots, m\}$, $i \neq j$. Robots do not know Z. Instead, each robot r_i has its own coordinate system Z_{r_i} centered at the current position of r_i. We assume *disoriented* robots *i.e.* they neither agree on an axis nor have a common unit distance. Observe that the Smallest Enclosing Circle (SEC) is independent of the coordinate system.

We consider the FSYNC model in which at each time instant t, called round, each robot r_i looks, computes and then moves with respect to its local coordinate system Z_{r_i}, synchronously with all the other robots. During the Look phase, r_i observes the positions of all the other robots and builds the set $V_{r_i}(t) = \{p_1(t), \ldots, p_m(t)\}$ ($m \leq k$) where m is the number of occupied points in the plane and $p_i(t)$ refers to the coordinate of a robot or a collocated set of robots with respect to r_i's local coordinate system Z_{r_i} (translated by $-r_i$ so that r_i is always at the center). We call $V_{r_i}(t)$ the *local view* of r_i at time t. Note that robots have no way to distinguish positions occupied by a single robot from those occupied by more than one robot *i.e.* they have no multiplicity detection.

An algorithm A is a function mapping local views to destinations. When r_i is activated at time t, algorithm A outputs r_i's destination d in its local coordinate system Z_{r_i}. Robot r_i then moves towards the computed destination. We assume *non-rigid* movements *i.e.* when a robot moves towards a target destination computed during the Move phase, an adversary can prevent it from reaching it by stopping the robot anywhere along the straight path towards the destination. However, we assume that the robot travels at least a fixed positive distance δ. The value of δ is common to all robots but is unknown. It can be arbitrary small and does not change during the execution of the algorithm.

An execution $\mathcal{E} = (C_0, C_1, \ldots)$ of A is a sequence of configurations, where C_0 is an initial configuration, and every configuration C_{t+1} is obtained from C_t by applying A.

A robot is said to *crash* at time t if it is not activated at any time $t' \geq t$ *i.e.*, a crashed robot stops executing its algorithm and remains at the same position indefinitely.

The Stand Up Indulgent Gathering Problem. An algorithm solves the Stand Up Indulgent Gathering (SUIG) problem if, for any initial configuration C_0 and for any execution $\mathcal{E} = (C_0, C_1, \ldots)$ with up to one crashed location (location where robots crash), there exists a round t and a point p such that $C_{t'} = \{p\}$ for all $t' \geq t$. In other words, if one robot crashes, all non crashed robots go and join the crashed one; if no robot crashes, all robots gather in a finite number of rounds.

Since we consider oblivious robots and an arbitrary initial configuration, we can consider without loss of generality that the crash, if any, occurs at the start of the execution.

3   The SUIG Algorithm

The moves of our algorithm depend on how many occupied locations (also called *points* in the sequel) are seen by a robot and whether they are aligned or not. If two points are seen, we further divide the set of configurations depending on the distance between those points. More precisely, we partition the set *Conf* as follows:

$$Conf = \mathcal{T}_{SEC} \cup \mathcal{T}_{ext} \cup \bigcup_{k \geq 0} \left(\mathcal{A}^k \cup \mathcal{B}^k \cup \mathcal{C}_1^k \cup \mathcal{C}_2^k \cup \mathcal{C}_3^k \right)$$

- $\mathcal{T}_{ext}(p)$ (or simply $\mathcal{T}_{ext}$ when p is arbitrary) denotes the set of configurations where all robots are aligned, and a single extremal robot p is at distance e from the closest robot, with $\frac{e}{d} \in \{\frac{1}{9}, \frac{1}{8}, \frac{9}{80}, \frac{10}{81}, \frac{10}{18}, \frac{9}{16}, \frac{80}{81}\}$, where d denotes the distance between the two extremal robots.
- $\mathcal{T}_{SEC}$ denotes the set of configurations that do not consist in only two points, and that are not in $\mathcal{T}_{ext}$.
- The other sets of configurations form a partition of the set $Conf_2$ of configurations consisting in only two points. When a configuration consists in only two points, we define the *level* of a robot r as the number l_r such that $d_r \in [2^{-l_r}, 2^{-l_r+1})$, where d_r is the distance between the two points seen by robot r. Then we define for all $k \geq 0$

$$\begin{aligned}
\mathcal{A}^k &= \{C \in Conf_2 \mid S_k & \leq l_r < S_k + k\} \\
\mathcal{B}^k &= \{C \in Conf_2 \mid S_k + k & \leq l_r < S_k + 2k\} \\
\mathcal{C}_1^k &= \{C \in Conf_2 \mid S_k + 2k & \leq l_r < S_k + 2k + 1\} \\
\mathcal{C}_2^k &= \{C \in Conf_2 \mid S_k + 2k + 1 \leq l_r < S_k + 2k + 2\} \\
\mathcal{C}_3^k &= \{C \in Conf_2 \mid S_k + 2k + 2 \leq l_r < S_k + 2k + 3\}
\end{aligned}$$

Where $S_k = k(k+2)$, so that $S_{k+1} = S_k + 2k + 3$ and all the levels ≥ 0 are considered. Also, for simplicity, instead of being the empty set, we fix by convention $\mathcal{A}^0 = \{C \in Conf_2 \mid l_r < 1\}$. Doing so, the infinite sequence $\left(\mathcal{A}^k \cup \mathcal{B}^k \cup \mathcal{C}_1^k \cup \mathcal{C}_2^k \cup \mathcal{C}_3^k \right)_{k \geq 0}$ is a partition of $Conf_2$. One can notice that the deduced partition depends on the observing robot r i.e., two different robots may see a configuration in $Conf_2$ in different subsets at the same time, since they may have different distance units.

Algorithm Description. When the configuration consists in two points at distance d, we say a robot performs move Move (e) if it is ordered to move toward the other point for distance $e \times d$. We are now ready to describe our algorithm called SUIG for Stand-up Indulgent Gathering. The pseudo-code is given in Algorithm 1, and a visual representation is given in Fig. 1. When robots occupy only two points (*i.e.*, when the configuration is in $Conf_2$), a robot action depends on its own coordinate system. More precisely, a robot r orients the line passing through both occupied points using its coordinate system. If the other point (where the robot is not located) is located on the East or on the North (in case no point is at the East of the other), then r considers it is on the left of the other point, otherwise r sees itself on the right of the other point. In the illustration, we orient the line with an arrow and present the moves using bent arrows, depending on where the robot sees itself, on the right or on the left. In the pseudo code, we write

$$left \rightarrow \texttt{Move1}; right \rightarrow \texttt{Move2}$$

to notify that a robot that sees itself on the left, resp. on the right, should execute Move1, resp. Move2.

Algorithm 1: SUIG Algorithm

---
if $C \in \mathcal{A}^k$ **then** $\texttt{Move}\left(\frac{1}{2}\right)$
if $C \in \mathcal{B}^k$ **then** $left \rightarrow \texttt{Move}\left(\frac{1}{9}\right)$; $right \rightarrow \texttt{Move}\left(\frac{1}{10}\right)$
if $C \in \mathcal{C}_1^k$ **then** $\texttt{Move}\left(\frac{1}{2}\right)$
if $C \in \mathcal{C}_2^k$ **then** $left \rightarrow \texttt{Move}(1)$; $right \rightarrow \texttt{Move}\left(\frac{1}{2}\right)$
if $C \in \mathcal{C}_3^k$ **then** $left \rightarrow \texttt{Move}\left(\frac{1}{2}\right)$; $right \rightarrow \texttt{Move}(1)$
if $C \in \mathcal{T}_{ext}(p)$ **then** Move to p
else Move to the center of the smallest enclosing circle.

Lemma 1. *If robots do not gather, then they eventually remain at distance at most δ from each other.*

Proof. If the robots do not gather, then in each configuration there are at least two occupied locations. Let $D(t)$ be the distance between the two farthest robots at time t. Assume for the purpose of contradiction that for all $t \geq 0$, $D(t) > \delta$. Since robots never move outside of the convex hull they form, the function $t \mapsto D(t)$ is non-increasing, hence converges to a value $B \geq \delta$, and there is a time T such that,

$$\forall t > T, \qquad D(t) \in [B, B + \delta/10). \qquad (1)$$

Consider any such time $t > T$. By our algorithm, the robots either move to the center of the SEC, move to an extremity (when in phase $\mathcal{T}_{ext}$), or perform $\texttt{Move}(e)$, $e \in \{\frac{1}{10}, \frac{1}{9}, \frac{1}{2}, 1\}$. We consider different cases depending on what moves robots execute in configuration $C(t)$

- **Case A:** If robots are not in phase $\mathcal{T}_{ext}$ and no robot executes $\texttt{Move}(1)$, then the maximum distance among robots decreases by at least $\delta/10$, which contradicts Relation 1.
- **Case B:** If robots are in phase $\mathcal{T}_{ext}(p)$, then the configuration is not symmetric and all robots have the same target, point p. Let $q \neq p$ be the other extremity of the segment hosting all robots. If no robot is crashed at q, then

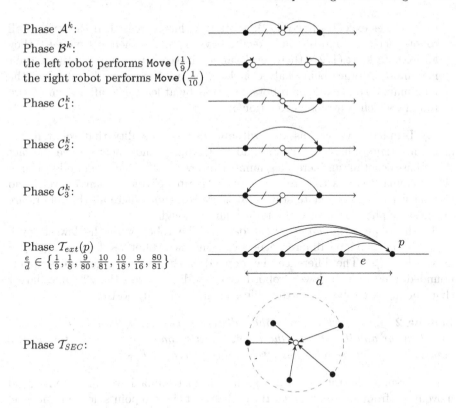

Phase $\mathcal{A}^k$:

Phase $\mathcal{B}^k$:
the left robot performs Move $\left(\frac{1}{9}\right)$
the right robot performs Move $\left(\frac{1}{10}\right)$

Phase $\mathcal{C}_1^k$:

Phase $\mathcal{C}_2^k$:

Phase $\mathcal{C}_3^k$:

Phase $\mathcal{T}_{ext}(p)$
$\frac{e}{d} \in \left\{ \frac{1}{9}, \frac{1}{8}, \frac{9}{80}, \frac{10}{81}, \frac{10}{18}, \frac{9}{16}, \frac{80}{81} \right\}$

Phase $\mathcal{T}_{SEC}$:

Fig. 1. Algorithm 1.

the maximum distance between robots decreases by at least $\delta/10$ (in the worst case, the crashed robot is at distance $9D(t)/10$ from p), which contradicts Relation 1. If there is a crashed robot at q, then in configuration $C(t+1)$ no correct robot is collocated with the crashed robot at q, and either case A or C applies to reach a contradiction.

- **Case C:** If some robots execute Move (1) in phase $\mathcal{C}_2^k$, or $\mathcal{C}_3^k$ ($C(t)$ consists of two points), and if there is a crashed robot and no correct robot is collocated with it, then all the correct robots move towards the crashed robot a distance at least $\delta/10$ (because some robots might be in other phases), so the maximum distance among robots decreases by at least $\delta/10$, which contradicts Relation 1.

- **Case D:** If there is no crashed robot, or if there is a crashed robot collocated with correct robots, then either there is a robot that executes a move different from Move (1), and the next configuration $C(t + 1)$ does not consist of only two points, and a previous case applies to reach a contradiction, or all robots execute Move (1) and configuration $C(t+1)$ consists in only two points. Then, if $D(t + 1)$ is still in the interval $[B, B + \frac{\delta}{10})$, then moving robots must have changed their side on the segment. This implies that, at time $t + 1$, each robot either executes Move $(1/2)$, or its level has increased. If the level of all robots increases, and they all execute Move (1) again, then at time $t + 2$ they all execute Move $(1/2)$ (their level cannot increase two times without their maximum distance being halved at least once in between). In all cases, the maximum distance among robots decreases by at least $\delta/2$, after at most two rounds, which contradicts Relation 1.   □

By Lemma 1, we can assume without loss of generality that robot movements are rigid. The next Lemma and its Corollary show how we use the fact that phases contain an increasing number of levels ($\mathcal{A}^{k+1}$ has 1 more level than $\mathcal{A}^k$). Lemma 2 states that robots cannot "jump up" more than 7 levels, and Corollary 1 uses this fact to state that there is a time where all the robots are in the same phase $\mathcal{A}^k$, resp. $\mathcal{B}^k$, for a k large enough.

In the sequel, the *lowest robot* denotes the robot with the lowest level. Δ_{level} is the maximal difference between any two robot levels, *i.e.*, $\Delta_{level} = \max_{r,r'} |l_r - l_{r'}|$. The difference may depend on the configuration but is upper-bounded. Indeed, if the lowest robot has a unit distance less than 2^c times larger than the highest robot, then the difference in level is at most c.

Lemma 2. *In any execution, either all robots gather, or there exists a level l such that for any level $l' \geq l$, the robots reach a configuration consisting in two points and the lowest robot has level in the interval $[l', l' + 7]$.*

Proof. Assume the robots do not gather, from Lemma 1 we can assume rigid movements from a given time t_0. If $C(t_0)$ consists in two points, let l be the level of the lowest robot in $C(t_0)$. Otherwise either all robots gather in $C(t_0 + 1)$, or $C(t_0 + 1)$ consists in two points, and let l be the level of the lowest robot in $C(t_0 + 1)$.

To prove the Lemma, it is sufficient to prove the following claim: if a configuration $C(t)$ at time t consists in two points at distance d, then either $C(t + 1)$ or $C(t + 2)$ consists in two points at distance $d' \geq \frac{d}{2^7}$, or all robots gather in $C(t + 1)$ or $C(t + 2)$. Indeed, this implies that the level between two consecutive configurations forming two points cannot increase by more than 7. This implies that, for any $l' \geq l$ we eventually reach a configuration where the lowest robot has a level in the interval $[l', l' + 7]$, or all robots gather.

We now prove the claim. After executing the algorithm from $C(t)$, either all robots gather, or $C(t + 1)$ consists in two points, or in three or more points. If $C(t + 1)$ consists in two points, the distance between any two points is at least $(\frac{1}{9} - \frac{1}{10})d = \frac{1}{90}d \geq \frac{1}{2^7}d$. So, the level increases by at most 7 between $C(t)$ and $C(t + 1)$.

If $C(t+1)$ consists in 3 points or more, the minimal interval containing three points is at least $\frac{1}{10}d$, so that the extremities (recall the robots are aligned) are at distance $d' \geq \frac{1}{10}d$. In $C(t + 1)$ the robots all move towards the same destination. If there is no crashed robot or if the crashed robot is already at the destination, then the next configuration $C(t + 2)$ is gathered. Otherwise, since the crashed robot is located at an extremity and the destination is either an extremity or the middle, then $C(t+2)$ consists in two points at distance $d'' \geq d'/2$. Hence we have $d'' \geq \frac{1}{20}d \geq \frac{1}{27}d$.

So the claim is proved and the Lemma follows.   □

Corollary 1. *For any $k \geq 0$, eventually either all robots gather, or the robots are all in phase $\mathcal{A}^{k'}$ with $k' \geq k$. The same is true with phase $\mathcal{B}$.*

Proof. Let l be defined by Lemma 2, and let $k > \Delta_{level} + 7$ such that $S_k \geq l$. We can now apply Lemma 2 with $l' = S_{k'}$, and $k' \geq k$ (clearly we have $l' > l$ so the lemma applies). Thus, we know that either the robots eventually gather, or reach a configuration where the lower robot has a level in the interval $[S_{k'}, S_{k'} + 7]$. Since $k' > \Delta_{level} + 7$, all the robots have a level in the interval $[S_{k'}, S_{k'} + k' - 1]$, and they all are in phase $\mathcal{A}^{k'}$.

A similar proof can be done replacing $\mathcal{A}^{k'}$ by $\mathcal{B}^{k'}$.   □

We are now ready to prove the correctness of our algorithm. We first prove that robots gather if no robot crashes (Lemma 3), and then when robots may crash at the same location (Lemma 4). For simplicity, we consider in the sequel, without loss of generality, that the movements are rigid (using Lemma 1).

Lemma 3. *If no robot crashes, all robots eventually gather at the same point.*

Proof. By Lemma 1, either the robots gather or all enter phase $\mathcal{A}^k$ for some $k > 0$. Hence, after one more round all robots move to the middle and gather. □

Lemma 4. *If robots crash at the same location, all robots eventually gather at the same point.*

Proof. Assume some robots crash at the same location. By Lemma 1, either the robots gather, or all enter phase $\mathcal{B}^k$ for some $k > 0$. Let d denotes the distance between the two points.

If some correct robots are located at the crashed location, then after one round, at least three points are formed. In the obtained configuration, all the robots remain on the same line, and the new distance d' between the two farthest robots depends on which move the robots performed (move to $\frac{1}{10}$, or move to $\frac{1}{9}$). In case 1, if at least one robot at the opposite of the crashed location performed a $\frac{1}{10}$ move, then $d' = \frac{9}{10}d$, otherwise, in case 2, $d' = \frac{8}{9}d$. Also, all the correct robots that were on the crashed location are now at distance $\frac{1}{10}d$ or $\frac{1}{9}d$ from the crashed location (again depending on what move they performed). So depending on the new value of d', the crashed location is at the extremity of the line, and its distance from the closest correct robot is either in $\left\{\frac{1}{9}d', \frac{10}{81}d'\right\}$ in case 1 (*e.g.*, $\frac{1}{9}d'$ is obtained by robots that performed a $\frac{1}{10}$ move *i.e.*, $\frac{1}{10}d = \frac{1}{10}\frac{10}{9}d' = \frac{1}{9}d'$), or in $\left\{\frac{9}{80}d', \frac{1}{8}d'\right\}$ in case 2.

Note that the robots at the other extremity of the line have a distance from the closest robot either $\frac{1}{81}d'$ (if there were at least two robots that moved differently) or is greater than $\frac{1}{2}d'$ (otherwise). All the possible cases are represented in Fig. 2.

Fig. 2. The possible destinations of robots after executing a move in phase B, assuming a single crashed location (on the right in this example). All the white nodes represent the possible destinations of the correct robots. We can see that regardless of where the robots end up, all the robots can detect where is the crashed location, using the ratio of the distance from an extremity to the closest robot.

In any case, all the robots can detect where the crashed location is located. The crashed location is at the extremity of the line such that the closest robot is at distance in $\{\frac{1}{9}d', \frac{9}{80}d', \frac{10}{81}d', \frac{1}{8}d'\}$, where d' is the length of the line (recall that the ratio does not depend on the value of d'). Thus, correct robots gather at the crashed location after one more round by performing move $\mathcal{T}_{ext}$.

If no correct robot is located at the crashed location, and some robots have different orientation, the same thing happens. The obtained configuration contains three points, two of them are at distance $\frac{1}{81}d'$, and the crashed location is at distance $\frac{80}{81}d'$ from the closest correct robot, so that correct robots gather at the crashed location after one more round by performing move $\mathcal{T}_{ext}$.

If no robot is located at the crashed location, and all the robots have the same orientation, then the correct robots come closer to the crashed location every round until one robot enters phase $\mathcal{C}_1^k$. If some correct robots are still in phase $\mathcal{B}^k$, then, similarly as the previous cases, the obtained configuration contains 3 or 4 points, and all correct robots can detect where the crashed location is, as it is the extremity with distance from the closest robot in $\{\frac{10}{18}d', \frac{9}{16}d'\}$. Thus, correct robots gather at the crashed location after one more round by performing move $\mathcal{T}_{ext}$.

If all correct robots enter phase $\mathcal{C}_1^k$ at the same time, then after one more round they all enter phase $\mathcal{C}_2^k$. If they are on the left of the crashed location, all correct robots gather at the crashed location, otherwise they all move to the middle, enter phase $\mathcal{C}_3^k$, and then move and gather at the crashed location.   □

From Lemma 3 and Lemma 4, the main theorem follows.

Theorem 1. *Algorithm 1 solves the SUIG problem in FSYNC, for any initial configuration, with $n \geq 1$ disoriented robots, without multiplicity detection, and with non-rigid movements.*

The round complexity of our algorithm depends on δ and on the ratio between the largest unit distance u_{max} and the smallest one u_{min}. It also depends on D the maximum distance between two robots in the initial configuration.

Theorem 2. *The round complexity of Algorithm 1 is*

$$O\left(\frac{D}{\delta} + \log\left(\frac{\delta}{u_{min}}\right) + \log^2\left(\frac{u_{max}}{u_{min}}\right)\right).$$

Proof. The complexity corresponds to the three steps of our algorithm, in the worst case. The first step is to reach a configuration where the maximum distance between robots is at most δ. The second step is to reach a configuration where the lowest robot (the robot with the smallest unit distance) sees other robots at distance at most 1. After the second step, the lowest robot has a level at least 0, and the third step requires the lowest robot to reach at worst level $C^{\Delta_{level}+7}$.

We saw in the proof of Lemma 1 that if the maximum distance between two robots is greater than δ, then this maximum distance decreases by at least $\delta/10$ every two rounds, so in $O\left(\frac{D}{\delta}\right)$ rounds all the robots are within distance at most δ from one another.

When such a configuration is reached, the movements are rigid and if robots do not gather, the number of rounds in each level is bounded (because, with the same argument as before, the maximum distance between two robots decreases by a factor at least $\frac{1}{10}$ every two rounds). The lowest robot has level at most

$$\left\lceil \log\left(\frac{\delta}{u_{min}}\right)\right\rceil,$$

where the log has base 2. Indeed, the lowest robot sees the distance δ as $\frac{\delta}{u_{min}}$ (a robot with half the unit distance, sees double the distances).

From there, the number of rounds to reach phase $\mathcal{B}^k$ *i.e.*, to reach level $S_k + k = k(k+2)$, is in $O(k^2)$. If the robots do not gather before, the lowest robot reaches level $\mathcal{B}^{\Delta_{level}+7}$ in $O\left(\Delta_{level}^2\right)$ rounds. When this level is reached, then, we saw in the proof of Lemma 4 that $O(\Delta_{level})$ rounds (that is, after reaching phase $C_3^{\Delta_{level}+7}$) are sufficient to terminate the gathering. Since

$$\Delta_{level} \leq \left\lceil \log\left(\frac{u_{max}}{u_{min}}\right)\right\rceil,$$

the theorem follows.   □

4 Concluding Remarks

We presented the first stand-up indulgent gathering (also know as strong fault-tolerant gathering in the literature) solution. Furthermore, our solution is self-stabilizing (the initial configuration may include multiplicity points, and even be bivalent), does not rely on extra assumptions such as multiplicity detection capacity, a common direction, orientation, or chirality, etc., and its running time is proportional to the maximum initial distance between robots.

The very weak capacities of the robots we considered make the problem unsolvable in more relaxed execution models, such as SSYNC. However, it may be possible to solve SUIG in SSYNC with a number of additional assumptions: non-bivalent initial configurations (otherwise, the impossibility for stand-up indulgent rendezvous applies [5]), multiplicity detection capacity (otherwise, the impossibility for classical gathering applies [13]), and persistent coordinate system (otherwise, the impossibility by Defago et al. [10] about SUIG applies). This open question is left for future research.

References

1. Agmon, N., Peleg, D.: Fault-tolerant gathering algorithms for autonomous mobile robots. SIAM J. Comput. **36**(1), 56–82 (2006)
2. Balabonski, T., Delga, A., Rieg, L., Tixeuil, S., Urbain, X.: Synchronous gathering without multiplicity detection: a certified algorithm. Theory Comput. Syst. **63**(2), 200–218 (2019)
3. Bhagat, S., Gan Chaudhuri, S., Mukhopadhyaya, K.: Fault-tolerant gathering of asynchronous oblivious mobile robots under one-axis agreement. In: Rahman, M.S., Tomita, E. (eds.) WALCOM 2015. LNCS, vol. 8973, pp. 149–160. Springer, Cham (2015). https://doi.org/10.1007/978-3-319-15612-5_14
4. Bouzid, Z., Das, S., Tixeuil, S.: Gathering of mobile robots tolerating multiple crash faults. In: Proceedings of 33rd IEEE International Conference on Distributed Computing Systems (ICDCS), pp. 337–346, July 2013
5. Bramas, Q., Lamani, A., Tixeuil, S.: Stand up indulgent rendezvous. In: Devismes, S., Mittal, N. (eds.) SSS 2020. LNCS, vol. 12514, pp. 45–59. Springer, Cham (2020). https://doi.org/10.1007/978-3-030-64348-5_4
6. Bramas, Q., Tixeuil, S.: Wait-free gathering without chirality. In: Scheideler, C. (ed.) SIROCCO 2014. LNCS, vol. 9439, pp. 313–327. Springer, Cham (2015). https://doi.org/10.1007/978-3-319-25258-2_22
7. Cohen, R., Peleg, D.: Convergence properties of the gravitational algorithm in asynchronous robot systems. SIAM J. Comput. **34**(6), 1516–1528 (2005)
8. Courtieu, P., Rieg, L., Tixeuil, S., Urbain, X.: Impossibility of gathering, a certification. Inf. Process. Lett. **115**(3), 447–452 (2015)
9. Défago, X., Gradinariu, M., Messika, S., Raipin-Parvédy, P.: Fault-tolerant and self-stabilizing mobile robots gathering. In: Dolev, S. (ed.) DISC 2006. LNCS, vol. 4167, pp. 46–60. Springer, Heidelberg (2006). https://doi.org/10.1007/11864219_4
10. Défago, X., Potop-Butucaru, M., Parvédy, P.R.: Self-stabilizing gathering of mobile robots under crash or byzantine faults. Distrib. Comput. **33**(5), 393–421 (2020)
11. Dolev, S.: Self-stabilization. MIT Press, Cambridge (2000)
12. Flocchini, P., Prencipe, G., Santoro, N. (eds.): Distributed Computing by Mobile Entities-Current Research in Moving and Computing. Lecture Notes in Computer Science, vol. 11340. Springer, Heidelberg (2019). https://doi.org/10.1007/978-3-030-11072-7
13. Prencipe, G.: Impossibility of gathering by a set of autonomous mobile robots. Theor. Comput. Sci. **384**(2–3), 222–231 (2007)
14. Suzuki, I., Yamashita, M.: Distributed anonymous mobile robots: formation of geometric patterns. SIAM J. Comput. **28**(4), 1347–1363 (1999)

Gathering a Euclidean Closed Chain of Robots in Linear Time

Jannik Castenow[✉], Jonas Harbig, Daniel Jung, Till Knollmann,
and Friedhelm Meyer auf der Heide

Heinz Nixdorf Institute and Computer Science Department, Paderborn University,
Paderborn, Germany
{janniksu,jharbig,jungd,tillk,fmadh}@mail.upb.de

Abstract. We focus on the following question about GATHERING of n autonomous, mobile robots in the Euclidean plane: Is it possible to solve GATHERING of robots that do not agree on their coordinate systems (disoriented) and see other robots only up to a constant distance (limited visibility) in linear time? Up to now, such a result is only known for robots on a two-dimensional grid [1,8]. We answer the question positively for robots that are connected in one closed chain (like [1]), i.e., every robot is connected to exactly two other robots, and the connections form a cycle. We show that these robots can be gathered by asynchronous robots ($\mathcal{A}$SYNC) in $\Theta(n)$ epochs assuming the $\mathcal{LUMI}$ model [12] that equips the robots with locally visible lights like in [1,8]. The lights are used to initiate and perform so-called runs along the chain, which are essential for the linear runtime. Starting of runs is done by determining locally unique robots (based on geometric shapes of neighborhoods). In contrast to the grid [1], this is not possible in every configuration in the Euclidean plane. Based on the theory of isogonal polygons by Grünbaum [18], we identify the class of isogonal configurations in which, due to a high symmetry, no locally unique robots can be identified. Our solution consists of two algorithms that might be executed in parallel: The first one gathers isogonal configurations without any lights. The second one works for non-isogonal configurations; it is based on the concept of runs using a constant number of lights.

1 Introduction

The GATHERING problem is one of the most studied and fundamental problems in the research area of distributed computing by mobile robots. GATHERING requires a set of initially scattered point-shaped robots to meet at the same (not predefined) position. This problem has been studied under several different robot and time models, all having in common that the capabilities of the individual robots are very restricted. The central questions among all

This work was partially supported by the German Research Foundation (DFG) under the project number 453112019; ME 872/14-1. A brief announcement about the result under the $\mathcal{F}$SYNC scheduler has appeared in [5] and a full version can be found online [6].

L. Gąsieniec et al. (Eds.): ALGOSENSORS 2021, LNCS 12961, pp. 29–44, 2021.
https://doi.org/10.1007/978-3-030-89240-1_3

models are: Which capabilities of robots are needed to solve GATHERING and how do these capabilities influence the runtime? One popular and well-studied model is the $\mathcal{OBLOT}$ model [15]. Its fundamental features are that the robots are *autonomous*, *identical* and *anonymous* (externally and internally identical), *homogeneous* (all robots execute the same algorithm), *silent* (no direct communication) and *oblivious* (no persistent memory). Additionally, the robots operate in discrete Look-Compute-Move cycles (rounds). Each cycle consists of three phases: first, robots take snapshots of their environment; afterward, they compute a target point and finally move there. The cycles of the robots can either be fully synchronous ($\mathcal{F}$SYNC), semi-synchronous ($\mathcal{S}$SYNC) or completely asynchronous ($\mathcal{A}$SYNC). Time is measured in *epochs*, i.e., the smallest number of rounds such that each robot has completed its cycle at least once. Another emerging model is the $\mathcal{LUMI}$ model [12,16] – it coincides in most parts with the $\mathcal{OBLOT}$ model. However, it does not demand the robots to be oblivious and silent. Instead, the robots are equipped with locally visible lights that are persistent. These lights can be used to communicate state information to local neighbors.

While it is nowadays well understood under which capabilities GATHER-ING is possible, much less is known concerning how the capabilities influence the runtime. The best known algorithm in the Euclidean plane considering disoriented robots with limited visibility and the $\mathcal{OBLOT}$ model is the GO-TO-THE-CENTER (GTC) algorithm that requires $\Theta(n^2)$ rounds under the $\mathcal{F}$SYNC scheduler [11]. It is conjectured that the runtime is optimal for the given robot model. The $\Omega(n^2)$ lower bound of GTC examines an initial configuration where the robots form a regular polygon with neighboring robots having a constant distance, the *viewing radius*. It is shown that GTC takes $\Omega(n^2)$ rounds until the robots start seeing more robots than their initial neighbors. This gives rise to a slightly different connectivity model, the *closed chain* [1]. Each robot has two direct chain neighbors it can distinguish, and the chain connections form a cycle in a closed chain. A robot can always see a constant number of chain neighbors in each direction along the chain. Based on the observations above, it can be seen that GTC has a runtime of $\Theta(n^2)$ for closed chains. Hence, it is also still open whether closed chains of disoriented robots with limited visibility can be gathered in linear time in the Euclidean plane. For robots that are located on a two-dimensional grid, the picture is different: a linear time algorithm for closed chains exists [1]. The algorithm is based on (at least) two main concepts: the distinction of *connectivity range* and *viewing range* and a locally sequential movement called *run* implemented with the help of the $\mathcal{LUMI}$ model. It is assumed that the distance between two direct neighbors in the chain is at most 1 (the connectivity range), but the robots can see the next 11 (the viewing range) robots in each direction along the chain. The larger viewing range significantly enhances the local views of the robots and is a commonly used tool in the context of efficient GATHERING algorithms, see, e.g., [1,8,24].

The second central concept behind the grid algorithm is the notion of a run (initially introduced in [22]). A run is a visible state (realized with lights) that is swapped along the chain and allows the robot with the state to move. In most rounds, $\Omega(n)$ runs are active, essential for the linear runtime. To start runs, locally unique robots – based on geometric shapes of neighborhoods – are determined. Therefore, the grid algorithm [1] benefits from an ever-present asymmetry of non-final configurations on the grid such that robots can always be identified to start runs (the "most symmetric" configuration w.r.t. the local views of the robots is the square). In the Euclidean plane, the picture is fundamentally different since classes of (non-final) configurations exist where every robot has the same view. The most obvious example is a configuration in which robots are located on the vertices of a regular polygon.

We show that closed chains of disoriented robots with limited visibility in the Euclidean plane can be gathered in linear time assuming the $\mathcal{LUMI}$ model. Our solution combines two algorithms: the first algorithm uses the notion of a run and identifies locally unique robots to start runs. The movement operations of robots with runs are inspired by [22], an algorithm for shortening open chains of robots in the Euclidean plane. In our model, and contrast to [22], runs might have different movement directions along the chain. The different directions introduce the additional challenge to handle runs with opposite movement directions located at direct neighbors. Another new challenge (compared to [22]) is to prevent runs from cycling multiple times around the chain. The second algorithm considers all configurations for which the concept of runs is not applicable due to the absence of locally unique robots. Based on the theory of *isogonal polygons* by Grünbaum [18], we characterize isogonal configurations in which no locally unique robots exist. With the help of the characterization, we introduce an algorithm that gathers isogonal configurations in linear time without using any light. We then demonstrate that running both algorithms in parallel, i.e., robots whose neighborhood fulfills the criterion of being an isogonal configuration, execute the algorithm for isogonal configurations while all others execute the asymmetric algorithm, solves GATHERING in linear time.

Related Work: Much research is devoted to GATHERING in various settings, mostly combined with an unbounded viewing radius. Due to space constraints, we focus on results that deal with the runtime of GATHERING algorithms. For a comprehensive overview of models, algorithms, and analyses, we refer the reader to the recent survey [14]. Additionally, see [13, 17, 23, 26] for practical applications of robot chains and [1, 7, 10, 20, 22, 25, 27] for more algorithmic results about robot chain problems.

In the $\mathcal{OBLOT}$ model, there is the GTC algorithm [2] that solves GATHERING of disoriented robots with local visibility in $\Theta\left(n^2\right)$ rounds assuming the $\mathcal{F}$SYNC scheduler [11]. The same runtime can be achieved for robots located on a two-dimensional grid [4]. It is conjectured that both algorithms are asymptotically optimal and thus, $\Omega\left(n^2\right)$ is also a lower bound for *any* algorithm that solves GATHERING in this model. The only proven non-trivial lower bound is $\Omega(D_G^2)$, where D_G denotes the diameter of the initial visibility graph [19]. However, this bound only holds for comparably small diameters $D_G \in \Theta(\sqrt{\log n})$. Faster runtimes could only be achieved in a continuous time model (see [21] for an overview), or by assuming agreement on one or two axes of the local coordinate systems or considering the $\mathcal{LUMI}$ model. In [24], an algorithm with runtime $\Theta(D_E)$ (ASYNC) for robots in the Euclidean plane assuming one-axis agreement in the $\mathcal{OBLOT}$ model is introduced. D_E denotes the initial config- uration's Euclidean diameter (the largest distance between any pair of robots). Assuming disoriented robots, the algorithms that achieve a runtime of $o(n^2)$ are developed under the $\mathcal{LUMI}$ model and assume robots that are located on a two-dimensional grid: There exist two algorithms having an asymptotically optimal runtime of $\mathcal{O}(n)$; one algorithm for *closed chains* [1] and another one for arbitrary (connected) swarms [8].

Our Contribution: In this work, we give the first asymptotically optimal algorithm, called CCH, that solves GATHERING of disoriented robots in the Euclidean plane. More precisely, we show that a closed chain of disoriented robots with limited visibility located in the Euclidean plane can be gathered in $\mathcal{O}(n)$ epochs assuming the $\mathcal{LUMI}$ model with a constant number of lights and the ASYNC scheduler. The number of epochs is asymptotically optimal since if the initial configuration forms a straight line with direct neighbors at a maximal distance, at least $\Omega(n)$ epochs are required by *any* algorithm.

Our algorithm assumes that direct chain neighbors are in distance at most 1 (the connectivity range is 1), and robots can always see the positions of 4 robots in each direction along the chain (the viewing range is 4). The viewing range of 4 is a significant improvement over the linear time GATHERING algorithm for closed chains of robots on a grid that uses a viewing range of 11 [1].

The visible lights help to exploit asymmetries in the chain to identify locally unique robots that generate *runs*. We characterize the class of *isogonal configura- tions* based on the theory of isogonal polygons by Grünbaum [18] and show that no locally unique robots exist in these configurations, in contrast to every other configuration. We believe that this characterization is of independent interest as highly symmetric configurations often cause a large runtime. For instance the lower bound of GTC holds for an isogonal configuration [11].

Our approach combines two algorithms into one: An algorithm inspired by [1,22] that gathers non-isogonal configurations in linear time using visible lights and another algorithm for isogonal configurations without using any lights. Note that there might be cases in which both algorithms are executed in parallel due to the limited visibility. An additional rule ensures that both algorithms can be interleaved without hindering each other.

In this version of the paper, we introduce CCH for the $\mathcal{F}$SYNC scheduler. Due to space constraints, the two-step synchronization procedure (mainly based on existing results [3,9]) to make the algorithm work under the ASYNC scheduler while maintaining the runtime of $\Theta(n)$ epochs can be found in the full version [6].

2   Model and Notation

Time Model: Robots operate in discrete LCM (Look, Compute, Move) cycles. Each robot takes a snapshot of its neighborhood during Look, computes a target point in Compute, and moves to this point in Move. We assume a *rigid* movement, robots always reach their target points during Move. A scheduler controls the timing of the executions of the LCM cycles: The cycles can be fully synchronous ($\mathcal{F}$SYNC), or only a subset of all robots participate ($\mathcal{S}$SYNC). Additionally, the cycles can be asynchronous ($\mathcal{A}$SYNC). The executions of the $\mathcal{S}$SYNC and $\mathcal{A}$SYNC schedulers are always fair: All robots execute their cycles infinitely often. The $\mathcal{S}$SYNC and $\mathcal{A}$SYNC schedulers are called to be *k-fair* if, between any two successive cycles of a robot, every other robot is activated at most k times. Time is measured in epochs, i.e., the smallest number of rounds until each robot processed at least one complete LCM cycle.

Robot Model: We consider n robots $r_0, \ldots, r_{n-1}$ located in $\mathbb{R}^2$. Each robot occupies a single point, and there can be multiple robots in the same location. Moreover, the robots are connected in a closed chain topology: Each robot r_i has two direct neighbors: r_{i-1} and r_{i+1} (mod n). The *connectivity range* is assumed to be 1, i.e., two direct neighbors are allowed to have a distance of at most 1. The robots are disoriented and thus do not agree on any axis of their local coordinate systems, and the latter can be arbitrarily rotated and inverted. However, the robots agree on unit distance and can measure distances precisely. Except for their direct neighbors, each robot can see the positions of 4 predecessors and successors along the chain. Moreover, we assume the $\mathcal{LUMI}$ model: Each robot is equipped with a constant number of lights $\ell_1, \ldots, \ell_k$ with color sets $C_1, \ldots, C_k$ and at every point in time each light can have a single color out of its color set (later on, we use names like ℓ_r).[1]

Notation: Let $p_i(t)$ be the position of r_i in round t in a global coordinate system (not known to the robots) and $d(p_i(t), p_j(t)) = \|p_i(t) - p_j(t)\|$. Furthermore, let $u_i(t) = p_i(t) - p_{i-1}(t)$ be the vector pointing from robot r_{i-1} to r_i in round t. The length of the chain is defined as $L(t) := \sum_{i=0}^{n-1} \|u_i(t)\|$. The angle created by anchoring $u_{i+1}(t)$ at the terminal point of $u_i(t)$ is denoted by $\alpha_i(t) = \angle(u_i(t), u_{i+1}(t)) \in [0, \pi]$, $\text{sgn}_i(\alpha_i(t)) \in \{-1, 0, 1\}$ denotes the orientation of $\alpha_i(t)$ from r_i's point of view and $\text{sgn}(\alpha_i(t))$ denotes the orientation in a global coordinate system. $N_i(t)$ denotes the neighborhood of a robot. Throughout the algorithm's execution, two robots may merge and continue to behave as a single robot. For simplicity, r_{i+1} represents the first robot with an index larger i that has not yet merged with r_i (r_{i-1} analogously).

3 Basics

This section explains the basics behind the two sub-algorithms that are part of the CCH. In Sect. 3.1 we characterize isogonal configurations. Section 3.2 explains the basic idea of the asymmetric algorithm: the notion of runs and the movement operations induced by them. The $\mathcal{F}$SYNC scheduler is considered.

---

[1] In the classical $\mathcal{LUMI}$ model [12] each robot is equipped with a single light and color set. Our assumption of multiple lights and color sets can be transferred to the classical setting by choosing a single light with a color set of size at most $2^{\sum_{i=1}^{k} |C_i|}$.

3.1   Isogonal Configurations

There are some configurations in which every robot locally has the same view. We classify these as the *isogonal configurations*. The most prominent example is a configuration where robots are located on the vertices of a regular polygon. However, there are more such configurations. Intuitively, a configuration is isogonal if all angles $\alpha_i(t)$ have the same size and orientation and either all vectors $u_i(t)$ have the same length, or there are two alternating vector lengths. More formally, for some round t, the set of all vectors $u_i(t)$ describes a polygon denoted as the *configuration polygon* of round t. A configuration is then called an *isogonal configuration* in case its configuration polygon is isogonal. Grünbaum classified the isogonal polygons as follows [18]: A polygon P is *isogonal* iff for each pair of vertices there is a symmetry of P that maps the first onto the second [18]. Examples of such polygons can be seen in Figs. 1 and 2. The set of isogonal polygons consists of the *regular stars* and polygons that can be obtained from them by a small translation of the vertices [18]. A *regular star* $\{n/d\}$ $(n, d \in \mathbb{N}, d \leq n)$ is constructed as follows: Consider a circle C and fix an arbitrary radius R of C. Place n points $A_1, \ldots, A_n$ such that A_j is placed on C and forms an angle of $2\pi d/n \cdot j$ with R and connect A_j to $A_{j+1} \bmod n$ by a segment. A configuration is called a *regular star configuration*, in case the configuration polygon is a regular star [18].

For odd n, every isogonal polygon is a regular star. For even n, isogonal polygons that are not regular stars can be constructed as follows: Take any regular star $\{n/d\}$ based on the circle C of radius R. Choose a parameter $0 < t < n/2$ and locate the vertex A_j such that its angle to R is $2\pi/n \cdot (j \cdot d + (-1)^j \cdot t)$. Choosing $t = \frac{n}{2}$ yields the polygon $\{n/d\}$ again. Larger values for t obtain the same polygons as in the interval $[0, \frac{n}{2}]$ [18].

Fig. 1. An isogonal configuration that has two alternating vector lengths and all angles are equal with $n = 12$.

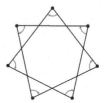

Fig. 2. An isogonal configuration of which the polygon is a star configuration with $n = 7$.

3.2   Sequential Movement with Run-States

A run-state (introduced first in [22]) is a light that is passed along the chain in a fixed direction associated to it. Robots with a run-state perform a movement operation while robots without do not. The movement is sequentialized in a way that in round t the robot r_i executes a movement operation (and neither r_{i-1} nor r_{i+1}), the robot r_{i+1} in round $t+1$ and so on (cf. Fig. 3). The movement of a run-state along the chain is denoted as a *run*. For ease of description, we use the term *run* (instead of run-state) for the rest of the paper. Due to the sequential passing of runs, any moving robot does not have to consider the movements of its direct neighbors since it knows that these do not change their positions. There is one exception: two runs with opposite directions might be located at two neighboring robots. In this case, the two robots move simultaneously. A run can be implemented with two lights: ℓ_r and ℓ_p. The light ℓ_r indicates that a robot has a run in the current round, and ℓ_p is active if a robot had a run in the last round. Thus, each run keeps a fixed direction along the chain; robots that have not activated the light ℓ_p and see one neighbor with an active light ℓ_r will take over the run in the next round by activating ℓ_r. After completing the movement based on the run, ℓ_r is switched off, and ℓ_p is activated such that the robot does not take over the same run in the next round. We use the following notation to speak about runs. For a robot r_i, $run(r_i, t) = true$ if r_i has a run in round t. Additionally, $run(N_i(t)) = \{r_j \in N_i(t)| \ run(r_j, t) = true\}$. Let κ denote an arbitrary run. $r(\kappa, t)$ denotes the robot that has run κ in round t.

Movement Operations Based on Runs: To preserve the connectivity of the chain, CCH ensures that at most two directly neighboring robots move in the same round. This is done by allowing the existence of only two patterns of runs at neighboring robots: Either r_i and neither r_{i-1} nor r_{i+1} has a run (*isolated run*) or r_i and r_{i+1} have runs heading in each other's direction while r_{i-1} and r_{i+2} do not have runs (*joint run-pair*). All other patterns, especially sequences of length at least 3 of neighboring robots having runs, are prohibited.

For robots with a run, there are three kinds of movement operations, the *merge*, the *shorten* and the *hop*. The purpose of the merge is to reduce the number of robots in the chain. It is executed by a robot r_i if its direct neighbors have a distance of at most 1. In this case, r_i is not necessary for the connectivity of the chain and can be safely removed. Removing r_i means that it moves to the position of its next neighbor in the direction of the run, the robots merge their neighborhoods, and both continue to behave as a single robot. The execution of a merge stops a run. The goal of a shorten is to reduce $L(t)$ by moving to the midpoint between the direct neighbors. After executing a shorten, the run stops. In case no significant progress can be made locally, a hop is executed. The purpose of a hop is to exchange two neighboring vectors in the chain. By this, each run is associated with a run-vector. The vector is swapped along the chain until it finds a position at which a merge or a shorten can be executed. For each of the three operations, there is also a *joint* one (*joint hop*, *joint shorten* and *joint merge*), which is a similar operation executed by a joint run-pair. We continue with introducing the formal definitions of all movement operations. For the ease of notation, we assume for an isolated run κ that $r(\kappa, t) = r_i$ and $r(\kappa, t+1) = r_{i+1}$.

(Joint) Hop: Consider the isolated run κ. If r_i executes a hop, $p_i(t + 1) = p_{i+1}(t) - u_i(t)$. The run continues in its direction. A *joint hop* is a similar operation executed by a joint run-pair κ_1 and κ_2 located at robots r_i and r_{i+1}. The new positions are $p_i(t+1) = p_{i-1}(t)+u_{i+2}(t)$ and $p_{i+1}(t+1) = p_{i+2}(t)-u_i(t)$. Both runs continue in their directions and skip the next robot, i.e., in round $t+1$, $r(\kappa_1, t+1) = r_{i+2}$ and $r(\kappa_2, t+1) = r_{i-1}$. See Fig. 4 for a visualization.

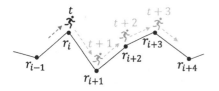

Fig. 3. A run at r_i in round t is passed along the chain.

Fig. 4. Visualization of a hop (above) and a joint hop (below).

(Joint) Shorten: In the *shorten*, a robot r_i with an isolated run moves to the midpoint between its direct neighbors: $p_i(t + 1) = \frac{1}{2} \cdot p_{i-1}(t) + \frac{1}{2} \cdot p_{i+1}(t)$. The run stops. In a *joint shorten* executed by two robots r_i and r_{i+1} with a joint run-pair, the vector $v(t) = p_{i+2}(t) - p_{i-1}(t)$ is subdivided into three parts of equal length. The new positions are $p_i(t + 1) = p_{i-1}(t) + \frac{1}{3} \cdot v(t)$ and $p_{i+1}(t + 1) = p_{i+2}(t) - \frac{1}{3} \cdot v(t)$. Both runs are stopped after executing a joint shorten. See Fig. 5 for a visualization of both operations.

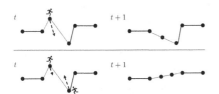
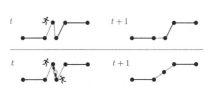

Fig. 5. Visualization of a shorten (above) and a joint shorten (below).

Fig. 6. Visualization of a merge (above) and a joint merge (below).

(Joint) Merge: If r_i executes a *merge*, it moves to $p_{i+1}(t)$. Afterward, the robots r_i and r_{i+1} merge such that their neighborhoods are identical, and they continue to behave like a single robot. In the *joint merge*, the robots r_i and r_{i+1} both move to $\frac{1}{2}p_i(t) + \frac{1}{2}p_{i+1}(t)$. The robots merge there such that they behave as a single robot in the future. All runs that participate in a (joint) merge are immediately stopped (Fig. 6).

4 Closed-Chain-Hopper

Next, we present the CLOSED-CHAIN-HOPPER (CCH) algorithm under the $\mathcal{F}$SYNC scheduler in detail. Our approach consists of two algorithms – one for asymmetric configurations (Sect. 4.2) and one for isogonal configurations (Sect. 4.3). All robots with an isogonal neighborhood move according to the symmetric algorithm. Other robots follow the asymmetric algorithm. To present the algorithm in the most comprehensible way, we use an incremental description. For the sake of completeness, a pseudocode can be found in the full version [6].

4.1 Intuition About the Asymmetric Algorithm

While Sect. 3.2 has already discussed the purpose of the individual movement operations, we add some intuition about how to handle runs in general.

Generation of Runs: In non-isogonal configurations, we identify robots that are regarding their local neighborhood geometrically unique. These robots are assigned an init-state (implemented with a light ℓ_{init}) allowing them to regularly generate new runs. The algorithm always ensures that at most two neighboring robots have an init-state to maintain the connectivity of the chain. Additionally, a robot r_i with an init-state only generates a new run in case no other run is present in its neighborhood.

Stopping of Runs After at Most n Rounds: For the linear runtime of the CCH algorithm, each run must stop after at most n rounds since otherwise the run could cycle multiple times around the chain and hinder other robots with init-states to generate new runs that potentially lead to progress. The following ideas are used to ensure this behavior. Robots with init-states generate two runs at the same time: one run heading in each direction of the chain. Additionally, the robot with the init-state moves to the midpoint between its two direct neighbors before generating the runs. As a consequence, both runs start with opposite run-vectors. Furthermore, a hop is only executed if the angle between two neighboring vectors is larger than $7/8\pi$. Now suppose that the robot starting the two runs lies in the origin of a global coordinate system, and after moving to the midpoint, one of its neighbors lies on the positive x-axis while the other one lies on the negative x-axis. The angle of $7/8\pi$ ensures that the run that starts along the positive x-axis can only move to the right in case of a (joint) hop while the other run can only move to the left. Hence, the two runs cannot meet each other again, and at least one run must stop via a (joint) merge or a (joint) shorten. See Fig. 7 for a visualization. Observe that a threshold of $\frac{\pi}{2}$ would be sufficient to ensure that only one run stops.

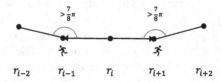

Fig. 7. Two runs generated by r_i with opposite run-vectors. Due to the threshold of $7/8\pi$, the run at r_{i-1} can only execute a hop if r_{i-2} is positioned to the left of r_{i-1} (mirrored for r_{i+1}).

A larger threshold is needed to guarantee that the second run stops after at most n rounds. Suppose the first run (w.l.o.g. the run that moves to the left) stops at the robot r_i. The algorithm needs to ensure that r_i cannot move to the right of the second run to ensure that the second run also stops. For this, the threshold of $7/8\pi$ is crucial as well as an additional rule to ensure that the chain structure cannot change significantly because of (joint) merges. The rule is defined as follows: Each run that leads to a (joint) merge stops all runs in its neighborhood. Additionally, for a constant number of rounds also no new run is generated in this neighborhood. This way, it is ensured that not too many (joint) merges occur during n rounds to guarantee also the second run to stop.

4.2   Asymmetric Algorithm in Detail

The asymmetric algorithm consists of two parts: The generation of new runs and the movement depending on such a run. We start by explaining the movement depending on runs. Assume that the number of robots in the chain is at least 6 and consider an isolated run κ in round t with $r(\kappa, t) = r_i$ and $r(\kappa, t+1) = r_{i+1}$. Then, r_i moves as described in Fig. 8. Given a joint run-pair at robots r_i and r_{i+1}, the robots r_i and r_{i+1} move according to Fig. 9. If the number of robots in the chain is at most 5 (robots can detect this since they can see 4 robots in each direction), the robots move towards the center of the smallest enclosing circle of their neighborhood while ensuring connectivity. More precisely, the robots execute GTC which ensures GATHERING after $\mathcal{O}(1)$ rounds [11].

1. If $d(p_{i-1}(t), p_{i+1}(t)) \leq 1$, r_i: merge.
2. If $d(p_i(t), p_{i+2}(t)) \leq 1$, r_i: Pass the run to r_{i+1}.
3. If $\alpha_i(t) \leq 7/8\pi$, r_i: shorten.
4. Otherwise, r_i: hop.

1. If $d(p_{i-1}(t), p_{i+2}(t)) < 2$,   both: joint merge.
2. If $\alpha_i(t) \leq 7/8\pi$ and $\alpha_{i+1}(t) \leq 7/8\pi$ both: joint shorten
3. If $\alpha_i(t) \leq 7/8\pi$, r_i: shorten.
4. If $\alpha_{i+1}(t) \leq 7/8\pi$, r_{i+1}: shorten.
5. If $\angle(u_i(t), -u_{i+2}(t)) \leq 7/8\pi$: both: joint shorten.
6. Otherwise,   both: joint hop.

Fig. 8. Movement of isolated runs.   **Fig. 9.** Movement of joint run-pairs.

Where to Start Runs? New runs are created by robots with init-states (realized with a light ℓ_{init}). We say $init(r_i) = true$ if r_i has an init-state. Moreover, $init(N_i(t)) = \{r_j \in N_i(t) \mid init(r_j) = true\}$. To generate new init-states, we aim at discovering structures in the chain that are asymmetric. When the surrounding robots observe such a structure, the robot closest to the structure is assigned an init-state. Our rules ensure that at most two neighboring robots have an init-state to keep the distance between runs (essential for maintaining the connectivity). A robot r_i only tries to assign itself a init-state if $init(N_i(t)) = \emptyset$. There are three sources of asymmetry in the chain: Sizes of angles, orientations

of angles, and lengths of vectors. For each source of asymmetry, we introduce
a set of patterns. The next class of patterns is only checked if a complete symmetry regarding the previous pattern is identified. More precisely, a robot only
checks orientation patterns if all angles $\alpha_i(t)$ in its neighborhood are identical.
Similarly, a robot only checks vector length patterns if all angles in its neighborhood have the same size and orientation. Whenever a pattern holds, the robot
observing the pattern assigns itself an init-state if there is no other robot already
assigned an init-state in its neighborhood. If two direct neighbors are assigned
an init-state, they fulfill the same type of pattern and form a *joint init-state*
together. For better readability, we omit the time parameter t, e.g., we write u_i
instead of $u_i(t)$.

Angle Patterns: A robot r_i is assigned an init-state if either $\alpha_{i-1}(t) > \alpha_i(t) \leq \alpha_{i+1}(t)$ or $\alpha_{i-1}(t) \geq \alpha_i(t) < \alpha_{i+1}(t)$ (Fig. 10).

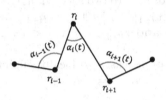

Fig. 10. A configuration in which r_i fulfills the first *Angle Pattern*, i.e., $\alpha_i(t)$ is a local minimum.

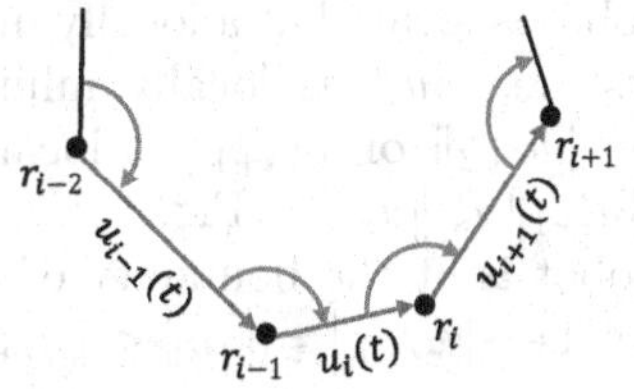

Fig. 11. A configuration in which r_i (and also r_{i-1}) fulfills the first *Vector Length Pattern*, i.e., the length of $u_i(t)$ is a local minimum.

Orientation Patterns: A robot r_i gets an init-state if one of the following patterns is fulfilled.

1. r_i is between three angles that have a different orientation than $\alpha_i(t)$:
   $\operatorname{sgn}_i(\alpha_{i-1}(t)) = \operatorname{sgn}_i(\alpha_{i+1}(t)) = \operatorname{sgn}_i(\alpha_{i+2}(t)) \neq \operatorname{sgn}_i(\alpha_i(t))$
   or $\operatorname{sgn}_i(\alpha_{i-2}(t)) = \operatorname{sgn}_i(\alpha_{i-1}(t)) = \operatorname{sgn}_i(\alpha_{i+1}(t)) \neq \operatorname{sgn}_i(\alpha_i(t))$ (Fig. 12).
2. r_i borders a sequence of at least two angles with the same orientation next to
   a sequence of at least three angles with the same orientation: $\operatorname{sgn}_i(\alpha_{i-1}(t)) = \operatorname{sgn}_i(\alpha_i(t)) \neq \operatorname{sgn}_i(\alpha_{i+1}(t)) = \operatorname{sgn}_i(\alpha_{i+2}(t)) = \operatorname{sgn}_i(\alpha_{i+3}(t))$ or $\operatorname{sgn}_i(\alpha_{i+1}(t)) = \operatorname{sgn}_i(\alpha_i(t)) \neq \operatorname{sgn}_i(\alpha_{i-1}(t)) = \operatorname{sgn}_i(\alpha_{i-2}(t)) = \operatorname{sgn}_i(\alpha_{i-3}(t))$ (Fig. 13).[2]

---

[2] Observe that the viewing range of 4 is based on this pattern: to identify the angles $\alpha_{i+3}(t)$ and $\alpha_{i-3}(t)$, r_i needs to be able to see r_{i-4} and r_{i+4}.

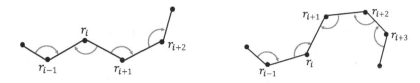

Fig. 12. A configuration in which r_i fulfills the first *Orientation Pattern*.

Fig. 13. A configuration in which r_i fulfills the second *Orientation Pattern*.

Vector Length Patterns: In the patterns, the term *locally minimal* occurs. $\|u_i\|$ is locally minimal means that all other vectors that can be seen by r_i are either larger or have the same length.

1. The robot is located at a locally minimal vector next to two succeeding larger vectors, i.e., $\|u_i\|$ is locally minimal **and** $\|u_{i-1}\| > \|u_i\| < \|u_{i+1}\|$ **and** $\|u_i\| < \|u_{i+2}\|$ **or** $\|u_{i+1}\|$ is locally minimal **and** $\|u_i\| > \|u_{i+1}\| < \|u_{i+2}\|$ **and** $\|u_{i+1}\| < \|u_{i+3}\|$ (Fig. 11).
2. The robot is at the boundary of a sequence of at least two locally minimal vectors, i.e., $\|u_{i-1}\| = \|u_i\| < \|u_{i+1}\|$ **or** $\|u_i\| > \|u_{i+1}\| = \|u_{i+2}\|$.

How to Start Runs? Robots with (joint) init-states try every 9 rounds (counted with a light ℓ_c) to start new runs. A robot r_i with $init(r_i) = true$ only starts a new run if $run(N_i(t)) = \emptyset$ to ensure sufficient distance between runs. The constant 9 is chosen to ensure that a robot (potentially) observes different runs in its neighborhoods each time it tries to start a new run. Additionally, r_i only starts new runs provided $d(p_{i-1}(t), p_{i+1}(t)) > 1$. Otherwise, it executes a merge. Given $d(p_{i-1}(t), p_{i+1}(t)) > 1$, r_i generates two new runs at its direct neighbors with opposite directions as follows: r_i executes a shorten and generates two new runs κ_1 and κ_2 with $r(\kappa_1, t+1) = r_{i+1}$ and $r(\kappa_2, t+1) = r_{i-1}$. Two robots r_i and r_{i+1} with a joint init-state proceed similarly: given $d(p_{i-1}(t), p_{i+2}(t)) \leq 2$, they directly execute a joint merge. Otherwise r_i and r_{i+1} execute a joint shorten and induce two new runs at their direct neighbors with opposite direction.

Blocking of Robots After (Joint) Merges: Suppose the robot r_i (and r_{i+1}) executes a merge (a joint merge). All runs in the neighborhood of r_i (and r_{i+1}) are immediately stopped and all robots in $N_i(t)$ do not start any further runs within the next 4 rounds (the robots are *blocked*, counted with a light ℓ_{block}). Special care has to be taken of init-states. Suppose that a robot r_i executes a merge into the direction of r_{i+1} while having an init-state. The init-state is handled as follows: In case $init(r_{i+2}) = false$ and r_{i+2} does not execute a merge in the same round and $init(r_{i+3}) = true$, the init-state of r_i is passed to r_{i+1}. Otherwise, the state is removed.

4.3   Symmetric Algorithm

A robot r_i moves according to the symmetric algorithm if its neighborhood is isogonal, i.e., all $\alpha_i(t)$ in its neighborhood have the same size and orientation, either all vectors $u_i(t)$ have the same length or have two alternating lengths, $init(N_i(t)) = \emptyset$ and $run(N_i(t)) = \emptyset$. Then, r_i performs one of the two following symmetrical operations. In case all vectors $u_i(t)$ have the same length, it performs a *bisector-operation*. The purpose of the bisector-operation is to move all robots towards the center of the circle surrounding the isogonal polygon described by the configuration. Otherwise, the robot executes a *star-operation*. The goal of the star-operation is to transform an isogonal configuration with two alternating vector lengths into a regular star configuration such that bisector-operations are applied afterward. More formally, in the *bisector-operation*, a robot r_i computes the angle bisector of vectors pointing to its direct neighbors (bisecting the angle of size less than π) and jumps to the point p on the bisector such that $d(p_{i-1}(t), p) = d(p_{i+1}(t), p) = 1$. If $d(p_i(t), p) > \frac{1}{5}$, the robot moves only a distance of $\frac{1}{5}$ towards p. Additionally, the *star-operation* works as follows: Let C be the circle induced by r_i's neighborhood and R its radius. If the diameter of C has a length of at most 2, r_i jumps to the midpoint of C. Otherwise, the robot r_i observes the two circular arcs $L_\alpha = \alpha \cdot R$ and $L_\beta = \beta \cdot R$ connecting itself to its direct neighbors. The angles α and β are the corresponding central angles measured from the radius R_i connecting r_i to the midpoint of C. W.l.o.g. assume $L_\alpha < L_\beta$. r_i jumps to the point on L_β such that L_α is enlarged by $R \cdot ((\beta - \alpha)/4)$.

4.4   Combination of the Algorithms

Intuitively, suppose some robots follow the asymmetric algorithm while others execute the symmetric algorithm. In that case, there are borders at which a robot r_i executes the symmetric algorithm while its direct neighbor does not move at all (since r_i moves according to the symmetric algorithm, the direct neighbor cannot have a run). At these borders, it can happen that the length of the chain increases. To prevent this from happening too often, we make use of an additional visible light ℓ_{sy}. Robots that move according to the symmetric algorithm store this via activating ℓ_{sy}. If any robot detects in the next round that ℓ_{sy} is activated, but its local neighborhood does not fulfill the criterion of being an isogonal configuration, it concludes that the chain is not entirely isogonal. The robot r_c closest to the asymmetry is assigned an init-state to ensure that this does not occur again. As a consequence, r_c and all robots that can see r_c will not execute the symmetric algorithm again until r_c executes a (joint) merge. Hence, this case can occur at most n times (for more details, see [6]).

4.5   Analysis Sketch

This section contains the analysis outline for proving the main theorem (Theorem 1) of the CCH algorithm. The proofs can be found in [6].

Theorem 1. *The* CCH-*algorithm gathers a closed chain of disoriented robots with a connectivity range of* 1 *and viewing range of* 4 *in* $\Theta(n)$ *rounds.*

One of the crucial properties for the correctness of the CCH-algorithm is that it maintains the connectivity of the chain.

Lemma 1. *In every round* t, *the configuration is connected.*

The asymmetric algorithm depends on the generation of runs. We prove that in every asymmetric configuration, at least one pattern is fulfilled.

Lemma 2. *A configuration without any init-state in round* t *becomes either isogonal or at least one init-state exists in round* $t + 1$.

The following is the key lemma of the asymmetric algorithm: Every run started at robot r_i will never visit r_i again in the future. See Sect. 4.1 for an intuition.

Lemma 3. *A run does not visit the same robot twice.*

Next, we count the number of required runs to gather all robots. There can be at most $n - 1$ (joint) merges. To count the number of (joint) shortens, one can see that a (joint) shorten either decreases $L(t)$ by a constant or a vector of length less than $\frac{1}{2}$ has a length of at least $\frac{1}{2}$ afterward. Both cases occur at most a linear number of times.

Lemma 4. *At most* $143\,n$ *runs are required to gather all robots.*

Additionally, we prove that a sufficient number of runs is generated by applying a witness argument. Consider an init-state. After 9 rounds, this state either creates a new run or waits since a run is in its neighborhood. This way, we can count each 9 rounds a new run: Either the robot with the init-state starts a new run or waits because of a different run. Roughly said, we can prove that in k rounds $\approx \frac{k}{9}$ runs exist. This holds until the init-state is removed due to a (joint) merge. Afterward, we continue counting at the next init-state in the direction of the run causing the (joint) merge.

Lemma 5. *A configuration that does not become isogonal gathers in* $\mathcal{O}(n)$ *rounds.*

The first step of the symmetric algorithm transforms an isogonal configuration into a regular star configuration.

Lemma 6. *Given an isogonal configuration with two alternating vector lengths in round* t, *the configuration is a regular star configuration in round* $t + 1$.

To prove a linear runtime for regular star configurations, we analyze the runtime for the regular polygon $\{n/1\}$. In all other regular star configurations, inner angles are smaller, and the robots can move farther towards the center of the surrounding circle.

Lemma 7. *Regular star configurations gather in at most* $30\,n$ *rounds.*

5   Concluding Remarks

For GATHERING of disoriented robots with limited visibility, still, no non-trivial lower runtime bound for oblivious robots is known. A slight exception might be the bound of [19] (see related work), which, however, only holds for comparably small diameters. We conjecture that the linear runtime of the CCH is only possible due to the visible lights, and thus, quadratic lower bounds hold for the oblivious case. However, proving a general lower bound seems to be quite challenging and is left for future research. Additionally, it is still open whether the result can be transferred to robot swarms without a chain topology. The main idea would be to apply the CCH algorithm to the boundaries of the swarm, which form cycles. First attempts show that this approach has problems with maintaining the connectivity to *inner* robots that are not part of a boundary.

References

1. Abshoff, S., Cord-Landwehr, A., Fischer, M., Jung, D., Meyer auf der Heide, F.: Gathering a closed chain of robots on a grid. In: 2016 IEEE International Parallel and Distributed Processing Symposium, IPDPS 2016, Chicago, IL, USA, 23–27 May 2016, pp. 689–699 (2016)
2. Ando, H., Oasa, Y., Suzuki, I., Yamashita, M.: Distributed memoryless point convergence algorithm for mobile robots with limited visibility. IEEE Trans. Robot. Autom. **15**(5), 818–828 (1999)
3. Awerbuch, B.: Complexity of network synchronization. J. ACM **32**(4), 804–823 (1985)
4. Castenow, J., Fischer, M., Harbig, J., Jung, D., Meyer auf der Heide, F.: Gathering anonymous, oblivious robots on a grid. Theor. Comput. Sci. **815**, 289–309 (2020)
5. Castenow, J., Harbig, J., Jung, D., Knollmann, T., Meyer auf der Heide, F.: Brief announcement: gathering in linear time: a closed chain of disoriented and luminous robots with limited visibility. In: Devismes, S., Mittal, N. (eds.) SSS 2020. LNCS, vol. 12514, pp. 60–64. Springer, Cham (2020). https://doi.org/10.1007/978-3-030-64348-5_5
6. Castenow, J., Harbig, J., Jung, D., Knollmann, T., Meyer auf der Heide, F.: Gathering a euclidean closed chain of robots in linear time. CoRR abs/2010.04424 (2021). https://arxiv.org/abs/2010.04424
7. Cohen, R., Peleg, D.: Local spreading algorithms for autonomous robot systems. Theor. Comput. Sci. **399**(1–2), 71–82 (2008)
8. Cord-Landwehr, A., Fischer, M., Jung, D., Meyer auf der Heide, F.: Asymptotically optimal gathering on a grid. In: Proceedings of the 28th ACM Symposium on Parallelism in Algorithms and Architectures, SPAA 2016, Asilomar State Beach/Pacific Grove, CA, USA, 11–13 July 2016, pp. 301–312 (2016)
9. Das, S., Flocchini, P., Prencipe, G., Santoro, N., Yamashita, M.: Autonomous mobile robots with lights. Theor. Comput. Sci. **609**, 171–184 (2016)
10. Degener, B., Kempkes, B., Kling, P., Meyer auf der Heide, F.: Linear and competitive strategies for continuous robot formation problems. ACM Trans. Parallel Comput. **2**(1), 2:1–2:18 (2015)

11. Degener, B., Kempkes, B., Langner, T., Meyer auf der Heide, F., Pietrzyk, P., Wattenhofer, R.: A tight runtime bound for synchronous gathering of autonomous robots with limited visibility. In: SPAA 2011: Proceedings of the 23rd Annual ACM Symposium on Parallelism in Algorithms and Architectures, San Jose, CA, USA, 4–6 June 2011, pp. 139–148. ACM (2011)
12. Di Luna, G., Viglietta, G.: Robots with lights. In: Distributed Computing by Mobile Entities, Current Research in Moving and Computing, pp. 252–277 (2019)
13. Dixon, C., Frew, E.W.: Maintaining optimal communication chains in robotic sensor networks using mobility control. Mob. Netw. Appl. **14**(3), 281–291 (2009)
14. Flocchini, P.: Gathering. In: Distributed Computing by Mobile Entities, Current Research in Moving and Computing, pp. 63–82 (2019)
15. Flocchini, P., Prencipe, G., Santoro, N.: Moving and computing models: robots. In: Distributed Computing by Mobile Entities, Current Research in Moving and Computing, pp. 3–14 (2019)
16. Flocchini, P., Santoro, N., Wada, K.: On memory, communication, and synchronous schedulers when moving and computing. In: OPODIS. LIPIcs, vol. 153, pp. 25:1–25:17. Schloss Dagstuhl - Leibniz-Zentrum für Informatik (2019)
17. Gao, Y., Chen, H., Li, Y., Lyu, C., Liu, Y.: Autonomous wi-fi relay placement with mobile robots. IEEE/ASME Trans. Mechatron. **22**(6), 2532–2542 (2017)
18. Grünbaum, B.: Metamorphoses of polygons. In: The Lighter Side of Mathematics, pp. 35–48 (1994)
19. Izumi, T., Kaino, D., Potop-Butucaru, M., Tixeuil, S.: On time complexity for connectivity-preserving scattering of mobile robots. Theor. Comput. Sci. **738**, 42–52 (2018)
20. Kling, P., Meyer auf der Heide, F.: Convergence of local communication chain strategies via linear transformations: or how to trade locality for speed. In: SPAA 2011: Proceedings of the 23rd Annual ACM Symposium on Parallelism in Algorithms and Architectures, San Jose, CA, USA, 4–6 June 2011, pp. 159–166 (2011)
21. Kling, P., Meyer auf der Heide, F.: Continuous protocols for swarm robotics. In: Flocchini, P., Prencipe, G., Santoro, N. (eds.) Distributed Computing by Mobile Entities. LNCS, vol. 11340, pp. 317–334. Springer, Cham (2019). https://doi.org/10.1007/978-3-030-11072-7_13
22. Kutylowski, J., Meyer auf der Heide, F.: Optimal strategies for maintaining a chain of relays between an explorer and a base camp. Theor. Comput. Sci. **410**(36), 3391–3405 (2009)
23. Nguyen, H.G., Pezeshkian, N., Raymond, S.M., Gupta, A., Spector, J.M.: Autonomous communication relays for tactical robots. In: Proceedings of the 11th International Conference on Advanced Robotics (ICAR), pp. 35–40 (2003)
24. Poudel, P., Sharma, G.: Universally optimal gathering under limited visibility. In: Spirakis, P., Tsigas, P. (eds.) SSS 2017. LNCS, vol. 10616, pp. 323–340. Springer, Cham (2017). https://doi.org/10.1007/978-3-319-69084-1_23
25. Regnault, D., Rémila, E.: Lost in self-stabilization: a local process that aligns connected cells. Theor. Comput. Sci. **736**, 41–61 (2018)
26. Tagliabue, A., Schneider, S., Pavone, M., Agha-mohammadi, A.: Shapeshifter: a multi-agent, multi-modal robotic platform for exploration of titan. CoRR abs/2002.00515 (2020). https://arxiv.org/abs/2002.00515
27. Tekdas, O., Plonski, P.A., Karnad, N., Isler, V.: Maintaining connectivity in environments with obstacles. In: IEEE International Conference on Robotics and Automation, ICRA 2010, Anchorage, Alaska, USA, 3–7 May 2010, pp. 1952–1957 (2010)

Centralised Connectivity-Preserving Transformations for Programmable Matter: A Minimal Seed Approach

Matthew Connor$^{(\boxtimes)}$, Othon Michail, and Igor Potapov

Department of Computer Science, University of Liverpool, Liverpool, UK
{M.Connor3,Othon.Michail,potapov}@liverpool.ac.uk

Abstract. We study a model of programmable matter systems consisting of n devices lying on a 2-dimensional square grid which are able to perform the minimal mechanical operation of rotating around each other. The goal is to transform an initial shape A into a target shape B. We investigate the class of shapes which can be constructed in such a scenario under the additional constraint of maintaining global connectivity at all times. We focus on the scenario of transforming nice shapes, a class of shapes consisting of a central line L where for all nodes u in S either $u \in L$ or u is connected to L by a line of nodes perpendicular to L. We prove that by introducing a minimal 3-node seed it is possible for the canonical shape of a line of n nodes to be transformed into a nice shape of $n-1$ nodes. We use this to show that a 4-node seed enables the transformation of nice shapes of size n into any other nice shape of size n in $O(n^2)$ time. We leave as an open problem the expansion of the class of shapes which can be constructed using such a seed to include those derived from nice shapes.

The full version of the paper with all omitted details is available on arXiv at: https://arxiv.org/abs/2108.09250.

Keywords: Programmable matter · Transformation · Reconfigurable robotics · Shape formation · Centralised algorithms

1 Introduction

Programmable matter refers to matter which can change its physical properties algorithmically. This means that the change is the result following the procedure of an underlying program. The implementation of the program can either be a system level external centralised algorithm or an internal decentralised algorithm executed by the material itself. The model for such systems can be further refined to specify properties that are relevant to real-world applications, for example connectivity, colour [1] and other physical properties. The result of this is the development of programmable materials such as self-assembling DNA molecules [2,3]. In addition, systems which rely on large collectives of identical robots have been developed, for example the Kilobot system [4] and the Robot Pebbles

© Springer Nature Switzerland AG 2021
L. Gąsieniec et al. (Eds.): ALGOSENSORS 2021, LNCS 12961, pp. 45–60, 2021.
https://doi.org/10.1007/978-3-030-89240-1_4

system [5]. Another interesting implementation is Millimotein [6], a system where programmable matter folds itself into arbitrary 3D shapes. The CATOMS system [7,8] is a further implementation which constructs 3D shapes by first creating a "scaffolding structure" as a basis for construction. It is expected that applications in further domains such as molecular computers and self-repairing machines may become apparent in the long-term.

As the development of these systems continues, it becomes increasingly necessary to develop theoretical models which are capable of describing and explaining the emergent properties, possibilities and limitations of such systems in an abstract and fundamental manner. To this end, models have been developed for programmable matter. For example, algorithmic self-assembly [2] focuses on programming molecules like DNA to grow in a controllable way, and the Abstract Tile Assembly Model [9,10], as well as the nubot model [11], have both been developed for this area. Network Constructors [12] uses the Population Protocol model [13] based on a population of finite-automata interacting randomly as the basis for a new model where the automata are able to create networks by forming connections with each other. The latter model is formally equivalent to a restricted version of chemical reaction networks, which "are widely used to describe information processing occurring in natural cellular regulatory networks" [14,15]. Finally there is extensive research into the amoebot model [16–19], where finite automata on a triangle lattice follows a distributed algorithm to achieve a desired goal.

Recent progress in this direction has been made in a previous paper [20], covering questions related to a specific model of programmable matter where nodes exist in the form of a shape on a 2D grid and are capable of performing two specific movements: rotation around each other and sliding a node across two other nodes. They presented 3 problems: transformations with only rotations (Rot-Transformability), transformations with rotations with the restriction that shapes must always remain connected (RotC-Transformability) and transformations with both rotation and sliding movements (RS-Transformability). For Rot-Transformability they prove universal transformation between any pair of colour-consistent shapes which are not blocked, however they leave universal RotC-Transformability as an open problem. Such transformations are highly desirable due to the large numbers of programmable matter systems which rely on the preservation of connectivity. Progress in a very similar direction was made in another paper [21], which used a similar model but allowed for a greater range of movement, for example "leapfrog" and "monkey" movements. They accomplished universal transformation in $O(n^2)$ movements using a "bridging" procedure which added up to 5 nodes during the procedure as necessary in a manner similar to the seed idea from the previous paper.

2   Contribution

We investigate which families of connected shapes can be transformed into each other via rotation movements without breaking connectivity.

We consider the case of programmable matter on a 2D grid which is only capable of performing rotation movements, defined as the 90° rotation of a node a around one of the two vertices of the edge it shares with a neighbouring edge-adjacent node b, so long as the goal and intermediate cells are empty. All nodes must be *edge connected*, meaning that at every time step there must be a path from any arbitrary node to any other node crossing only spaces occupied by nodes via edges. Our algorithms are *centralised*, using external procedures to transform shapes, and therefore focusing on the questions of the feasibility and complexity of the transformations.

We assume the existence of a *seed*, a group of nodes in a shape S which are placed in empty cells neighbouring a shape A to create a new connected shape which is the unification of S and A. Seeds allow shapes which are blocked or incapable of meaningful movement to perform otherwise impossible transformations. The use of seeds was established in a previous work [22], and more recently shown to enable universal reconfiguration in the context of connectivity preserving transformations [21], however to our knowledge there has been no attempt to investigate this problem using a seed which is a connected shape fully introduced before the transformation is initiated.

We first study blocked shapes, where our goal is to define the class of shapes which are *blocked*, or incapable of moving any node without a seed. We show that shapes of this class consist of nodes which are surrounded by diagonal lines in the shape of a rhombus, or overlapping rhombuses which may be connected by lines. We then investigate the transformation of nice shapes. A *Nice Shape* (defined in [20]) is a shape S which has a central line L where for all nodes u in S either $u \in L$ or u is connected to L by a line of nodes perpendicular to L. We provide a lower bound of $\Omega(n^2)$ for transforming a line of n nodes into a nice shape. We show that it is possible to transform such a line into a nice shape of $n - 1$ nodes using a 3-node seed in $O(n^2)$ time. We then demonstrate that it is possible to transform nice shapes of size n into other nice shapes of size n by using the canonical shape of a line and a 4-node seed in $O(n^2)$ time. We provide an algorithm to implement this transformation and give time bounds for it. We then provide further directions for research.

In Sect. 3, we formally define the model of connectivity-preserving programmable matter used in this paper. In Sect. 4 we give our lower bounds. In Sect. 5 we provide our algorithm for the construction of nice shapes where the colour of nodes added to each side of the line always alternates, then generalise first to all nice shapes and second to the class of shapes made up of nice shapes. In Sect. 6 we conclude and give directions for potential future research.

3   Model

The programmable matter systems considered in this paper operate on a 2D square grid, with each cell being uniquely referred to by its $y \geq 0$ and $x \geq 0$ coordinates. Such a system consists of a set S of n modules, called nodes throughout. Each node may be viewed as a spherical module fitting inside a cell. At any given time, each node $u \in S$ occupies a cell in the grid $o(u) = (o_y(u), o_x(u)) = (i, j)$

(where i corresponds to a row and j to a column of the grid) and no two nodes may occupy the same cell. At any given time t, the positioning of nodes on the grid defines an undirected neighboring relation $E(t) \subset S \times S$, where $\{u, v\} \in E$ iff $o_y(u) = o_y(v)$ and $|o_x(u) - o_x(v)| = 1$ or $o_x(u) = o_x(v)$ and $|o_y(u) - o_y(v)| = 1$, that is, if u and v are either horizontal or vertical neighbors on the grid, respectively. We say that two nodes are *edge-adjacent* if such a relation exists between them. A more informative and convenient way to define the system at any time t is the mapping $P_t : \mathbb{N}_{\geq 0} \times \mathbb{N}_{\geq 0} \to \{0, 1\}$, where $P_t(i, j) = 1$ iff cell (i, j) is occupied by a node. At any given time t, $P_t^{-1}(1)$ defines a shape. Such a shape is called *connected* if $(S, E(t))$ defines a connected graph.

In general, shapes can *transform* to other shapes via a sequence of one or more movements of individual nodes. We consider only one type of movement: rotation. In this movement, a single node moves relative to one or more neighboring nodes. A single rotation movement of a node u is a $90°$ rotation of u around one of its neighbors. Let (i, j) be the current position of u and let its neighbor be v occupying the cell $(i - 1, j)$ (i.e., lying below u). Then u can rotate $90°$ clockwise (counterclockwise) around v iff the cells $(i, j+1)$ and $(i-1, j+1)$ $((i, j-1)$ and $(i - 1, j - 1))$, respectively) are both empty. By rotating the whole system $90°$, $180°$, and $270°$, all possible rotation movements are defined analogously.

Let A and B be two connected shapes. We say that A transforms to B via a rotation r, denoted $A \xrightarrow{r} B$, if there is a node u in A such that if u applies r, then the shape resulting after the rotation is B. We say that A transforms in one step to B (or that B is reachable in one step from A), denoted $A \to B$, if $A \xrightarrow{r} B$ for some rotation r. We say that A transforms to B (or that B is reachable from A) and write $A \rightsquigarrow B$, if there is a sequence of shapes $A = C_0, C_1, ..., C_t = B$, such that $C_i \to C_{i+1}$ for all $0 \leq i < t$. Rotation is a reversible movement, a fact that we use in our results.

A line is a connected shape where every node lies on the same column or the same row. A nice shape N is defined as a shape which has a central line L where for all nodes u either $u \in L$ or u is connected to L by a line of nodes perpendicular to L.

Consider a black and red checkered colouring of the 2D grid, like that of a chessboard. Then any shape S consists of $b(S)$ nodes which lie on black cells and $r(S)$ nodes which lie on red cells. Two shapes A and B are *colour consistent* if $b(A) = b(B)$ and $r(A) = r(B)$. Because rotations are the only permissible move, it is impossible for a node to change colour. Therefore, any two shapes for which a solution to Rot-Transformability (and by extension RotC-Transformability) exists must be colour-consistent. If S is not a nice shape and $S = A \cup B$ where A is a nice shape, we call B the *waste* of the shape S. A *configuration* of a shape is an arrangement of the nodes of the shape on a 2D grid where each node is uniquely identifiable.

4   Infeasible Transformations and the Time Lower Bound

In this section, we cover a series of transformations which are infeasible, meaning that they rely on the ability to move $O(n)$ nodes but exist in a scenario where moving at most $O(1)$ is possible. We first define the class of shapes which are *blocked*, meaning there is no potential movement available for any node. We show that it is necessary for a seed to have at least 3 nodes if it is to be connected and to enable the movement of more than 5 nodes in a horizontal line. Finally, we provide a lower bound of $\Omega(n^2)$ movements for the problem of transforming a line into a nice shape.

Two nodes are *vertex-adjacent* if their cells share a common vertex. A node w is an *interior* node if for each of the cells x edge-adjacent to w either there is a node occupying x or there are two nodes y and z such that y and z are edge-adjacent to x and vertex-adjacent to w. A node is an *exterior* node if it is not an interior node.

Theorem 1. *An arbitrary shape A which does not have to preserve connectivity is blocked if and only if there is only 1 node or every exterior node has no edge connections to any other exterior node.*

Proof. A shape with one node is trivially blocked because there is nothing for it to rotate around.

Otherwise, a shape consists of interior nodes connected to each other with the possibility of one-node gaps, surrounded by exterior nodes which form diagonal lines due to the edge-adjacency restriction.

Interior nodes are blocked by the nodes that surround them, either because the grid space is filled by an edge-adjacent node or the two vertex-adjacent nodes block the rotation movement.

Exterior nodes can only rotate around nodes which are edge-connected, which must be interior nodes. The nodes which surround an interior node, whether edge or vertex connected, always block an exterior node from moving, regardless of whether they are interior or exterior nodes themselves.

Conversely, if there is an exterior node which is edge-connected to an exterior node, the exterior node can rotate into the empty space which it provides. □

Theorem 2. *An arbitrary shape B is blocked under the condition of connectivity preservation if it is formed of lines connecting shapes blocked under the conditions of Theorem 1.*

Proof. By Theorem 1, each of the blocked shapes is incapable of movement. Lines are capable of movement, however if any node except the end nodes moves the resulting shape will not be connected. In addition, the nodes within a line do not enable the movement of nodes in a blocked shape as the only node which is capable of new movement is responsible for maintaining connectivity between the blocked shape and the line. Therefore, so long as the end nodes of a line are blocked as they form part of the blocked shape, the nodes of such a shape cannot be moved without breaking connectivity. □

This creates a shape which is similar to one or more overlapping rhombuses. In addition, with the additional condition of connectivity preservation, it is possible for these shapes to be connected by straight lines resembling a geometric cactus form of a cactus graph with these shapes instead of cycles.

4.1   Time and Seed Lower Bounds for Line Transformations

We now give a lower bound on the running time of any strategy which transforms a line into a nice shape.

Lemma 1. *There exists a nice shape such that any strategy which transforms a line of n nodes into the nice shape requires $\Omega(n^2)$ time steps in the worst case.*

Proof. Our goal is to transform the line of length n into a nice shape with two lines of length $n/2$, one horizontal line and one vertical line above and perpendicular to the node in the center of the horizontal line.

Let c be the node in the line which the vertical line will be constructed above.

To avoid breaking connectivity, it is necessary for M to transfer nodes from the ends of the line the space above c. Each of these nodes must perform $\lceil n/2 \rceil$ movements assisted by M. While the distance to the c grows shorter with each node transferred, the line above c grows longer. Therefore, given that $\lceil n/2 \rceil$ nodes must move towards and onto the vertical line, the total number of movements m is given by $\lceil n/2 \rceil \cdot \lceil n/2 \rceil = \Omega(n^2)$.   □

We define a *connected* seed to be a seed which is a connected shape by itself. We next show that a connected seed of size $s < 3$ on a line of length n occupying the grid spaces $(0,0)$ to $(n-1,0)$ can only move a constant number of nodes (5). Note that if the seed is disconnected a 2-node seed is able to enable non-trivial movement by taking positions such that they can work with both ends of the line at the same time. The position of the seed can also be symmetrical so long as the destination of the pairs is also mirrored.

Lemma 2. *Any line of nodes S of length n can move at most five nodes from the line with any k-seed of size $k < 3$ nodes.*

Proof. A line without seeds, with the connectivity preserving condition and with only rotation movements cannot do anything other than rotate the two nodes at each end point. With a one node seed, the only possible action is for the node to be positioned in the cell $(2,1)$ (or any equivalent symmetrical position) and rotate the end node at $(0,0)$ to $(1,1)$ to form a pair. This is equivalent to having a two node seed on a line of length $n-1$. With a two node seed, it can only interact with an end node and with each node in the positions $(0,1),(1,1)$ or $(1,1),(2,1)$ (or any symmetrical position). In the former case, the end node can only rotate around the node in $(0,1)$ because it depends on it to maintain connectivity. In the latter case, the end node can rotate to $(0,1)$. This allows the node in $(1,0)$ and the node next to it (i.e. in $(2,0)$) to rotate. However, they cannot move much without breaking connectivity thanks to a reliance on the nodes in $(3,0)$ and $(3,1)$ for connectivity which restricts movement.

Therefore, if we start with a one node seed, form a two node pair, rotate the node in $(0,1)$ to $(2,1)$, move the two nodes in $(1,0)$ and $(2,0)$ and the node at the other end of the line, we have exhausted all possibilities to maximise the number of moving nodes without using a seed of size $k \geq 3$.   □

5   Transformation for Nice Shapes

In this section, we investigate the possibilities related to the transformation of shapes which are connectivity preserving. We focus on the problem of converting a nice shape of $O(n)$ nodes into any other nice shape of $O(n)$ nodes using an $O(1)$ seed. We do this by showing we can transform the canonical shape of a line with $O(n)$ nodes into any nice shape. Due to reversibility, it follows that any nice shape can be transformed into such a line, and then into another nice shape. More specifically, we first provide a solution for the variant of this problem (which we call M) where all the lines perpendicular to a central line L in the nice shape are such that the node at the end of each line is the opposite colour to the node at the end of its nearest neighbouring lines. We then prove that slight modifications to the method of construction allow for the class of all nice shapes to be constructed. Our methods construct a shape which is a union of a nice shape with constant waste $O(1)$.

We start with a shape S which is a line of length n occupying the cells $(0,0)$ to $(n-1,0)$. We add a connected 3-node seed to the line as this is the minimum size which allows us to move more than 5 nodes without breaking connectivity. It is possible for our results to apply to a disconnected 2-node seed with a slightly modified procedure but with higher waste. We place the seed in a specific position as the connected 3-node seed is incapable of movement. We sketch the line to nice shape proof in the following subsection.

5.1   Line to Nice Shape

Our first result is the following theorem:

Theorem 3. *A line of length n can be transformed to any given nice shape in the class M_{n_1} using a 3-node seed in $O(n^2)$ time.*

To solve this problem, we follow a strategy of having nodes rotate onto the horizontal line with the help of the 3 node seed and then constructing lines perpendicular to the horizontal line using the nodes. Additionally, we move 4 nodes below the line and on the opposite side to the seed. These nodes can then replicate the behaviour of the seed on the other side of the line, allowing for construction to occur below as well as above the line. Because their behaviour is the same, we refer to the seed and the group of nodes on the other side of the line as *builders*. As a result, the horizontal line becomes the central line L of the nice shape, and the vertical lines become the lines of nodes perpendicular to L. Finally, the seed and a single node which aid construction cannot be incorporated into the final shape and are discarded as waste.

To prove that this is possible, we define three algorithmic procedures. The first procedure, *RaiseNodes*, allows a builder to move two nodes at a time from the horizontal line. These nodes combine with the builder to form a 5 node cluster. This cluster can be broken if necessary into a 3 node line and a 2 node line, allowing the 2 node line to move by having each node rotate around the other. The second procedure, *MirrorSeed*, is the procedure for creating the second builder below the horizontal line. It accomplishes this by moving two of the 2 node lines to the end of the horizontal and then rotating nodes in such a way that the four nodes are "pushed" through the horizontal and to the other side. The final procedure, *DepositNodes*, collects nodes from the horizontal line and deposits them in any reachable location. We will show that the set of reachable locations enables the construction of any nice shape.

5.2 RaiseNodes

We use a 3 node seed in the cells $(1,1)$, $(2,1)$, $(3,1)$ for our operations as, by Lemma 2, a two node seed is incapable of helping nodes to move.

We call the first operation *RaiseNodes*. For this operation we use the 3 node seed to move nodes from the horizontal line such that they are on top of the horizontal line as a pair. In the process, the 3 node seed moves along the horizontal line such that each node moves from its original position $(x,1)$ to $(x+1,1)$. The result can also be interpreted as a shape consisting of 5 nodes, which we refer to as a 5-node seed. Moving the pair of nodes once they are on the line is a trivial process. Each node rotates around the other node, alternating their relative positions within the two node shape. As a result, the process can be repeated so long as the pair of nodes on the line can be moved out of the way by rotating around each other to create space.

The following lemma shows that these operations are possible.

Lemma 3. *Using a 3 node seed in the cells $(1,1)$ to $(3,1)$, it is possible to move 2 nodes from the line such that the 3-node seed is converted into a 5-node seed.*

Figure 1 below depicts the process.

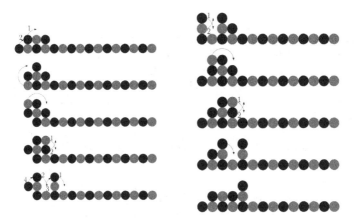

Fig. 1. Raising nodes from the line. Red nodes, used throughout the paper, appear grey in print. (Color figure online)

5.3   MirrorSeed

We now use RaiseNodes for our next operation, *MirrorSeed*, to place four nodes at the opposite side of the line (i.e. $(n-4,1)$ to $(n-1,1)$) and then push them through and below the line, creating a four node mirror of our original seed in the cells $(n-4,-1)$ to $(n-1,-1)$. Having a mirror of the original seed allows us to perform construction operations on the bottom of the horizontal line. We do this in 3 steps: raise four nodes using RaiseNodes twice, position the four nodes at the end of the line and rotate the nodes and those at the end of the line such that the four nodes move through (not around) the line and to the other side.

Lemma 4. *Using a 3 node seed in the cells $(1,1)$ to $(3,1)$, above a line L of length n it is possible to create a 4-node line in the cells immediately below the nodes $(n-4,0)$ to $(n-1,0)$.*

Proof. We first move the 4 leftmost nodes in S, S_0 to S_3 to the top of the line. We do this by raising S_0 and S_1, and then repeat the procedure a second time with the next two nodes S_2 and S_3. We now have 4 nodes a square above the end of the line. By rotating them around each other in pairs we can place them in the cells $(n-4,1)$ to $(n-1,1)$. We can then "push" the nodes to the other side of S by follow the procedure depicted in Fig. 2. The result is four nodes in the cells $(n-4,-1)$ to $(n-1,-1)$ □

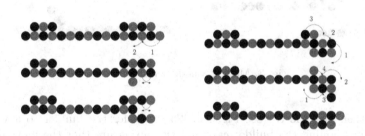

Fig. 2. Pushing the nodes through the line.

5.4   DepositNode

Next, we present *DepositNode*, a sub-procedure using the 3 node seed to create a 5 node shape and move a node from the horizontal line to any empty cell which the shape can reach, provided the 5 node shape has the correct colouring, defined as having 3 nodes of the colour which will fill the cell.

We raise two nodes from the line, use this shape to deposit a node and move the other 4 nodes as a square back to the left. By leaving the cells above and below the two leftmost nodes in the line empty we can rotate the leftmost node, merging with the square to create a new 5 node shape. We can therefore repeat the process of moving for each node one at a time. In addition, this sub-procedure can be applied to the builder on the other side of the line.

Our strategy is to demonstrate that the moves each builder can make are sufficient to be able to construct a nice shape. We do this by providing examples of the situations which appear when constructing such shapes and proving that the movement we intend to accomplish is possible. In this example, we show that it is possible to deposit the node at the end of the horizontal line.

Lemma 5. *A 3 node seed on any line S of length n, where n is an even number, can transfer a node the other end of the line.*

See Fig. 3 for an example execution.

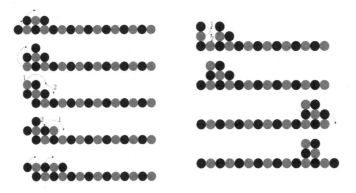

Fig. 3. Moving a node across the line.

It is then possible to (see Fig. 6 in [23]) transfer the builder to a vertical line. By positioning the builder carefully we can ensure that the movement is equivalent to crossing a line of even length. Therefore the process of adding another node can be performed on vertical lines, such as the ones we will build for our nice shapes.

To build any vertical line, we must first show that it is possible for DepositNode to construct lines of length 4 above the horizontal line. After that, because it is possible for the builders to shift onto a 4 node line, the situation becomes that of depositing a node at the end of a line.

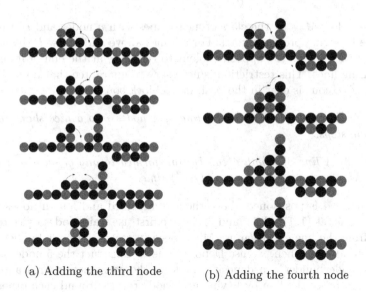

(a) Adding the third node   (b) Adding the fourth node

Fig. 4. Adding the last two nodes.

Lemma 6. *Using a 3 node seed in the cells $(1,1)$ to $(3,1)$, above a line L of length n it is possible to create another line of length 4 above any $u_i \in L$.*

Proof. For this situation we have two scenarios: one where the colouring is correct and another where it is incorrect. We first consider the correct colouring and then show how to deal with the incorrect colouring.

For the first node, we simply deposit the node using DepositNode above u_i. The next node is deposited above u_{i-1} and rotated to be above the first. The next two nodes are more difficult, so we have provided Fig. 4 to illustrate the process.

In the case where the colouring is incorrect, we deposit the incorrect node anywhere to the right directly above L and collect a second node from L. We can then merge the 5 node shape with the node we deposited temporarily to create 6 node shape. Then 5 nodes of the correct colouring can split from the shape we created and deposit the node.

The 4 node square can then return to the node that was left behind and use it as the next node for depositing. In this way, the 5 node shape is capable of "selecting" its colouring.   □

5.5   Construction of a Subset of Nice Shapes

We now have all of the lemmas that are necessary to prove that it is possible to construct a specific subset of the class of nice shapes. We first present an upper bound on the time for constructing nice shapes using our algorithm. We then prove that using our sub-procedures we can construct a nice shape using a line and a 3-node seed, and finally we show that process is reversible using a

4-node seed. Let M_{n_w} be the class of nice shapes with n nodes and w waste for which the following property holds: For all lines above and below L the node at the end of each line is the opposite colour to the node at the end of its nearest neighbouring lines. This restriction is necessary to guarantee that no node with the "wrong" colour is ever in the position to block construction.

Lemma 7. *The transformation of a line of n nodes into a nice shape requires $O(n^2)$ time steps.*

Theorem 3. *A line of length n can be transformed to any given nice shape in the class M_{n_1} using a 3-node seed in $O(n^2)$ time.*

Proof. The seed is positioned above the second, third and fourth nodes in the horizontal line, at $(1, 1)$, $(2, 1)$, and $(3, 1)$. We first use RaiseNodes twice to raise 4 nodes from the line and then use MirrorSeed to create a 4 node builder below the horizontal line. Then, we use DepositNode to construct the 5 node builder.

The 5 node builder can deposit a node in the construction area and move back to the end of the line by having each node rotate around each other. It is then able to take another node from the horizontal line by positioning itself two node spaces away from the end of the line and rotating the last node such that it is connected to the seed.

We are therefore able to follow a procedure for constructing vertical lines one node at a time. The construction proceeds for each side of L in phases $0 \leq i \leq |L|$, where phase i corresponds to the construction of the column above the node L_i.

The entire process is mirrored for the bottom of the shape using DepositNode for the builder on the bottom. The builder on the bottom waits until the builder on the top is finished and then starts lifting nodes from the same side of the line. By moving the other builder slightly it is possible to avoid the situation where it disconnects from the line.

Finally, one of the builders places the nodes of the other builder, and is then discarded, leading to a waste of 1 node. By Lemma 7, the whole process is completed in $O(n^2)$ time.   □

Theorem 4. *A nice shape in the class M_n can be transformed to any given nice shape from M_n using a 4-node seed in $O(n^2)$ time.*

Proof. The transformation can be made reversible by assuming that the 4 nodes which are discarded at the end of the transformation constitute a 4 node seed for transforming the nice shape into a line. We can then construct a line of length n by following the process in reverse, and from there construct a nice shape of size n.   □

5.6   Construction of Any Nice Shape

We now show how to extend this to the class of all nice shapes. We follow a broadly similar procedure to the one in Theorem 3. The key difference is that we first create the *foundation*, a layer of nodes above and below the horizontal line. We place a node at the start of every vertical line which starts with the same node colour that the previous vertical line built would end with. We then proceed as normal. First we prove that the foundation is sufficient for constructing any colour-consistent nice shape. Then we prove that the 5 node builder is capable of crossing the foundation to deposit nodes.

Lemma 8. *For any nice shape constructed from a line, for all lines perpendicular to L with an odd number of nodes there is at most one line which cannot be paired with another line which ends in the other colour.*

Proof. We have the initial line which is either odd or even. We can move nodes out in pairs to build lines. It is possible to build lines which are odd by splitting a pair and distributing its nodes between two odd lines. Such lines can therefore be paired.

However, there are two ways that an extra odd line can be created. First, when the horizontal line is odd, we can support one odd vertical line by extracting the extra node. Second, when the horizontal line is even, we can also split a pair with the horizontal, making it odd. If both are attempted at the same time the resulting lines will end in different colours and therefore can be paired. As a result, at most one line which is odd cannot be paired. □

Lemma 9. *Any 5 node builder which is constructing lines can cross the foundation to do so.*

Proof. When moving a builder carrying a node across the foundation, there are 3 scenarios the builder can encounter.

In the first scenario, there is a node in (x, y) which is the same colour as the node being carried in $(x - 2, y)$. In this case, the builder must deposit the node in $(x - 4, y)$ and collect the node it has encountered. Then, when the builder is returning without carrying a node, it must shift the node it deposited from $(x - 4, y)$ to (x, y).

In the second scenario, the node at (x, y) is a different colour and the cell $(x + 1, y)$ is empty. For this scenario, the node which is being carried rotates into $(x + 1, y)$. Then the builder's nodes rotate around each other to be above $(x - 1, y - 1)$ and $(x - 2, y - 1)$. Then the top two nodes in $(x - 1, y + 1)$ and $(x - 2, y + 1)$ rotate around each other such that the node in $(x + 1, y)$ is the node being carried by the 5 node builder.

In the third scenario, there is a series of nodes beginning with the node (x, y), with alternating colours blocking the builder. In this case, we first identify the node n which is the node furthest right in the series with the same colour as the node the builder is carrying. Then the top two nodes of the builder in $(x - 2, y + 1)$ and $(x - 3, y + 1)$ rotate until they are positioned such that they form a 5 node builder with n.

Any foundation must consist of any of these three scenarios arranged in a sequence. Therefore, by following the correct process in the scenario the builder

crosses the foundation and places a node of the correct colour. Then while returning any nodes deposited can be shifted, creating a new foundation which is
equivalent to the original.   □

We are now in the position to prove our main results, that it is possible to
construct any nice shape from any other nice shape using a seed of size 4. Let N_n
be the subclass of nice shapes which is colour consistent to a line of length n.

Theorem 5. *A line of length n can be transformed to any given nice shape*
N_{n-1} using a 3-node seed in $O(n^2)$ time.

Proof. The initial steps of the procedure are as in Theorem 3. When we have
created both builders, we then create the foundation by placing each node in the
foundation from right to left. We alternate between the builders as necessary.
By Lemma 8, we know that the scenario where the colours we need to place
do not match what is available will never occur. By Lemma 9, we know that
the existence of the foundation does not impede construction. We are then able
to follow a procedure for constructing vertical lines as before. Finally, the last
builder is discarded as before.   □

Theorem 6. *A nice shape of n nodes can be transformed to any given nice shape*
N_n using a 4-node seed in $O(n^2)$ time.

6 Conclusions

Some open problems follow from the findings of our work. The most obvious is
expanding the class of shapes which can be constructed using minimal seeds to
those which can be derived from nice shapes. This could possibly be expanded by
transferring nodes along the perimeter of a nice shape with the help of bridging
nodes or by compressing them. In the long run this could lead to characterisa-
tions of the classes of connectivity-preserving shapes which can be constructed
using only rotation for a given seed. Another important question is the impact
that switching to a decentralised model of transformations will have on the
results, especially because most programmable matter systems which model real-
world applications implement programs in this way. This in turn could lead to
real-world applications for the efficient transformation of programmable matter
systems.

References

1. Chen, X., et al.: Magnetochromatic polydiacetylene by incorporation of Fe3O4
   nanoparticles. Angew. Chem. Int. Ed. **50**(24), 5486–5489 (2011)
2. Doty, D.: Theory of algorithmic self-assembly. Commun. ACM **55**, 78–88 (2012)
3. Rothemund, P.W.K.: Folding DNA to create nanoscale shapes and patterns. Nature
   440, 297–302 (2006)
4. Rubenstein, M., Cornejo, A., Nagpal, R.: Programmable self-assembly in a
   thousand-robot swarm. Science **345**, 795–799 (2014)

5. Gilpin, K., Knaian, A., Rus, D.: Robot pebbles: one centimeter modules for programmable matter through self-disassembly. In: 2010 IEEE International Conference on Robotics and Automation, pp. 2485–2492, May 2010. ISSN: 1050–4729

6. Knaian, A.N., et al.: The Milli-Motein: a self-folding chain of programmable matter with a one centimeter module pitch. In: 2012 IEEE/RSJ International Conference on Intelligent Robots and Systems, pp. 1447–1453, October 2012. ISSN: 2153–0866

7. Thalamy, P., Piranda, B., Bourgeois, J.: Distributed self-reconfiguration using a deterministic autonomous scaffolding structure. In: Proceedings of the 18th International Conference on Autonomous Agents and MultiAgent Systems, AAMAS 2019, (Montreal QC, Canada), pp. 140–148. International Foundation for Autonomous Agents and Multiagent Systems, May 2019

8. Thalamy, P., Piranda, B., Bourgeois, J.: 3D coating self-assembly for modular robotic scaffolds. In: 2020 IEEE/RSJ International Conference on Intelligent Robots and Systems (IROS), pp. 11688–11695, October 2020. ISSN: 2153–0866

9. Rothemund, P.W., Winfree, E.: The program-size complexity of self-assembled squares (extended abstract). In: Proceedings of the Thirty-Second Annual ACM Symposium on Theory of Computing, STOC '00, (Portland, Oregon, USA), pp. 459–468. Association for Computing Machinery, May 2000

10. Winfree, E.: Algorithmic self-assembly of DNA. Ph.D. thesis, California Institute of Technology, June 1998

11. Woods, D., Chen, H.L., Goodfriend, S., Dabby, N., Winfree, E.: Active self-assembly of algorithmic shapes and patterns in polylogarithmic time. In: Proceedings of the 4th Conference on Innovations in Theoretical Computer Science, ITCS '13, (Berkeley, California, USA), pp. 353–354. Association for Computing Machinery, January 2013

12. Michail, O., Spirakis, P.G.: Simple and efficient local codes for distributed stable network construction. Distrib. Comput. **29**(3), 207–237 (2015). https://doi.org/10.1007/s00446-015-0257-4

13. Angluin, D., Aspnes, J., Diamadi, Z., Fischer, M.J., Peralta, R.: Computation in networks of passively mobile finite-state sensors. Distrib. Comput. **18**, 235–253 (2006)

14. Soloveichik, D., Cook, M., Winfree, E., Bruck, J.: Computation with finite stochastic chemical reaction networks. Nat. Comput. **7**, 615–633 (2008). https://doi.org/10.1007/s11047-008-9067-y

15. Doty, D.: Timing in chemical reaction networks. In: Proceedings of the 2014 Annual ACM-SIAM Symposium on Discrete Algorithms (SODA), Proceedings, pp. 772–784. Society for Industrial and Applied Mathematics, December 2013

16. Derakhshandeh, Z., Dolev, S., Gmyr, R., Richa, A.W., Scheideler, C., Strothmann, T.: Amoebot - a new model for programmable matter. In: Proceedings of the 26th ACM Symposium on Parallelism in Algorithms and Architectures, SPAA '14, (Prague, Czech Republic), pp. 220–222. Association for Computing Machinery, June 2014

17. Daymude, J.J., et al.: On the runtime of universal coating for programmable matter. Nat. Comput. **17**(1), 81–96 (2017). https://doi.org/10.1007/s11047-017-9658-6

18. Derakhshandeh, Z., Gmyr, R., Richa, A.W., Scheideler, C., Strothmann, T.: An algorithmic framework for shape formation problems in self-organizing particle systems. In: Proceedings of the Second Annual International Conference on Nanoscale Computing and Communication, NANOCOM' 15, (Boston, MA, USA), pp. 1–2. Association for Computing Machinery, September 2015

19. Derakhshandeh, Z., Gmyr, R., Richa, A.W., Scheideler, C., Strothmann, T.: Universal shape formation for programmable matter. In: Proceedings of the 28th ACM Symposium on Parallelism in Algorithms and Architectures, SPAA 2016, (Pacific Grove, California, USA), pp. 289–299. Association for Computing Machinery, July 2016

20. Almethen, A., Michail, O., Potapov, I.: Pushing lines helps: Efficient universal centralised transformations for programmable matter. Theoret. Comput. Sci. **830–831**, 43–59 (2020)

21. Akitaya, H.A., et al.: Universal reconfiguration of facet-connected modular robots by pivots: the O(1) Musketeers. Algorithmica **83**, 1316–1351 (2021)

22. Michail, O., Skretas, G., Spirakis, P.: On the transformation capability of feasible mechanisms for programmable matter. J. Comput. Syst. Sci. **102**, 18–39 (2019)

23. Connor, M., Michail, O., Potapov, I.: Centralised connectivity-preserving transformations for programmable matter: a minimal seed approach. arXiv:2108.09250 [cs], August 2021

Distributed Coloring and the Local Structure of Unit-Disk Graphs

Louis Esperet[1]([✉]), Sébastien Julliot[1], and Arnaud de Mesmay[2]

[1] Laboratoire G-SCOP, CNRS, Univ. Grenoble Alpes, Grenoble, France
louis.esperet@grenoble-inp.fr
[2] LIGM, CNRS, Univ. Gustave Eiffel, ESIEE Paris, 77454 Marne-la-Vallée, France
arnaud.de-mesmay@univ-eiffel.fr

Abstract. Coloring unit-disk graphs efficiently is an important problem in the global and distributed settings, with applications in radio channel assignment problems when the communication relies on omni-directional antennas of the same power. In this context it is important to bound not only the complexity of the coloring algorithms, but also the number of colors used. In this paper, we consider two natural distributed settings. In the location-aware setting (when nodes know their coordinates in the plane), we give a constant time distributed algorithm coloring any unit-disk graph G with at most $(3 + \epsilon)\omega(G) + 6$ colors, for any constant $\epsilon > 0$, where $\omega(G)$ is the clique number of G. This improves upon a classical 3-approximation algorithm for this problem, for all unit-disk graphs whose chromatic number significantly exceeds their clique number. When nodes do not know their coordinates in the plane, we give a distributed algorithm in the LOCAL model that colors every unit-disk graph G with at most $5.68\omega(G)$ colors in $O(\log^3 \log n)$ rounds. Moreover, when $\omega(G) = O(1)$, the algorithm runs in $O(\log^* n)$ rounds. This algorithm is based on a study of the local structure of unit-disk graphs, which is of independent interest. We conjecture that every unit-disk graph G has average degree at most $4\omega(G)$, which would imply the existence of a $O(\log n)$ round algorithm coloring any unit-disk graph G with (approximatively) $4\omega(G)$ colors.

Keywords: Distributed algorithms · Graph coloring · Unit-disk graphs

1 Introduction

A *unit-disk graph* is a graph G whose vertex set is a collection of points $V \subseteq \mathbb{R}^2$, and such that two vertices $u, v \in V$ are adjacent in G if and only if

The authors are partially supported by ANR Projects GATO (ANR-16-CE40-0009-01), GrR (ANR-18-CE40-0032), MIN-MAX (ANR-19-CE40-0014) and SoS (ANR-17-CE40-0033), and by LabEx PERSYVAL-lab (ANR-11-LABX-0025). The full version of the paper is available on arXiv [7]. It contains some proofs that are omitted in this version together with an additional appendix discussing a Fourier analytical approach toward Conjecture 1.

© Springer Nature Switzerland AG 2021
L. Gąsieniec et al. (Eds.): ALGOSENSORS 2021, LNCS 12961, pp. 61–75, 2021.
https://doi.org/10.1007/978-3-030-89240-1_5

$\|u - v\| \leqslant 1$, where $\| \cdot \|$ denotes the Euclidean norm. Unit-disk graphs are a classical model of wireless communication networks, and are a central object of study in distributed algorithms (see the survey [23] for an extensive bibliography on this topic). A classical way to design distributed communication protocols avoiding interferences is to find a proper coloring of the underlying unit-disk graph: the protocol then lets each vertex of the first color communicate with their neighbors, then each vertex of the second color, etc. Clearly the efficiency of the protocol depends on the number of colors used, so it is important to minimize the total number of colors (in addition to optimizing the complexity of the distributed coloring algorithm).

The *chromatic number* of a graph G, denoted by $\chi(G)$, is the smallest number of colors in a proper coloring of G. The *clique number* of G, denoted by $\omega(G)$, is the largest size of a clique (a set of pairwise adjacent vertices) in G. Note that for any graph G we have $\omega(G) \leqslant \chi(G)$, but the gap between the parameters can be arbitrarily large in general (see [22] for a recent survey on the relation between ω and χ for various graph classes). However, for unit-disk graphs it is known that $\chi(G) \leqslant 3\omega(G) - 2$ [19] (see also [11] for a different proof), and improving the multiplicative constant 3 is a longstanding open problem. It should be noted that while computing $\chi(G)$ for a unit-disk graph G is NP-hard, computing $\omega(G)$ for a unit-disk graph G can be done in polynomial time [5].

In the LOCAL model, introduced by Linial [16], the graph G that we are trying to color models a communication network: its vertices are processors of infinite computational power and its edges are communication links between (some of) these nodes. The vertices exchange messages with their neighbors in a certain number of synchronous rounds of communication (the round complexity), and then (in the case of graph coloring) each vertex outputs its color in a proper coloring of G. When in addition each vertex knows its coordinates in the plane, we call the model the location-aware LOCAL model (more details about these models will be given in Sect. 2.1).

In the location-aware LOCAL model, the following is a classical result [13, 14, 25, 26] (see also [23] for a survey on *local algorithms*, which are algorithms that run in a constant number of rounds).

Theorem 1. ([13,14,25,26]). *A coloring of any unit-disk graph G with at most $3\chi(G)$ colors can be obtained in a constant number of rounds by a deterministic distributed algorithm in the location-aware LOCAL model.*

We prove the following complementary result, which improves the number of colors as soon as $\omega(G)$ is sufficiently large, and $\chi(G)$ itself is significantly larger than $\omega(G)$. This result can be seen as an efficient distributed implementation of the proof of [11] that unit-disk graphs satisfy $\chi \leqslant 3\omega$.

Theorem 2. *For any $\epsilon > 0$, a coloring of any unit-disk graph G with at most $(3 + \epsilon)\omega(G) + 6$ colors can be computed in $O(1/\epsilon)$ rounds by a deterministic deterministic algorithm in the location-aware LOCAL model.*

As mentioned above we have $\chi(G) \geqslant \omega(G)$ for any graph G, so this result improves upon Theorem 1 as soon as $\omega(G)$ is sufficiently large and $\chi(G) \geqslant (1 + \delta)\omega(G)$, for some fixed $\delta > 0$. It was proved that for different models of random unit-disk graphs the ratio between the chromatic number and the clique number is equal to $\frac{2\sqrt{3}}{\pi} \approx 1.103$ with high probability [17,18], so this shows that Theorem 2 outperforms Theorem 1 for almost all unit-disk graphs (with respect to these distributions).

Given two integers $p \geqslant q \geqslant 1$, a $(p:q)$-coloring of a graph G is an assignment of q-element subsets of $[p]$ to the vertices of G, such that the sets assigned to any two adjacent vertices are disjoint. The fractional chromatic number $\chi_f(G)$ is defined as the infimum of $\{\frac{p}{q} \mid G$ has a $(p:q)$-coloring$\}$ [21] (it can be proved that this infimum is indeed a minimum). Observe that a $(p:1)$-coloring is a (proper) p-coloring, and that for any graph G, $\omega(G) \leqslant \chi_f(G) \leqslant \chi(G)$. The fractional chromatic number is often used in scheduling as an alternative to the chromatic number when resources are fractionable, which is the case for communication protocols. It was proved in [8] that for any unit-disk graph G, $\chi_f(G) \leqslant 2.155\,\omega(G)$. Here we give an efficient distributed implementation of this result, up to a small additive constant.

Theorem 3. *For any sufficiently large integer q, a $(p:q)$-coloring of any unit-disk graph G with $\frac{p}{q} \leqslant 2.156\,\omega(G) + 4.31$ can be computed in $O(1)$ rounds by a deterministic distributed algorithm in the* **location-aware LOCAL** *model.*

We now turn to the abstract setting, where vertices do not have access to their coordinates in the plane. For a real number $n > 0$, let $\log^* n$ be the number of times we have to iterate the logarithm, starting with n, to reach a value in $(0,1]$. Since paths are unit-disk graphs and coloring n-vertex paths with a constant number of colors takes $\Omega(\log^* n)$ rounds in the **LOCAL** model [16], coloring unit-disk graphs of bounded clique number with a bounded number of colors also takes $\Omega(\log^* n)$ rounds in the **LOCAL** model. Recalling that for any unit-disk graph G, $\omega(G) \leqslant \chi(G) \leqslant 3\omega(G)$, a natural question is the following.

Question 1. What is the minimum real $c > 0$ such that a coloring of any n-vertex unit-disk graph G with $c \cdot \omega(G)$ colors can be obtained in $O(\log^* n)$ rounds in the **LOCAL** model?

Using the folklore result that any unit-disk graph G has maximum degree at most $6\omega(G)$ (see [11]), it can be proved that unit-disk graphs can be colored with $6\omega(G)$ colors efficiently in the **LOCAL** model. We obtain the following improved version by studying the local structure of unit-disk graphs, using techniques that might be of independent interest.

Theorem 4. *Every unit-disk graph G can be colored with at most $5.68\,\omega(G)$ colors by a randomized distributed algorithm in the* **LOCAL** *model, running in $O(\log^3 \log n)$ rounds w.h.p. Moreover, if $\omega(G) = O(1)$, the coloring can be obtained deterministically in $O(\log^* n)$ rounds.*

In relation to Question 1, it is natural to study the power of graph coloring algorithms in unit-disk graphs in a different (less restrictive) range of round complexity.

Question 2. What is the minimum real $c > 0$ such that a coloring of any n-vertex unit-disk graph G with $c \cdot \omega(G)$ colors can be obtained in $O(\log n)$ rounds in the LOCAL model?

An interesting property of the $O(\log n)$ range of round complexity (compared to the $O(\log^* n)$ range) is that it allows to solve coloring problems for graphs of bounded average degree (rather than bounded maximum degree). The *average degree* of a graph G is the average of its vertex degrees. The *maximum average degree* of a graph G is the maximum average degree of a subgraph H of G. In [1], Barenboim and Elkin gave, for any $\epsilon > 0$, a deterministic distributed algorithm coloring n-vertex graphs of maximum average degree d with at most $(1+\epsilon)d+3$ colors in $O(\frac{d}{\epsilon} \log n)$ rounds (the result was proved in terms of arboricity rather than average degree).

While the chromatic number and degeneracy of unit-disk graphs (as a function of the clique number) are well studied topics, it seems that little is known about the average degree of unit-disk graphs. We conjecture the following:

Conjecture 1. Every unit-disk graph G has average degree at most $4\,\omega(G)$.

It can be checked that the constant 4 would be best possible by considering uniformly distributed points in the plane. In this case each vertex has degree equal to some density constant $c > 0$ times the area of a disk of radius 1, so the average degree is $c \cdot \pi$. On the other hand any clique is contained in a region of diameter at most 1, and the area of such a region is known to be maximized for a disk of radius $\frac{1}{2}$ [3], i.e., the graph has clique number $c \cdot \pi/4$, giving a ratio of 4 between the average degree and the clique number.

Using the result of Barenboim and Elkin [1] mentioned above, Conjecture 1 would imply the existence of a deterministic distributed coloring algorithm using $(4+\epsilon)\,\omega(G)$ colors in $O(\frac{\omega(G)}{\epsilon} \log n)$ (for fixed $\epsilon > 0$ and sufficiently large $\omega(G) = \Omega(1/\epsilon)$).

Unfortunately we are quite far from proving Conjecture 1 at the moment. Our best result so far is the following.

Theorem 5. *Every unit-disk graph G has average degree at most $5.68\,\omega(G)$.*

Organization of the Paper
We start with a presentation of the LOCAL model and some basic results on coloring and unit-disk graphs in Sect. 2. Section 3 is devoted to proving our main results in the location-aware setting, Theorems 2 and 3. In Sect. 4, we study the local structure of unit-disk graphs and deduce our coloring result in the LOCAL model, Theorem 4, together with our upper bound on the average degree of unit-disk graphs, Theorem 5 above. Some proofs are omitted due to the space limitation. They are included in the full version of the paper [7].

2   Preliminaries

2.1   Distributed Models of Communication

All our results are proved in the LOCAL model, introduced by Linial [16]. The underlying network is modelled as an n-vertex graph G whose vertices have unbounded computational power, and whose edges are communication links between the corresponding vertices. In the case of deterministic algorithms, each vertex of G starts with an arbitrary unique identifier (an integer between 1 and n^c, for some constant $c \geqslant 1$, such that all integers assigned to the vertices are distinct). For randomized algorithms, each vertex starts instead with a collection of (private) random bits. The vertices then exchange messages (possibly of unbounded size) with their neighbors in synchronous rounds, and after a fixed number of rounds (the *round complexity of the algorithm*), each vertex v outputs its local "part" of a global solution to a combinatorial problem in G, for instance its color $c(v)$ in some proper k-coloring c of G.

It turns out that with the assumption that messages have unbounded size, after t rounds we can assume without loss of generality that each vertex v "knows" its neighborhood $B_t(v)$ at distance t (the set of all vertices at distance at most t from v). More specifically v knows the labelled subgraph of G induced by $B_t(v)$ (where the labels are the identifiers of the vertices), and nothing more, and the output of v is based solely on this information.

The goal is to minimize the round complexity. Since nodes have infinite computational power, the paragraph above shows that any problem can be solved in a number of rounds equal to the diameter of the graph, which is at most n when G is connected. The goal is to obtain algorithms that are significantly more efficient, i.e., of round complexity $O(\log n)$, or even $O(\log^* n)$.

If in addition, the n-vertex graph modelling the communication network is a unit-disk graph embedded in the plane, and every vertex knows its coordinates in the embedding, this stronger communication model is called the location-aware LOCAL model.

2.2   Distributed Coloring

Consider a graph G with maximum degree Δ, and some $\epsilon > 0$. In the $(\deg + \epsilon\Delta)$-*list coloring problem*, each vertex v is given a list $L(v)$ of colors such that $|L(v)| \geqslant d(v) + \epsilon\Delta$, where $d(v)$ denotes the degree of v in G, and the goal is to color each vertex with a color from its list, so that any two adjacent vertices receive different colors. In the $(\deg + 1)$-*list coloring problem*, the setting is the same, except that each vertex v has a list of at least $d(v) + 1$ colors. The union of all the lists in a coloring problem is called *the color space*, and in some results below it will be convenient to assume that it has bounded size.

The following result can be obtained by combining the approach of [2,6] with a more recent result of Ghaffari and Kuhn [10] (note that recent breakthrough results on network decompositions [9,20] can also be used instead, giving a slightly larger round complexity).

Theorem 6. ([2,6,10]). *For any fixed $\epsilon > 0$, there exists a randomized distributed algorithm in the* LOCAL *model that solves the* $(\deg + \epsilon\Delta)$*-list coloring problem in n-vertex graphs of maximum degree Δ in $O(\log^3 \log n)$ rounds w.h.p.*

Proof. If $\Delta = \Omega(\log^2 n)$, Theorem 4.1 in [6] gives an algorithm running in $O(\log^* \Delta) = O(\log^* n)$ rounds. Assume now that $\Delta = O(\log^2 n)$. The shattering algorithm of Theorem 5.1 in [2] solves the $(\deg+1)$-list coloring problem (which is stronger than the $(\deg + \epsilon\Delta)$-list coloring problem) in $O(\log \Delta) + \mathsf{Det}_d(\Delta^2 \log n)$ rounds, where $\mathsf{Det}_d(n')$ is the deterministic round complexity of the $(\deg + 1)$-list coloring problem in graphs of n' vertices. Using the recent result from [10] that $\mathsf{Det}_d(n') = O(\log^3 n')$, we obtain that if $\Delta = O(\log^2 n)$, the $(\deg + 1)$-list coloring problem (and thus the $(\deg + \epsilon\Delta)$-list coloring problem) can be solved by a randomized algorithm running in $O(\log \Delta + \log^3(\Delta^2 \log n)) = O(\log^3 \log n)$ rounds, as desired.

A graph G has *neighborhood independence* less than k if for any vertex $v \in G$ and set S of k neighbors of v, the set S contains two adjacent vertices. It was proved that when each list $L(v)$ contains at least $d(v) + 1$ colors and G has bounded neighborhood independence, the problem can be solved even more efficiently (and deterministically) when Δ is small.

Theorem 7. ([15]). *There exists a deterministic distributed algorithm in the* LOCAL *model that solves the* $(\deg + 1)$*-list coloring problem in any n-vertex graph of bounded neighborhood independence and maximum degree Δ, with a color space of size* $\mathrm{poly}(\Delta)$, *in* $2^{O(\sqrt{\log \Delta})} + O(\log^* n)$ *rounds.*

It is easy to check that unit-disk graphs have neighborhood independence at most 5, which yields the following immediate corollary.

Corollary 1. *There exists a deterministic distributed algorithm in the* LOCAL *model that solves the* $(\deg + 1)$*-list coloring problem in any n-vertex unit-disk graph of maximum degree Δ, with a color space of size* $\mathrm{poly}(\Delta)$, *in* $2^{O(\sqrt{\log \Delta})} + O(\log^* n)$ *rounds.*

2.3 Unit-Disk Graphs

For $0 \leqslant r \leqslant 1$, and a point v let $D_r(v)$ be the disk of radius r centered in v and let $C_r(v)$ the circle of radius r centered in v. Given a unit-disk graph G embedded in the plane, a vertex v, and a real $0 \leqslant r \leqslant 1$, we denote by $d_r(v)$ the number of neighbors of v lying in $D_r(v)$, and by $x_r(v)$ the number of neighbors of v lying on $C_r(v)$. Note that $d_1(v)$ is precisely $d(v)$, the degree of v in G, and for every $0 \leqslant r \leqslant 1$, $d_r(v) = \sum_{s \in [0,r]} x_s(v)$ (note that since $s \mapsto x_s(v)$ has finite support, this sum is well defined).

It is well known that a disk of radius 1 can be covered by 6 regions of diameter 1 (see [11]), and thus the neighborhood of each vertex of G can be covered by 6 cliques (and thus $d(v) \leqslant 6\omega(G)$ for each vertex v of G). A *Reuleaux triangle* is the intersection of 3 disks of radius 1, centered in the three vertices of an equilateral triangle of side length 1 (see the green region in Fig. 1). Note that Reuleaux triangles have diameter 1, and 6 Reuleaux triangles are enough to cover a disk of radius 1. Moreover, points close to the center of the disk are covered by more triangles than points on the outer circle. This can be used to prove the following.

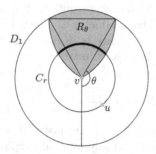

Fig. 1. The intersection (in bold) of a circle C_r of radius r with a Reuleaux triangle R_θ (the green region). (Color figure online)

Lemma 1. *For each vertex v of a unit-disk graph G embedded in the plane,* $\sum_{r \in [0,1]} (2-r) x_r(v) \leqslant 6\omega(G)$.

The (simple) proof is omitted due to the space limitation, it can be found in the full version of the paper [7].

The following is a direct consequence of Lemma 1.

Corollary 2. *For each vertex v of a unit-disk graph G embedded in the plane and $r \in [0,1]$, $d(v) + (1-r)d_r(v) \leqslant 6\omega(G)$. In particular $d_{1/2}(v) \leqslant 12\omega(G) - 2d(v)$.*

Proof. By Lemma 1, $6\omega(G) \geqslant \sum_{s \in [0,1]} (2-s)x_s(v) = \sum_{s \in [0,r]} (2-s)x_s(v) + \sum_{s \in [r,1]} (2-s)x_s(v) \geqslant (2-r)d_r(v) + d(v) - d_r(v) = (1-r)d_r(v) + d(v)$. By taking $r = \frac{1}{2}$, we obtain $d(v) + \frac{1}{2}d_{1/2}(v) \leqslant 6\omega(G)$, and thus $d_{1/2}(v) \leqslant 12\omega(G) - 2d(v)$, as desired. □

In the next section will need the following useful observation of [11] (see also [8]).

Lemma 2. *([11]). Let G be a unit-disk graph embedded in the plane, such that the y-coordinates of any two vertices of G differ by at most $\sqrt{3}/2$. Then $\chi(G) = \omega(G)$.*

We deduce the following easy corollary (which holds in the LOCAL model, so it does not require nodes to know their own coordinates in the plane).

Corollary 3. *Let G be a unit-disk graph embedded in the plane, such that the y-coordinates of any two vertices of G differ by at most $\sqrt{3}/2$, and the x-coordinate differ by at most ℓ, for some real number ℓ. Then G can be colored with $\chi(G) = \omega(G)$ colors by a deterministic distributed algorithm running in $O(\ell)$ rounds in the LOCAL model.*

Proof. Take any shortest path $P = v_1, v_2, \ldots, v_k$ in G. Then for any $1 \leqslant i \leqslant k-2$, $\|v_i - v_{i+2}\| > 1$, since otherwise P would not be a shortest path in G. Since y-coordinates differ by at most $\sqrt{3}/2$, it follows that the x-coordinates of v_i and v_{i+2} differ by at least $\frac{1}{2}$, and the x-coordinates of the vertices v_i with i odd are monotone (say increasing with loss of generality). Hence, the x-coordinates of v_1 and v_k differ by at least $k/4$, and by definition, $k \leqslant 4\ell$. As a consequence, any connected component of G has diameter at most 4ℓ, and thus any connected component can be colored optimally by a deterministic distributed algorithm running in $O(\ell)$ rounds in the LOCAL model. $\qquad\square$

3   Location-Aware Coloring

The techniques we use in this section are inspired by the work of Halldórsson and Konrad [12], who proved that any interval graph G can be colored with at most $(1 + \epsilon)\omega(G)$ colors (for any $\epsilon > 0$) in $O(\frac{1}{\epsilon} \log^* n)$ rounds in the LOCAL model.

A *layering* of a graph G is a partition $L_0, L_1, L_2, \ldots, L_\ell$ of $V(G)$ into (possibly empty) sets (called *layers*), such that for any edge uv of G, either u and v lie in the same layer, or u and v lie in consecutive layers, i.e. layers L_i and L_{i+1}, for some $0 \leqslant i \leqslant \ell - 1$.

For any integer k, we denote by $[k]$ the set $\{1, 2, \ldots, k\}$. We say that a coloring c_1 of a graph G extends a coloring c_2 of an induced subgraph $G[S]$ of G if for any $v \in S$, $c_1(v) = c_2(v)$.

We start by proving the following recoloring lemma, which is inspired by the work of [12,24] on (circular-)interval graphs, but holds in greater generality.

Lemma 3. *Let G be a k-colorable graph, and let $L_0, L_1, \ldots, L_\ell$ be a layering of G such that $G[L_0]$ and $G[L_\ell]$ are complete graphs. Then any k-coloring of $G[L_0 \cup L_\ell]$ can be extended to a coloring of G with at most $k + \frac{4k}{\ell-2} + 2$ colors.*

Proof. Let c_0 be the target coloring of $G[L_0 \cup L_\ell]$, and let c_1 be any k-coloring of G. Since L_0 is a clique, the colors of the vertices of L_0 are pairwise distinct, so by permuting the names of the k colors in c_1 we can assume without loss of generality that for any $v \in L_0$, $c_1(v) = c_0(v)$. It remains to recolor the vertices of L_ℓ to map them to their target color from c_0.

Let $A = \{a_1, a_2, \ldots, a_t\}$ be a subset of $[k]$ and let $\phi : A \to B$ be a bijection such that $B = \phi(A)$ is also a subset of $[k]$. Let $1 \leqslant i \leqslant \ell-1$, and let c be a proper coloring of G. By *swapping A and $\phi(A)$ in c at depth i*, we mean performing the following modification in the coloring c. In L_i, for any $1 \leqslant j \leqslant t$, each vertex colored a_j is recolored with color $k + j$ and if $\phi(a_j) \notin A$, each vertex colored $\phi(a_j)$ is recolored with color $k+t+j$. Then, in $\bigcup_{i'>i} L_{i'}$, for any $1 \leqslant j \leqslant t$, each vertex colored a_j is recolored with color $\phi(a_j)$. Note that the vertices of L_i now use colors from $[k + 2t]$, but all the vertices in further layers still use colors from $[k]$. Note also that if c is a proper coloring before the swap and L_{i-1} only uses colors from $[k]$, then c is still proper after the swap. Moreover, by definition, for each vertex $v \in L_\ell$, if $c(v) = a_j$ before the swap, then $c(v) = \phi(a_j)$ after the swap.

We now order arbitrarily the elements of $c_1(L_\ell) \subseteq [k]$ as $a_1, a_2, \ldots, a_p$. Since L_ℓ is a clique, for any $1 \leqslant i \leqslant p$, there is a unique vertex $v \in L_\ell$ with $c_1(v) = a_i$. Let $\phi(a_i) := c_0(v)$ (note that ϕ is a permutation of $c_1(L_\ell)$). Our goal is thus to replace each color a_i by $\phi(a_i)$ in L_ℓ, by maintaining the property that the coloring c_1 is proper, and without changing the colors of the elements of L_0. We do this as follows: we partition $c_1(L_\ell)$ into $s = \lfloor \ell/2 \rfloor$ sets $A_1, A_2, \ldots, A_s$ of size at most $\lceil k/s \rceil \leqslant \frac{k}{\lfloor \ell/2 \rfloor} + 1 \leqslant \frac{2k}{\ell-2} + 1$, and for each $i = 1, \ldots, s$ in increasing order, we swap A_i and $\phi(A_i)$ in c_1 at depth $2i - 1$.

Since we do not perform any color swapping in sets L_i with i even, we indeed have the property that for any L_i where a color swapping is performed, only colors from $[k]$ are used in L_{i-1}. It thus follows from the observations above that after performing these s color swappings, we obtain a proper coloring c_1 coinciding with c_0 in $L_0 \cup L_\ell$, and using at most $k + 2t \leqslant k + \frac{4k}{\ell-2} + 2$ colors, as desired. □

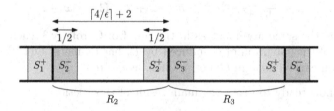

Fig. 2. The division of a stripe into rectangles R_i (proof of Lemma 4).

Note that the hypothesis that $G[L_0]$ and $G[L_\ell]$ are complete graphs can be replaced by the weaker condition that all the vertices of L_0 have distinct colors in the target coloring, and similarly for L_ℓ.

Using Lemma 3 and Corollary 3, we now prove the following lemma, which will be used in the proofs of Theorems 8 and 9.

Lemma 4. *Let G be a unit-disk graph embedded in the plane, such that the y-coordinates of any two vertices of G differ by at most $\sqrt{3}/2$. Then for any $0 < \epsilon \leqslant 1$, G can be colored with at most $(1+\epsilon)\omega(G)+2$ colors by a deterministic distributed algorithm running in $O(1/\epsilon)$ rounds in the location-aware LOCAL model.*

Proof. Let $\omega = \omega(G)$. We can assume that all the vertices of G are contained in some horizontal stripe S of height $\sqrt{3}/2$. We divide S into a sequence of rectangles $R_1, R_2, \ldots$ of height $\sqrt{3}/2$ and width $\lceil 4/\epsilon \rceil + 2 > 2$. The regions bounded by these rectangles are denoted by $R_1, R_2, \ldots$, and in the location-aware LOCAL model each vertex has access to its own coordinates and thus knows in which rectangle R_i it lies. For any rectangle R_i, we denote by S_i^- the subset of

R_i consisting of all the points at distance at most $\frac{1}{2}$ from the left side of R_i, and similarly we denote by S_i^+ the subset of R_i consisting of all the points at distance at most $\frac{1}{2}$ from the right side of R_i (see Fig. 2). Note that S_i^+ and S_i^- are rectangles of height $\sqrt{3}/2$ and width $\frac{1}{2}$. For any rectangles R_i and R_{i+1}, the right side of R_i coincides with the left side of R_{i+1}. By Corollary 3, the union of the regions $S_i^+ \cup S_{i+1}^-$ can be colored deterministically in $O(1)$ rounds with ω colors (here we use the fact that S_i^+ and S_i^- are at distance more than $2 - \frac{1}{2} - \frac{1}{2} = 1$ apart, so there are no edges between them).

Note that for every $i \geqslant 1$, R_i has a natural layering $L_0, L_1, \ldots, L_k$ where $L_0 = S_i^-$ and $L_k = S_i^+$, and $k = \lceil 4/\epsilon \rceil + 2$. It suffices to divide $R_i \setminus (S_i^- \cup S_i^+)$ into consecutive rectangles $L_1, \ldots, L_{k-1}$ of height $\sqrt{3}/2$ and width 1 (for convenience we identify each rectangle L_j with the subset of vertices of G lying in L_j). We assume for convenience that these rectangles L_j are closed on their left side and open on their right side, so all the edges are inside a rectangle L_j or between two consecutive rectangles L_j and L_{j+1}, and thus the partition $L_0, \ldots, L_k$ is indeed a layering of R_i. We can thus apply Lemma 3 and extend the coloring of $S_i^- \cup S_i^+$ to R_i, using at most

$$\omega + \frac{4\omega}{\lceil 4/\epsilon \rceil + 2 - 2} + 2 \leqslant \omega + \epsilon\omega + 2 = (1 + \epsilon)\omega + 2$$

colors. Using the same argument as in the proof of Corollary 3, each connected component of the subgraph of G induced by R_i has diameter $O(1/\epsilon)$, and thus the extension can be done in $O(1/\epsilon)$ rounds, as desired. $\square$

We are now ready to prove the main result of this section.

Theorem 8. *For any $0 < \epsilon \leqslant 1$, a coloring of any unit-disk graph G with at most $(3+\epsilon)\omega(G)+6$ colors can be computed in $O(1/\epsilon)$ rounds by a deterministic distributed algorithm in the* location-aware LOCAL *model.*

Proof. Let $\omega = \omega(G)$. We start by covering $V(G)$ by consecutive horizontal stripes $\mathcal{S}_1, \mathcal{S}_2, \ldots$, each of height $\sqrt{3}/2$ (see Fig. 3, left). Note that any two stripes $\mathcal{S}_j$ and $\mathcal{S}_{j+3}$ are at distance at least $2 \cdot \sqrt{3}/2 = \sqrt{3} > 1$ apart, so there are no edges connecting a vertex lying in $\mathcal{S}_j$ and a vertex lying in $\mathcal{S}_{j+3}$. It follows from this observation and Lemma 2 that for each $i \in \{0, 1, 2\}$, the set of vertices lying in the union of all stripes $\mathcal{S}_j$ with $j \equiv i \pmod 3$ induces a graph of chromatic number at most ω. We will color each of these 3 graphs with a disjoint set of at most $(1 + \epsilon/3)\omega + 2$ colors (this will give a coloring of G with at most $3 \cdot (1+\epsilon/3)\omega + 6 = (3+\epsilon)\omega + 6$ colors, as desired. As there are no edges between the vertices lying in $\mathcal{S}_j$ and the vertices lying in $\mathcal{S}_{j+3}$, it is enough to color the vertices of each stripe with at most $(1+\epsilon/3)\omega + 2$ colors, in parallel (recall that in the location-aware LOCAL model, each vertex has access to its own coordinates and thus knows in which stripe it lies). Using Lemma 4, this can be done in $O(1/\epsilon)$ rounds of communication, which concludes the proof of Theorem 8. $\square$

It was proved in [8] that for any unit-disk graph G, $\chi_f(G) \leqslant 2.155\,\omega(G)$. Using the same ideas as in the proof of Theorem 8, we give an efficient distributed version of this result.

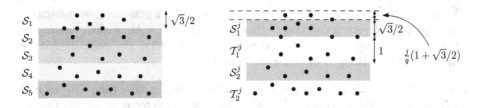

Fig. 3. Covering $V(G)$ by horizontal stripes in the proof of Theorem 8 (left) and Theorem 9 (right).

Theorem 9. *For any sufficiently large integer q, a $(p:q)$-coloring of any unit-disk graph G with $\frac{p}{q} \leqslant 2.156\omega(G) + 4.31$ can be computed in $O(1)$ rounds by a deterministic distributed algorithm in the* location-aware LOCAL *model.*

Proof. Let $\omega = \omega(G)$. We start by covering $V(G)$ by consecutive horizontal stripes $\mathcal{S}_1, \mathcal{T}_1, \mathcal{S}_2, \mathcal{T}_2, \ldots$, such that the stripes $\mathcal{S}_i$ have height $\sqrt{3}/2$ and the stripes $\mathcal{T}_i$ have height 1. It will be convenient to assume that each stripe contains its top boundary and excludes its bottom boundary. For any $i \geqslant 1$ and $j \geqslant 0$, we denote by $\mathcal{S}_i^j$ and $\mathcal{T}_i^j$ the stripes $\mathcal{S}_i$ and $\mathcal{T}_i$ translated by the vector $(0, -\frac{j}{q} \cdot (1 + \frac{\sqrt{3}}{2}))$ (see Fig. 3, right). Note in particular that $\mathcal{S}_i^q = \mathcal{S}_{i+1}$ and $\mathcal{T}_i^q = \mathcal{T}_{i+1}$.

As in the proof of Theorem 8, it follows from Lemma 4 that for any $0 \leqslant j \leqslant q - 1$, the subgraph of G induced by the set X_j of vertices lying in $\bigcup_{i \geqslant 1} \mathcal{S}_i^j$ can be colored with at most $(1 + \epsilon)\omega + 2$ colors in $O(1/\epsilon)$ rounds, for any $\epsilon > 0$. Consider such a coloring of these vertices with a set C_j of at most $(1 + \epsilon)\omega + 2$ colors, and assume that all sets C_j $(0 \leqslant j \leqslant q - 1)$ are pairwise disjoint, so in total at most $q(1 + \epsilon)\omega + 2q$ colors are used. Note that each vertex of G is covered by at least $\left\lfloor \frac{\sqrt{3}/2}{(1+\sqrt{3}/2)/q} \right\rfloor \geqslant 0.4641q$ sets X_j (where the inequality holds for any sufficiently large q), and thus any vertex receives at least $0.4641q$ distinct colors. As $\frac{q(1+\epsilon)\omega+2q}{0.4641q} \leqslant 2.155\omega + 4.31$ for any sufficiently small (but constant) $\epsilon > 0$, the result follows. $\square$

4   Coloring Without Coordinates

We start by giving a bound on the average degree of two adjacent vertices.

Lemma 5. *For every two vertices u and v in a unit-disk graph G embedded in the plane such that $\frac{1}{2} \leqslant \|u - v\| \leqslant 1$, we have $\frac{1}{2}(d(u) + d(v)) \leqslant 5.675\,\omega(G)$.*

Due to the space limitation, the proof of Lemma 5 is omitted in this version (the reader is invited to read the full version of the paper [7]).

This bound easily implies that there is an efficient distributed algorithm coloring G with at most $5.68\,\omega(G)$ colors.

Theorem 10. *Every unit-disk graph G can be colored with at most $5.68\,\omega(G)$ colors by a randomized distributed algorithm in the LOCAL model, running in $O(\log^3 \log n)$ rounds w.h.p. Moreover, if $\omega(G) = O(1)$, the coloring can be obtained deterministically in $O(\log^* n)$ rounds.*

Proof. Let $\omega = \omega(G)$, let A be the set of vertices of degree more than $5.675\,\omega$, and let B be the remaining vertices. We claim that any connected component of $G[A]$, the subgraph of G induced by A, is a clique. Indeed, any two adjacent vertices in $G[A]$ are at distance at most $\frac{1}{2}$ by Lemma 5 and thus if $G[A]$ contains a path uvw, then u and w are at distance $\frac{1}{2} + \frac{1}{2} \leqslant 1$, and so u and w are adjacent. Since $G[A]$ is a union of cliques, it can be colored with at most ω colors in $O(1)$ rounds (each connected component has diameter at most 2, and contains at most ω vertices). For each vertex $v \in B$, let $L(v)$ be the set of colors from $1, 2, \ldots, 5.68\,\omega$ that do not appear among the colored neighbors of v. Let us denote by $d_A(v)$ and $d_B(v)$ the number of neighbors of v in A and B, respectively. Note that for each $v \in B$, $|L(v)| \geqslant 5.68\,\omega - d_A(v) \geqslant d_B(v) + \epsilon\Delta$ for a sufficiently small (but constant) $\epsilon > 0$, since $d_A(v) + d_B(v) \leqslant 5.675\,\omega$ and $\omega \geqslant \Delta/6$. This is an instance of the $(\deg + \epsilon\Delta)$-list coloring problem, which can be solved in $O(\log^3 \log n)$ rounds w.h.p in general (Theorem 6), and deterministically in $2^{O(\sqrt{\log \omega})} + O(\log^* n)$ rounds (Corollary 1). The resulting coloring is a coloring of G with at most $5.68\,\omega$ colors, as desired. $\square$

A natural problem is to prove a 3-vertex version of Lemma 5, in the hope of obtaining a better bound on the average degree of three pairwise adjacent vertices (compared to the average degree of two adjacent vertices). However the number of inequalities and the volume of pairwise distances increases significantly, so the problem becomes quickly difficult to solve by hand. It might be the case that everything can be automatized and solved efficiently by a computer program, in which case the following result would provide a (hopefully significant) improvement on Theorem 4.

Theorem 11. *Assume that for every three vertices u, v, w in a unit-disk graph G embedded in the plane, at pairwise distance at least $\frac{1}{2}$ and at most 1 apart, we have $\frac{1}{3}(d(u) + d(v) + d(w)) \leqslant (6 - \kappa)\,\omega(G)$, for some $\kappa > 0$. Then for any $\epsilon > 0$, every unit-disk graph G can be colored with at most $\max\{(10\kappa + \epsilon)\,\omega(G), (6 - \kappa + \epsilon)\,\omega(G),\}$ colors by a randomized distributed algorithm in the LOCAL model, running in $O(\log^3 \log n)$ rounds w.h.p. Moreover, if $\omega(G) = O(1)$, the coloring can be obtained deterministically in $O(\log^* n)$ rounds.*

Proof. Let $\omega = \omega(G)$, let A be the set of vertices of degree more than $(6 - \kappa)\omega$, and let B be the remaining vertices. We first color $G[A]$ with at most $(10\kappa + \epsilon)\,\omega$ colors, and then extend the coloring to B. Consider a vertex $v \in A$, and a maximal set S of neighbors of v in $G[A]$, at distance at least $\frac{1}{2}$ from v, and such that any two vertices of S are at distance at least $\frac{1}{2}$ apart. Consider the set of angles between two consecutive elements of S (viewed from v). These angles sum to 2π, so if $|S| \geqslant 6$, then there are two consecutive elements of S, say u and w, that are at distance at most one apart. Since u, v, w are pairwise at distance at least $\frac{1}{2}$ and at most 1 apart, this would contradict the property that u, v, w have average degree at most $(6-\kappa)\omega$. Thus, $|S| \leqslant 5$. Since S is maximal, any neighbor of v at distance at least $\frac{1}{2}$ from v is at distance at most $\frac{1}{2}$ from one of the elements of S, Thus the neighborhood of v in $G[A]$ is contained in the union of the disks of radius $\frac{1}{2}$ centered in the elements of $S \cup \{v\}$. By Corollary 2 and the definition of A, each such disk contains at most $2\kappa\omega$ elements, and thus v has degree at most $10\kappa\omega$ in $G[A]$. It follows that $G[A]$ has maximum degree at most $10\kappa\omega$, and thus it can be colored with at most $(10\kappa + \epsilon)\omega$ colors by a randomized algorithm running $O(\log^3 \log n)$ rounds (Theorem 6), and deterministically in $O(2^{O(\sqrt{\log \omega})} + \log^* n)$ (Corollary 1).

Each vertex of B has degree at most $(6-\kappa)\omega$, so as in the proof of Theorem 4, we can then extend the coloring of A to B in the same number of rounds, using $\max\{(10\kappa + \epsilon)\omega, (6 - \kappa + \epsilon)\omega, \}$ colors. $\qquad\square$

For instance, if one can prove that any triple of vertices that are pairwise at distance at least $1/2$ and at most 1 apart has average degree at most $5.5\,\omega(G)$, say, then Theorem 11 implies that G can be colored efficiently with at most $(5.5 + \epsilon)\omega(G)$ colors, for any $\epsilon > 0$.

As an interesting application of Lemma 5, we now obtain an improved upper bound on the average degree of any unit-disk graph.

Theorem 12. *Every unit-disk graph G has average degree at most $5.68\,\omega(G)$.*

Proof. Set $\epsilon = 6 - 5.675 = 0.325$ (all the computations in the proof are with respect to this specific choice of ϵ) and $\omega = \omega(G)$, and consider a fixed embedding of G in the plane. By Lemma 5, any two vertices u, v with $\|u - v\| \in [\frac{1}{2}, 1]$ have average degree at most $(6 - \epsilon)\omega$.

Each vertex v of G starts with a charge $w(v) = d(v)/\omega$, so that the average charge is precisely the average degree of G divided by ω. The charge is then moved according to the following rule: for any $\delta \geqslant 0$, each vertex with degree $(6-\epsilon-\delta)\omega$ takes $\frac{\delta}{(6-\epsilon-\delta)\omega}$ from the charge of each neighbor. For each $v \in V(G)$, let $w'(v)$ be the resulting charge of v. Note that the total charge has not changed and thus the average of $w'(v)$ over $v \in V$ is still the average degree of G divided by ω. We now prove that $w'(v) \leqslant 6 - \epsilon + 0.005 = 5.68$ for each vertex $v \in V$, which directly implies that G has average degree at most $5.68\,\omega$.

Consider first a vertex v of degree at most $(6 - \epsilon)\omega$. Then $d(v) = (6-\epsilon-\delta)\omega$ for some $\delta \geqslant 0$. By the discharging rule, v takes $\frac{\delta}{(6-\epsilon-\delta)\omega}$ from the charge of each of its $(6-\epsilon-\delta)\omega$ neighbors. Thus $w'(v) = 6-\epsilon-\delta + (6-\epsilon-\delta)\omega\frac{\delta}{(6-\epsilon-\delta)\omega} = 6-\epsilon$.

Consider now a vertex v of degree at least $(6 - \epsilon)\omega$. Then $d(v) = (6-\epsilon+\delta)\omega$ for some $0 \leqslant \delta \leqslant \epsilon$. By Corollary 2, $d_{1/2}(v) \leqslant 2(\epsilon - \delta)\omega$, and thus $D = D_1(v) \setminus D_{1/2}(v)$ contains at least $(6 - \epsilon + \delta)\omega - 2(\epsilon - \delta)\omega \geqslant (6 - 3\epsilon + 3\delta)\omega$ vertices.

By Lemma 5, each vertex of D has degree at most $(6 - \epsilon - \delta)\omega$. Observe that the function $x \mapsto \frac{x}{6-\epsilon-x}$ is increasing for our choice of ϵ and for $x \in [0, \epsilon]$, thus each vertex of D takes at least $\frac{\delta}{(6-\epsilon-\delta)\omega}$ from the charge of v. It follows that

$$w'(v) \leqslant 6 - \epsilon + \delta - (6 - 3\epsilon + 3\delta)\omega\frac{\delta}{(6-\epsilon-\delta)\omega} = 6 - \epsilon + \frac{2\epsilon\delta - 4\delta^2}{6-\epsilon-\delta} \leqslant 5.68,$$

for any $0 \leqslant \delta \leqslant \epsilon$ (for our choice of ϵ). $\qquad\square$

5   Conclusion

Given a sequence of pairs $\mathcal{P} = (p_i, r_i)_{1 \leqslant i \leqslant n}$, where each p_i is a point in the plane and each r_i is a positive real, the *disk graph* on $\mathcal{P}$ is the graph with vertex set $\{p_1, p_2, \ldots, p_n\}$, in which two vertices p_i and p_j are adjacent if and only if $\|p_i - p_j\| \leqslant r_i + r_j$. Disk graphs model wireless communication networks using omni-directional antennas of possibly different powers (where the power of the i-th antenna is proportional to the real number r_i), and disk graphs where all the reals r_i are equal are precisely unit-disk graphs. A natural question is whether results similar to the result we obtain here can be proved for disk graphs. A major difference is that disk graphs do not have maximum degree bounded by a function of the clique number ω (the class of disk graphs contains the class of all trees for instance). However disk graphs have average degree bounded by a constant times ω, and this can be used to obtain $O(\log n)$ round algorithms coloring these graphs with few colors [1]. In the same spirit as Question 2 we can ask what is the minimum real $c > 0$ such that a coloring of any n-vertex disk graph G with $c \cdot \omega(G)$ colors can be obtained in $O(\log n)$ rounds in the LOCAL model.

A final comment is that all the results and techniques developed in this paper also hold for unit-disk graphs embedded on the torus (rather than the plane), provided the area of the torus is sufficiently large (see [4] for more on unit-disk graphs on the torus). It does not seem to be known that for these graphs $\chi(G) \leqslant 3\omega(G)$. The best that can be achieved using existing techniques seems to be $\chi(G) \leqslant (3 + \epsilon)\omega(G)$, where $\epsilon \to 0$ as the area of the torus tends to ∞ (regardless of complexity concerns). It follows that with our current approach, avoiding the ϵ in the bound Theorem 2 might be a difficult task.

Acknowledgement. The authors would like to thank Wouter Cames van Batenburg and François Pirot for the interesting discussions. The authors would also like to thank the reviewers of the conference version of the paper for their comments and suggestions, and Mohsen Ghaffari for his kind explanations on the status of the (deg + $\epsilon\Delta$)-list coloring and (deg + 1)-list coloring problems.

References

1. Barenboim, L., Elkin, M.: Sublogarithmic distributed MIS algorithm for sparse graphs using Nash-Williams decomposition. Distrib. Comput. **22**(5–6), 363–379 (2010)
2. Barenboim, L., Elkin, M., Pettie, S., Schneider, J.: The locality of distributed symmetry breaking. J. ACM **63**(3), 20:1–20:45 (2016)
3. Bieberbach, L.: Über eine Extremaleigenschaft des Kreises. Jahresber. Deutsch. Math.-Verein. **24**, 247–250 (1915)
4. Cho, S.Y., Adjih, C., Jacquet, P.: Heuristics for network coding in wireless networks. In: Proceedings of the 3rd International Conference on Wireless Internet (WICON '07), Article 6, pp. 1–5 (2007)
5. Clark, B.N., Colbourn, C.J., Johnson, D.S.: Unit disk graphs. Discret. Math. **86**(1–3), 165–177 (1990)

6. Elkin, M., Pettie, S., Su, H.-H.: $(2\Delta-1)$-edge-coloring is much easier than maximal matching in the distributed setting. In: Proceedings of the ACM-SIAM Symposium on Discrete Algorithms (SODA'15), pp. 355–370 (2015)
7. Esperet, L., Julliot, J., de Mesmay, A.: Distributed coloring and the local structure of unit-disk graphs. arXiv:2106.12322 (2021)
8. Gerke, S., McDiarmid, C.J.H.: Graph imperfection. J. Combin. Theory Ser. B **83**(1), 58–78 (2001)
9. Ghaffari, M., Grunau, C., Rozhoň, V.: Improved deterministic network decomposition. In: Proceedings of the ACM Symposium on Discrete Algorithms (2021)
10. Ghaffari, M., Kuhn, F.: Deterministic distributed vertex coloring: simpler, faster, and without network decomposition. arXiv:2011.04511 (2020)
11. Gräf, A., Stumpf, M., Weißenfels, G.: On coloring unit disk graphs. Algorithmica **20**, 277–293 (1998)
12. Halldórsson, M., Konrad, C.: Improved distributed algorithms for coloring interval graphs with application to multicoloring trees. Theoret. Comput. Sci. **811**, 29–41 (2020)
13. Hassinen, M., Kaasinen, J., Kranakis, E., Polishchuk, V., Suomela, J., Wiese, A.: Analysing local algorithms in location-aware quasi-unit-disk graphs. Discrete Applied Math. **159**(15), 1566–1580 (2011)
14. Kuhn, F.: The price of locality: exploring the complexity of distributed coordination primitives. Ph.D. thesis, ETH Zurich (2005)
15. Kuhn, F.: Faster deterministic distributed coloring through recursive list coloring. In: Proceedings of the ACM-SIAM Symposium on Discrete Algorithms (2020)
16. Linial, N.: Locality in distributed graph algorithms. SIAM J. Comput. **21**, 193–201 (1992)
17. McDiarmid, C.J.H.: Random channel assignment in the plane. Random Struct. Algorithms **22**(2), 187–212 (2003)
18. McDiarmid, C.J.H., Reed, B.: Colouring proximity graphs in the plane. Discret. Math. **199**(1–3), 123–137 (1999)
19. Peeters, R.: On coloring j-unit sphere graphs. FEW 512, Department of Economics, Tilburg University (1991)
20. Rozhoň, V., Ghaffari, M.: Polylogarithmic-time deterministic network decomposition and distributed derandomization. In: Proceedings 52nd ACM Symposium on Theory of Computing (STOC), pp. 350–363 (2020)
21. Scheinerman E.R., Ullman, D.H.: Fractional Graph Theory: A Rational Approach to the Theory of Graphs. Dover Publications (2013)
22. Scott, A., Seymour, P.: A survey of χ-boundedness. J. Graph Theory **95**, 473–504 (2020)
23. Suomela, J.: Survey of local algorithms. ACM Comput. Surv. **45**(2), Article 24 (2013)
24. Valencia-Pabon, M.: Revisiting Tucker's algorithm to color circular arc graphs. SIAM J. Comput. **32**(4), 1067–1072 (2003)
25. Wiese, A.: Local approximation algorithms in unit disk graphs. Master's thesis, Technische Universität Berlin (2007)
26. Wiese, A., Kranakis, E.: Local construction and coloring of spanners of location aware unit disk graphs. Discret. Math. Algorithms Appl. **1**(4), 555–588 (2009)

Evacuating from ℓ_p Unit Disks in the Wireless Model
(Extended Abstract)

Konstantinos Georgiou$^{(\boxtimes)}$, Sean Leizerovich, Jesse Lucier, and Somnath Kundu

Department of Mathematics, Ryerson University, Toronto, ON M5B 2K3, Canada
{konstantinos,sleizerovich,jesse.lucier,
somnath.kundu}@ryerson.ca

Abstract. The search-type problem of evacuating 2 robots in the wireless model from the (Euclidean) unit disk was first introduced and studied by Czyzowicz et al. [DISC'2014]. Since then, the problem has seen a long list of follow-up results pertaining to variations as well as to upper and lower bound improvements. All established results in the area study this 2-dimensional search-type problem in the Euclidean metric space where the search space, i.e. the unit disk, enjoys significant (metric) symmetries.

We initiate and study the problem of evacuating 2 robots in the wireless model from ℓ_p unit disks, $p \in [1,\infty)$, where in particular robots' moves are measured in the underlying metric space. To the best of our knowledge, this is the first study of a search-type problem with mobile agents in more general metric spaces. The problem is particularly challenging since even the circumference of the ℓ_p unit disks have been the subject of technical studies. In our main result, and after identifying and utilizing the very few symmetries of ℓ_p unit disks, we design *optimal evacuation algorithms* that vary with p. Our main technical contributions are two-fold. First, in our upper bound results, we provide (nearly) closed formulae for the worst case cost of our algorithms. Second, and most importantly, our lower bounds' arguments reduce to a novel observation in convex geometry which analyzes trade-offs between arc and chord lengths of ℓ_p unit disks as the endpoints of the arcs (chords) change position around the perimeter of the disk, which we believe is interesting in its own right. Part of our argument pertaining to the latter property relies on a computer assisted numerical verification that can be done for non-extreme values of p.

Keywords: Search · Evacuation · Wireless model · ℓ_p metric space · Convex and computational geometry

1 Introduction

In the realm of mobile agent computing, search-type problems are concerned with the design of searchers' (robots') trajectories in some known search space to locate a

K. Georgiou—Research supported in part by NSERC.
J. Lucier—Research supported by a NSERC USRA.

© Springer Nature Switzerland AG 2021
L. Gąsieniec et al. (Eds.): ALGOSENSORS 2021, LNCS 12961, pp. 76–93, 2021.
https://doi.org/10.1007/978-3-030-89240-1_6

hidden object. Single searcher problems have been introduced and studied as early as the 60's by the mathematics community [11,12], and later in the late 80's and early 90's by the theoretical computer science community [8]. The previously studied variations focused mainly on the type of search domain, e.g. line or plane or a graph, and the type of computation, e.g. deterministic or randomized. Since search was also conducted primarily by single searchers, termination was defined as the first time the searcher hit the hidden object. In the last decade with the advent of robotics, search-type problems have been rejuvenated within the theoretical computer science community, which is now concerned with novel variations including the number of searchers (mobile agents), the communication model, e.g. face-to-face or wireless, and robots' specifications, e.g. speeds or faults, including crash-faults or byzantine faults. As a result of the multi-searcher setup, termination criteria are now subject to variations too, and these include the number or the type of searchers that need to reach the hidden item (for a more extended discussion with proper citations, see Sect. 1.1).

One of the most studied search domains, along with the line, is that of a circle, or a disk. In a typical search-type problem in the disk, the hidden item is located on the perimeter of the unit circle, and searchers start in its center. Depending on the variation considered, and combining all specs mentioned above, a number of ingenious search trajectories have been considered, often with counter-intuitive properties. Alongside the hunt for upper bounds (as the objective is always to minimize some form of cost, e.g. time or traversed space or energy) comes also the study of lower bounds, which are traditionally much more challenging to prove (and which rarely match the best known positive results).

Search on the unbounded plane as well as in other 2-dimensional domains, e.g. triangles or squares, has been considered too, giving rise to a long list of treatments, often with fewer tight (optimal) results. While the list of variations for searching on the plane keeps growing, there is one attribute that is common to all previous results where robots' trajectories lie in $\mathbb{R}^2$, which is the underlying Euclidean metric space. In other words, distances and trajectory lengths are all measured with respect to the Euclidean ℓ_2 norm. Not only the underlying geometric space is well understood, but it also enjoys symmetries, and admits standard and elementary analytic tools from trigonometry, calculus, and analytic geometry.

We deviate from previous results, and to the best of our knowledge, we initiate the study of a search-type problem with mobile agents in $\mathbb{R}^2$ where the underlying metric space is induced by any ℓ_p norm, $p \geq 1$. The problem is particularly challenging since even "highly symmetric" shapes, such as the unit circle, enjoy fewer symmetries in non-Euclidean spaces. Even more, robot trajectories are measured with respect to the underlying metric, giving rise to technical mathematical expressions for measuring the performance of an algorithm. In particular, we consider the problem of reaching (evacuating from) a hidden object (the exit) placed on the perimeter of the ℓ_p unit circle. Our unit-speed searchers start from the center of the circle, placed at the origin of the Cartesian plane $\mathbb{R}^2$, and are controlled by a centralized algorithm that allows them to communicate their findings instantaneously. Termination is determined by the moment that the last searcher reaches the exit, and the performance analysis is evaluated against a deterministic worst case adversary. For this problem we provide *optimal evacuation algorithms*. Apart from the novelty of the problem, our contributions pertain to (a) a technical analysis of search (optimal) algorithms that have to vary with p, giving rise to our upper bounds, and to (b) an involved geometric argument that also uses, to the best of our knowledge, a novel observation on convex geometry that relates a given ℓ_p unit circle's arcs to its chords, giving rise to our matching lower bounds.

1.1 Related Work

Our contributions make progress in Search-Theory, a term that was coined after several decades of celebrated results in the area, and which have been summarized in books [3,5,6,53]. The main focus in that area pertains to the study of (optimal) searchers' strategies who compete against (possibly hidden) hider(s) in some search domain. An even wider family of similar problems relates to exploration [4], terrain mapping, [48], and hide-and-seek and pursuit-evasion [49].

The traditional problem of searching with one robot on the line [8] has been generalized with respect to the number of searchers, the type of searchers, the search domain, and the objective, among others. When there are multiple searchers and the objective is that all of them reach the hidden object, the problem is called an *evacuation problem*, with the first treatments dating back to over a decade ago [10,35]. The evacuation problem that we study is a generalization of a problem introduced by Czyzowicz et al. [21] and that was solved optimally. In that problem, a hidden item is placed on the (Euclidean) unit disk, and is to be reached by two searchers that communicate their findings instantaneously (wireless model). Variations of the problem with multiple searchers, as well as of another communication model (face-to-face) was considered too, giving rise to a series of follow-up papers [15,25,32]. Searching the boundary of the disc is also relevant to so-called Ruckle-type games, and closely related to our problem is a variation mentioned in [9] as an open problem, in which the underlying metric space is any ℓ_p-induced space, $p \geq 1$, as in our work.

The search domain of the unit circle that we consider is maybe one of the most well studied, together with the line [18]. Other topologies that have been considered include multi-rays [16], triangles [20,27], and graphs [7,14]. Search for a hidden object on an unbounded plane was studied in [47], later in [34,46], and more recently in [1,33].

Search and evacuation problems with faulty robots have been studied in [22, 39,50] and with probabilistically faulty robots in [13]. Variations pertaining to the searcher's speeds appeared in [36,38] (immobile agents), in [45] (speed bounds) and in [26] (terrain dependent speeds). Search for multiple exits was considered in [28,51], while variation of searching with advice appeared in [41]. Some variations of the objective include the so-called priority evacuation problem [23,30] and its generalization of weighted searchers [40]. Randomized search strategies have been considered in [11,12] and later in [42] for the line, and more recently in [19] for the disk. Finally, turning costs have been studied in [31] and an objective of minimizing a notion pertaining to energy (instead of time) was studied in [29,44], just to name a few of the developments related to our problem. The reader may also see recent survey [24] that elaborates more on selected topics.

1.2 High Level of New Contributions and Motivation

The algorithmic problem of searching in arbitrary metric spaces has a long history [17], but the focus has been mainly touching on database management. In our work, we extend results of a search-type problem in mobile agent computing first appeared in [21]. More specifically, we provide optimal algorithms for the search-type problem of evacuating two robots in the wireless model from the ℓ_p unit disk, for $p \geq 1$ (previously considered only for the Euclidean space $p = 2$). The novelty of our results is multi-fold. First, to the best of our knowledge, this is the first result in mobile agent computing in which a search problem is studied and optimally solved in ℓ_p metric spaces. Second, both our upper and lower bound arguments rely on technical arguments. Third, part of our lower bound argument relies on an interesting property of unit circles in convex geometry, which we believe is interesting in its own right.

The algorithm we prove to be optimal for our evacuation problem is very simple, but it is one among infinitely many natural options one has to consider for the underlying problem (one for each deployment point of the searchers). Which of them is optimal is far from obvious, and the proof of optimality is, as we indicate, quite technical.

Part of the technical difficulty of our arguments arises from the implicit integral expression of arc lengths of ℓ_p circles. Still, by invoking the Fundamental Theorem of Calculus we determine the worst case placement of the hidden object for our algorithms. Another significant challenge of our search problem pertains to the limited symmetries of the unit circle in the underlying metric space. As a result, it is not surprising that the behaviour of the provably optimal algorithm does depend on p, with $p = 2$ serving as a threshold value for deciding which among two types of special algorithms is optimal. Indeed, consider an arbitrary contiguous arc of some fixed length of the ℓ_p unit circle with endpoints A, B. In the Euclidean space, i.e. when $p = 2$, the length of the corresponding chord is invariant of the locations of A, B. In contrast, for the unit circle hosted in any other ℓ_p space, the slope of the chord AB does determine its length. The relation to search and evacuation is that the arc corresponds to a subset of the search domain which is already searched, and points A, B are the locations of the searchers when the exit is reported. Since searchers operate in the wireless model in our problem (hence one searcher will move directly to the other searcher when the hidden object is found), their trajectories are calculated so that their ℓ_p distance is the minimum possible for the same elapsed search time.

Coming back to the ℓ_p unit disks, we show an interesting property which may be of independent interest (and which we did not find in the current literature). More specifically, and in part using computer assisted numerical calculations for a wide range of values of p, we show that for any arc of fixed length, the placement of its endpoint A, B that minimizes the ℓ_p length of chord AB is when AB is parallel to the $y = 0$ or $x = 0$ lines, for $p \leq 2$, and when AB is parallel to the $y = x$ or $y = -x$ lines for $p \geq 2$. The previous fact is coupled by a technical extension of a result first sketched in [21], according to which at a high level, as long as searchers have left any part of the unit circle of cumulative length α unexplored (not necessarily contiguous), then there are at least two unexplored points of arc distance *at least* α.

All omitted proofs from this extended abstract can be found in the full version of the paper [37].

2 Problem Definition, Notation and Nomenclature

For a vector $x = (x_1, x_2) \in \mathbb{R}^2$, we denote by $\|x\|_p$ the vector's ℓ_p norm, i.e. $\|x\|_p = (|x_1|^p + |x_2|^p)^{1/p}$. The ℓ_p *unit circle* is defined as $\mathscr{C}_p := \{x \in \mathbb{R}^2 : \|x\|_p = 1\}$, see also Fig. 2a for an illustration. We equip $\mathbb{R}^2$ with the metric d_p induced by the ℓ_p norm, i.e. for $x, y \in \mathbb{R}^2$ we write $d_p(x, y) = \|x - y\|_p$. Similarly, if $r : [0, 1] \mapsto \mathbb{R}^2$ is an injective and continuously differentiable function, it's ℓ_p *length* is defined as $\mu_p(r) := \int_0^1 \|r'(t)\|_p \, dt$. As a result, a unit speed robot can traverse $r([0, 1])$ in metric space $(\mathbb{R}^2, d_p)$ in time $\mu_p(r)$.

We proceed with a formal definition of our search-type problem. In problem WE_p (*Wireless Evacuation in ℓ_p space, $p \geq 1$*), two unit-speed robots start at the center of a unit circle $\mathscr{C}_p$ placed at the origin of the metric space $(\mathbb{R}^2, d_p)$. Robots can move anywhere in the metric space, and they operate according to a centralized algorithm. An *exit* is a point P on the perimeter of $\mathscr{C}_p$. An *evacuation algorithm* A consists of robots trajectories, either of which may depend on the placement of P only after at least one of the robots passes through P (*wireless model*).[1] For each exit P, we define the evacuation cost of the algorithm as the first instance that the last robot reaches P. The *cost of algorithm* A is defined as the supremum, over all placements P of the exit, of the evacuation time of A with exit placement P. Finally, the *optimal evacuation cost of* WE_p is defined as the infimum, over all evacuation algorithms A, of the cost of A.

Next we show that $\mathscr{C}_p$ has 4 axes of symmetry (and of course $\mathscr{C}_2$ has infinitely many, i.e. any line $ax + by = 0, a, b \in \mathbb{R}$).

Lemma 1. *Lines $y = 0, x = 0, y = x, y = -x$ are all axes of symmetry of $\mathscr{C}_p$. Moreover, the center of $\mathscr{C}_p$ is its point of symmetry.*

Proof. Reflection of point $P = (a, b)$ across lines $y = 0, x = 0, y = x, y = -x$ give points $P_1 = (a, -b), P_2 = (-a, b), P_3 = (b, a), P_4 = (-b, -a)$, respectively. It is easy to see that setting $\|P\|_p = 1$ implies that $\|P_i\|_p = 1, i = 1, 2, 3, 4$.

---

[1] An underlying assumption is also that robots can distinguish points (x, y) by their coordinates, and they can move between them at will. As a byproduct, robots have a sense of orientation. This specification was not mentioned explicitly before for the Euclidean space, since all arguments were invariant under rotations (which is not the case any more). However, even in the ℓ_2 case this specification was silently assumed by fixing the cost of the optimal offline algorithm to 1 (a searcher that knows the location of the exit goes directly there), hence all previous results were performing competitive analysis by just doing worst case analysis.

We use the generalized trigonometric functions $\sin_p(\cdot), \cos_p(\cdot)$, as in [52], which are defined as $\sin_p(\phi) := \sin(\phi)/N_p(\phi)$, $\cos_p(\phi) := \cos(\phi)/N_p(\phi)$, where $N_p(\phi) := \left(|\sin(\phi)|^p + |\cos(\phi)|^p\right)^{1/p}$. By introducing $\rho_p(\phi) := \left(\cos_p(\phi), \sin_p(\phi)\right)$, which is injective and continuously differentiable function in each of the 4 quadrants, we have the following convenient parametric description of the ℓ_p unit circle; $\mathcal{C}_p = \{\rho_p(\phi) : \phi \in [0, 2\pi)\}$. In particular, set $Q_1 = [0, \pi/2), Q_2 = [\pi/2, \pi), Q_3 = [\pi, 3\pi/2), Q_4 = [3\pi/2, 2\pi)$, and define for each $U \subseteq \mathcal{C}_p$ it's *length* (measure) as

$$\mu_p(U) = \sum_{i=1}^{4} \int_{t \in Q_i : \rho_p(t) \in U} \left\|\rho'_p(t)\right\|_p \, dt.$$

It is easy to see that $\mu_p(\cdot)$ is indeed a measure, hence it satisfies the principle of inclusion-exclusion over $\mathcal{C}_p$. Also, by Lemma 1 it is immediate that for every $U \subseteq \mathcal{C}_p$, and for $\overline{U} = \{\rho_p(t + \pi) : \rho(t) \in U\}$, we have that $\mu_p(U) = \mu_p(\overline{U})$ (both observations will be used later in Lemma 7). As a corollary of the same lemma, we also formalize the following observation.

Lemma 2. *For any* $\phi \in \{k \cdot \pi/4 : k = 0, 1, 2, 3, 4\}$ *and* $\theta \in [0, \pi]$, *let* $U_+ = \{\rho_p(\phi + t) : t \in [0, \theta]\}$ *and* $U_- = \{\rho_p(\phi - t) : t \in [0, \theta]\}$. *Then, we have that* $\mu_p(U_+) = \mu_p(U_-)$.

The perimeter of the ℓ_p unit circle can be computed as

$$\mu_p(\mathcal{C}_p) = \sum_{i=1}^{4} \int_{Q_i} \left\|\rho'_p(t)\right\|_p \, dt = 4 \int_0^{\pi/2} \left\|\rho'_p(t)\right\|_p \, dt := 2\pi_p.$$

By Lemma 2, we also have $\int_0^{\pi/2} \left\|\rho'_p(t)\right\|_p \, dt = 2 \int_0^{\pi/4} \left\|\rho'_p(t)\right\|_p \, dt = \pi_p/2$. Clearly $\mu_2(\mathcal{C}_2)/2 = \pi_2 = \pi = 3.14159\ldots$, while the rest of the values of π_p, for $p \geq 1$, do not have known number representation, in general. However, it is easy to see that $\pi_1 = \pi_\infty = 4$. More generally we have that $\pi_p = \pi_q$ whenever $p, q \geq 1$ satisfy $1/p + 1/q = 1$ [43]. As expected, $\pi_2 = \pi$ is also the minimum value of π_p, over $p \geq 1$ [2], see also Fig. 2b for the behavior of π_p.

For every $\phi, \theta \in [0, 2\pi)$, let $A = \rho(\phi), B = \rho(\phi + \theta)$ be two points on the ℓ_p unit circle. The *chord* $\overline{AB}$ is defined as the line segment with endpoints A, B. From the previous discussion we have $\mu_p\left(\overline{AB}\right) = d_p(A, B)$. The *arc* $\widehat{AB}$ is defined as the curve $\{\rho(\phi + t) : t \in [0, \theta]\}$, hence arcs identified by their endpoints are read counterclockwise. The length of the same arc is computed as $\mu_p\left(\widehat{AB}\right)$.

Finally, the *arc distance* of two points $A, B \in \mathcal{C}_p$ is defined as $\widehat{d_p}(A, B) := \min\left\{\mu_p\left(\widehat{AB}\right), \mu_p\left(\widehat{BA}\right)\right\}$, which can be shown to be a metric. By definition, it follows that $\widehat{d_p}(A, B) \in [0, \pi_p]$.

Next we present an alternative parameterization of the ℓ_p unit circle that will be convenient for some of our proofs. We define

$$r_p(s) := \left(-s, \left(1 - |s|^p\right)^{1/p}\right), \tag{1}$$

and we observe that $r_p(s) \in \mathcal{C}_p$, for every $s \in [-1, 1]$. It is easy to see that as s ranges from -1 to 1, we traverse the upper 2 quadrants of the unit circle with the same direction as $\rho_p(t)$, when t ranges from 0 to π. Moreover, for every $t \in [0, \pi]$, there exists unique $s = s(t)$, with $s \in [-1,1]$ such that $\rho_p(t) = r_p(s)$, and $s(t)$ strictly increasing in t with $s(0) = -1, s(\pi/4) = -2^{-1/p}, s(\pi/2) = 0, s(3\pi/4) = 2^{-1/p}$ and $s(\pi) = 1$.

3   Algorithms for Evacuating 2 Robots in ℓ_p Spaces

First we present a family of algorithms Wireless-Search$_p(\phi)$ for evacuating 2 robots from the ℓ_p unit circle $\mathscr{C}_p$. The family is parameterized by $\phi \in \mathbb{R}$, see also Fig. 4a for two examples, Algorithm Wireless-Search$_{1.5}(0)$ and Wireless-Search$_3(\pi/4)$.

Algorithm 1. Wireless-Search$_p(\phi)$

1: Both robots move to point $\rho_p(\phi)$.
2: Robots follow trajectories $\rho_p(\phi \pm t)$, $t \geq 0$, till the exit is found and communicated.
3: Finder stays put, and non-finder moves to finder's location along the shortest chord (line segment).

Our goal is to prove the following.

Theorem 1
For all $p \in [1,2]$, Algorithm Wireless-Search$_p(0)$ is optimal.
For all $p \in [2,\infty)$, Algorithm Wireless-Search$_p(\pi/4)$ is optimal.

Figure 4b depicts the performance of our algorithms as $p \geq 1$ varies. Our analysis is formal, however we do rely on computer-assisted numerical calculations to verify certain analytical properties in convex geometry (see proof of Lemma 5 on page 14, and proof of Lemma 9 on page 9) that effectively contribute a part of our lower bound argument for bounded values of p, as well as $p = \infty$. For large values of p, e.g. $p \geq 1000$, where numerical verification is of limited help, we provide provable upper and lower bounds that differ by less than 0.042% , multiplicatively (or less than 0.0021, additively).

Recall that as ϕ ranges in $[0, 2\pi)$, then $\rho_p(\phi)$ ranges over the perimeter of $\mathscr{C}_p$. In particular, for any execution of Algorithm 1, the exit will be reported at some point $\rho_p(\phi \pm t)$, where $t \in [0, \pi]$. Since in the last step of the algorithm, the non-finder has to traverse the line segment defined by the locations of robots when the exit is found, we may assume without loss of generality that the exit is always found at some point $\rho_p(\phi \pm t)$, where $t \in [0, \pi]$, say by robot #1. Note that even though Algorithm 1 is well defined for all $[0, 2\pi)$ (in fact all reals), due to Lemma 1 it is enough to restrict to $\phi \in [0, \pi/4]$.

In the remaining of this section, we denote by $\mathscr{E}_{p,\phi}(\tau)$ the evacuation time of Algorithm Wireless-Search$_p(\phi)$, given that the exit is reported after robots have spent time τ searching in parallel. We also denote by $\delta_{p,\phi}(\tau)$ the distance of the two robots at the same moment, assuming that no exit has been reported previously. Hence,

$$\mathscr{E}_{p,\phi}(\tau) = 1 + \tau + \delta_{p,\phi}(\tau). \tag{2}$$

Since $\mu_p(\mathscr{C}_p) = 2\pi_p$ and the two robots search in parallel, an exit will be reported for some $\tau \in [0, \pi_p]$. Hence, the worst case evacuation time $E_{p,\phi}$ of Algorithm Wireless-Search$_p(\phi)$ is given by[2]

$$E_{p,\phi} := \max_{\tau \in [0,\pi_p]} \mathscr{E}_{p,\phi}(\tau).$$

3.1 Worst Case Analysis of Algorithm Wireless-Search$_p(\phi)$

It is important to stress that parameter t in the description of robots' trajectories in Algorithm Wireless-Search$_p(\phi)$ does not represent the total elapsed search time. Even more, and for an arbitrary value of ϕ, it is not true that robots occupy points $\rho_p(\phi \pm t)$ simultaneously. To see why, recall that from the moment robots deploy to point $\rho_p(\phi)$, they need time $\alpha_{1,2}(\phi, t) := \mu_p(\{\rho_p(\phi + s) : s \in [0, t]\})$ in order to reach points $\rho_p(\phi \pm t)$. Moreover, $\alpha_1(\phi, t) \neq \alpha_2(\phi, t)$, unless $\phi = k \cdot \pi/4$ for some $k = 0, 1, 2, 3$, as per Lemma 2. We summarize our observation with a lemma.

Lemma 3. *Let $\phi \in \{0, \pi/4\}$, and consider an execution of Algorithm 1. When one robot is located at point $\rho_p(\phi + t)$, for some $t \in [-\pi, \pi]$, then the other robot is located $\rho_p(\phi - t)$, and in particular $\alpha_1(\phi, t) = \alpha_2(\phi, t)$.*

Now we provide worst case analysis of two Algorithms for two special cases of metric spaces. The proof is a warm-up for the more advanced argument we employ later to analyze arbitrary metric spaces.

Lemma 4. $E_{1,0} = E_{\infty, \pi/4} = 5$.

Proof. First we study Algorithm Wireless-Search$_1(0)$ for evacuating 2 robots from the ℓ_1 unit disk. By (2), if the exit is reported after time τ of parallel search, then $\mathscr{E}_{1,0}(\tau) = 1 + \tau + \delta_{1,0}(\tau)$. Note that $\pi_1 = 4$, so the exit is reported no later than parallel search time 4. First we argue that $\mathscr{E}_{1,0}(\tau)$ is increasing for $\tau \in [0, 2]$. Indeed, in that time window robot #1 is moving from point $(1, 0)$ to point $(0, 1)$ along trajectory $(1 - \tau/2, \tau/2)$ (note that this parameterization induces speed 1 movement). By Lemma 3, robot #2 at the same time is at point $(1 - \tau/2, -\tau/2)$. It follows that $\delta_{1,0}(\tau) = \tau$, so indeed $\mathscr{E}_{1,0}(\tau)$ is increasing for $\tau \in [0, 2]$. Finally we show that $\mathscr{E}_{1,0}(\tau) = 5$, for all $\tau \in [2, 4]$. Indeed, note that for the latter time window, robot #1 moves from point $(0, 1)$ to point $(-1, 0)$ along trajectory $(-(\tau - 2)/2, 1 - (\tau - 2)/2)$. By Lemma 3, robot #2 at the same time is at point $(-(\tau - 2)/2, -1 + (\tau - 2)/2)$. It follows that $\delta_{1,0}(\tau) = |-(\tau - 2)/2 + (\tau - 2)/2| + |1 - (\tau - 2)/2 + 1 - (\tau - 2)/2| = 4 - \tau$, and hence $\mathscr{E}_{1,0}(\tau) = 1 + \tau + \delta_{1,0}(\tau) = 5$, as wanted.

Next we study Algorithm Wireless-Search$_\infty(\pi/4)$ for evacuating 2 robots from the ℓ_∞ unit disk. By (2), if the exit is reported after time τ of parallel search, then $\mathscr{E}_{\infty, \pi/4}(\tau) = 1 + \tau + \delta_{\infty, \pi/4}(\tau)$. As before, $\pi_\infty = 4$, so the exit is reported no later than parallel search time 4. We show again that $\mathscr{E}_{\infty, \pi/4}(\tau)$ is increasing for $\tau \in [0, 2]$. Indeed, in that time window robot #1 is moving from point $(1, 1)$ to point $(-1, 1)$ along trajectory $(1 - \tau, 1)$ (note that this induces speed 1 movement). By Lemma 3, robot #2 at the

---

[2] For arbitrary algorithms one should define the cost as the supremum over all exit placements. Since in Algorithm Wireless-Search$_p(\phi)$ the searched space remains contiguous and its boundaries keep expanding with time, the maximum always exists.

same time is at point $(1, 1-\tau)$. It follows that $\delta_{\infty,\pi/4}(\tau) = \max\{|1-\tau-1|, |1-1+\tau|\} = \tau$, so indeed $\mathscr{E}_{\infty,\pi/4}(\tau)$ is increasing for $\tau \in [0,2]$. Finally we show that $\mathscr{E}_{\infty,\pi/4}(\tau) = 5$, for all $\tau \in [2,4]$. Indeed, note that for the latter time window, robot #1 moves from point $(-1,1)$ to point $(-1,-1)$ along trajectory $(-1, 1-(\tau-2))$. By Lemma 3, robot #2 at the same time is at point $(1-(\tau-2),-1)$. It follows that $\delta_{\infty,\pi/4}(\tau) = \max\{|-1-1+(\tau-2)|, |1-(\tau-2)+1|\} = 4-\tau$, and hence $\mathscr{E}_{\infty,\pi/4}(\tau) = 1+\tau+\delta_{\infty,\pi/4}(\tau) = 5$, as wanted.

It is interesting to see that the algorithms of Lemma 4 outperform algorithms with different choices of ϕ. For example, it is easy to see that $E_{1,\pi/4} \geq 6$. Indeed, note that Algorithm Wireless-Search$_1(\pi/4)$ deploys robots at point $(1/2, 1/2)$. Robot reaches point $(0,1)$ after 1 unit of time, and it reaches point $(-1,0)$ after an additional 2 units of time. The other robot is then at point $(0,-1)$, at an ℓ_1 distance of 2. So, the placement of the exit at point $(-1,0)$ induces cost $1+1+2+2 = 6$. A similar argument shows that $E_{\infty,0} \geq 6$ too.

We conclude this section with a summary of our positive results, introducing at the same time some useful notation.

Theorem 2. *Let w_p be the unique root to equation $w^p + 1 = 2(1-w)^p$, and define*

$$
s_p := \begin{cases} \left((2^p-1)^{\frac{1}{p-1}} + 1\right)^{-1/p}, & p \in (1,2] \\ \left(w_p^{p/(p-1)} + 1\right)^{-1/p}, & p \in (2,\infty). \end{cases}
$$

For every $p \in (1,2]$, the placement of the exit inducing worst case cost for Algorithm Wireless-Search$_p$ (0) results in the total explored portion of $\mathscr{C}_p$ with measure

$$
e_p^- := \pi_p + 2 \int_0^{s_p} \left(z^{p^2-p}(1-z^p)^{1-p} + 1\right)^{1/p} dz.
$$

Also, when the exit is reported, robots are at distance $\gamma_p^- := 2(1-s_p^p)^{1/p}$.

For every $p \in [2,\infty)$, the placement of the exit inducing worst case cost for Algorithm Wireless-Search$_p$ ($\pi/4$) results in the total explored portion of $\mathscr{C}_p$ with measure

$$
e_p^+ := \pi_p + 2 \int_{2^{-1/p}}^{s_p} \left(z^{p^2-p}(1-z^p)^{1-p} + 1\right)^{1/p} dz.
$$

Also, when the exit is reported, robots are at distance $\gamma_p^+ := 2^{1/p}\left((1-s_p^p)^{1/p} + s_p\right)$.

We also set e_p (and γ_p) to be equal to e_p^- (and γ_p^-) if $p \leq 2$, and equal to e_p^+ (and γ_p^+) if $p > 2$, and in particular $e_p \in (\pi_p, 2\pi_p]$.

Quantities e_p, γ_p, and some of their properties are depicted in Figs. 3a, 3b, and discussed in Sect. 4. One can also verify that $\lim_{p\to 2^-} e_p^- = \lim_{p\to 2^+} e_p^+ = 4\pi/3$, and that $\lim_{p\to 2^-} \gamma_p^- = \lim_{p\to 2^+} \gamma_p^+ = \sqrt{3}$. In order to justify that indeed $e_p \in (\pi_p, 2\pi_p]$, recall that by robots' positions during the first $\pi_p/2$ search time (after robots reach perimeter in time 1) is an increasing function. Since the rate of change of time is constant (it remains strictly increasing) for the duration of the algorithm, it follows that the evacuation cost of our algorithms remains increasing till some additional search time. Since robots search in parallel and in different parts of $\mathscr{C}_p$, and since

e_p is the measure of the combined explored portion of the unit circle, it follows that for $e_p > 2\pi_p/2 = \pi_p$. At the same time, the unit circle has circumference $2\pi_p$, hence $e_p \leq 2\pi_p$.

In other words, γ_p^- is the length of chord with endpoints on $\mathscr{C}_p$, $p \in (1,2]$, defining an arc of length e_p^-. Similarly, γ_p^+ is the length of a chord with endpoints on $\mathscr{C}_p$, $p \in (2,\infty)$, defining an arc of length e_p^+. Unlike the Euclidean unit disks, in ℓ_p unit disks, arc and chord lengths are not invariant under rotation. In other words, arbitrary chords of length γ_p^-, γ_p^+ do not necessarily correspond to arcs of length e_p^-, and e_p^+, respectively, and vice versa. The claim extends also to the ℓ_1, ℓ_∞ spaces. For a simple example, consider points $A = \rho_1(\pi/4) = (1/2,1/2), B = \rho_1(3\pi/4) = (-1/2,1/2), C = \rho_1(0) = (1,0), D = \rho_1(\pi/2) = (0,1)$. It is easy to see that $d_p(A,B) = 1$ and $d_p(C,D) = 2$, while $\widehat{d_p}(A,B) = \widehat{d_p}(C,D) = \pi_1/2 = 2$, in other words two arcs of the same length identify chords of different length. We are motivated to introduce the following definition.

Definition 1. *For every $p \in [1,\infty)$, and for every $u \in [0,2\pi_p)$, we define*

$$\mathscr{L}_p(u) := \min_{A,B\in\mathscr{C}_p} \left\{ \|A - B\|_p : \ \mu_p\left(\widehat{AB}\right) = u \right\}.$$

In other words $\mathscr{L}_p(u)$ is the length of the shortest line segment (chord) with endpoints in $\mathscr{C}_p$ at arc distance u (and corresponding to an arc of measure u), and hence $\mathscr{L}_p(u) = \mathscr{L}_p(2\pi_p - u)$ for every $u \in (0,2\pi_p)$. As a special example, note that $\mathscr{L}_2(u) = 2\sin(u/2)$, as well as $\mathscr{L}_p(\pi_p) = 2$, for all $p \in [1,\infty)$.

Lemma 5. *For every $p \in (1,\infty)$, function $\mathscr{L}_p(u)$ is increasing in $u \in [0,\pi_p]$.*

The intuition behind Lemma 5 is summarized in the following proof sketch. Assuming, for the sake of contradiction, that the lemma is false, there must exist an interval of arc lengths, and some $p \geq 1$ for which $\mathscr{L}_p(u)$ is strictly decreasing. By first-order continuity of $\|A - B\|_p$, and in the same interval of arc-lengths, chord $\|A - B\|_p$ must be decreasing in $\mu_p\left(\widehat{AB}\right)$ even when points A, B are conditioned to define a line with a fixed slope (instead of admitting a slope that minimizes the chord length). However, the last statement gives a contradiction. Indeed, consider points A, B, A', B' such that $\widehat{d_p}(A,B) = u, \widehat{d_p}(A',B') = u'$, with $u < u' \leq \pi_p$. It should be intuitive that $d_p(A,B) \leq d_p(A',B) \leq d_p(A',B')$.

For fixed values of p, Lemma 5 can also be verified with confidence of at least 6 significant digits in MATHEMATICA. Due to precision limitations, the values of p cannot be too small, neither too big, even though a modified working precision can handle more values of p. With standard working precision, any p in the range between 1.001 and 45 can be handled within a few seconds. As we argue later, for large values of p, Lemma 5 bears less significance, since in that case we have an alternative way to prove the (near) optimality of algorithms Wireless-Search$_p(\phi)$, as per Theorem 1. Next we provide a visual analysis of function $\mathscr{L}_p$ that effectively justifies Lemma 5, see Fig. 1.

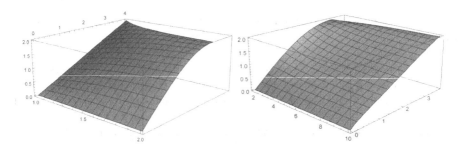

Fig. 1. Figures depict $\mathscr{L}_p(u)$ for various values of p and for $u \in [0, \pi_p]$. Left-hand side figure shows increasing function $\mathscr{L}_p(u)$ for $p \in (1,2]$. Right-hand side figure shows increasing function $\mathscr{L}_p(u)$ for $p \in [2,10]$. Recall that $\mathscr{L}_2(u) = 2\sin(u/2)$, $\mathscr{L}_p(\pi_p) = 2$, for all $p \in [1,\infty)$, as well as that $\pi_1 = \pi_\infty = 4$ and $\pi_p < 4$ for $p \in (1,\infty)$.

4   Visualization of Key Concepts and Results

In this section we provide visualizations of some key concepts, along with visualizations of our results. The Figures are referenced in various places in our manuscript but we provide self-contained descriptions.

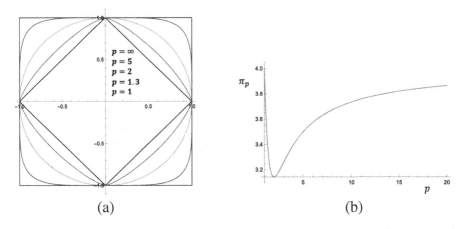

(a)   (b)

Fig. 2. (a) Unit circles $\mathscr{C}_p$, for $p = 1, 1.3, 2, 5, \infty$, induced by the ℓ_p norm. Circles are nested, starting from $p = 1$ for the inner diamond-shaped circle, moving monotonically to $p = \infty$ for the outer square-shaped circle. (b) The behavior of π_p as p ranges from 1 up to ∞, where $\pi_1 = \pi_\infty = 4$ and $\pi_2 = \pi$ is the smallest value of π_p.

Figures 3a and 3b depict quantities pertaining to algorithm Wireless-Search$_p(\phi)$ (where $\phi = 0$, if $p \in [1,2)$ and $\phi = \pi/4$, if $p \in (2,\infty)$) for the placement of the hidden exit inducing the worst case cost. Moreover Fig. 3a depicts quantities $e_p/2, \gamma_p$, as per Theorem 2. In particular, for each p, quantity $e_p/2$ is the time a searcher has spent searching the perimeter of $\mathscr{C}_p$ till the hidden exit is found (in the worst case). Therefore, e_p represents the portion of the perimeter that has been explored till the exit is found. Quantity γ_p is the distance of the two robots at the moment the hidden exit is found so that the total cost of the algorithm is $1 + e_p/2 + \gamma_p$. By [21] we know that $e_2 = 4\pi/3$ and $\gamma_2 = \sqrt{3}$. Our numerical calculations also indicate that $\lim_{p \to 1} e_p = 12/5$, $\lim_{p \to 1} \gamma_p = 8/5$, and $\lim_{p \to \infty} e_p = \lim_{p \to \infty} \gamma_p = 2$.

Figure 3b depicts quantities $e_p/2\pi_p$, which equals the explored portion of the unit circle $\mathscr{C}_p$, relative to its circumference, of Algorithm Wireless-Search$_p(\phi)$ (where $\phi = 0$, if $p \in [1,2)$ and $\phi = \pi/4$, if $p \in (2,\infty)$) when the worst case cost inducing exit is found. By [21] we know that $e_2/2\pi_2 = (4\pi/3)/2\pi = 2/3$. Interestingly, quantity $e_p/2\pi_p$ is maximized when $p = 2$, that is in the Euclidean plane searchers explore the majority of the circle before the exit is found, for the placement of the exit inducing worst case cost. Also, numerically we obtain that $\lim_{p \to 1} e_p/2\pi_p = 3/5$, and $\lim_{p \to \infty} e_p/2\pi_p = 1/2$. The reader should contrast the limit valuations with Lemma 4 according which in both cases $p = 1, \infty$ the cost of our search algorithms is constant and equal to 5 for all placements of the exit that are found from the moment searchers have explored half the unit circle and till the entire circle is explored.

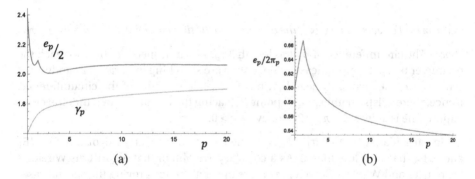

Fig. 3. (a) Perimeter search time $e_p/2$ and distance γ_p between searchers when worst case cost inducing exit is found as a function of p, see also Theorem 2. (b) Explored portion $e_p/2\pi_p$ as a function of p.

Figure 4b shows the worst case performance analysis of Algorithm Wireless-Search$_p(\phi)$ (where $\phi = 0$, if $p \in [1,2)$), which is also optimal for problem WE$_p$. As per Lemma 4, the evacuation cost is 5 for $p = 1$ and $p = \infty$. The smallest (worst case) evacuation cost when $p \in [1,2]$ is 4.7544 and is attained at $p \approx 1.5328$. The smallest (worst case) evacuation cost when $p \in [2,\infty]$ is 4.7784 and is attained at $p \approx 2.6930$. As per [21], the cost is $1 + \sqrt{3} + 2\pi/3 \approx 4.82644$ for the Euclidean case $p = 2$.

5   Lower Bounds and the Proof of Theorem 1

First we prove a weak lower bound that holds for all ℓ_p spaces, $p \geq 1$ (see also Fig. 2b for a visualization of π_p).

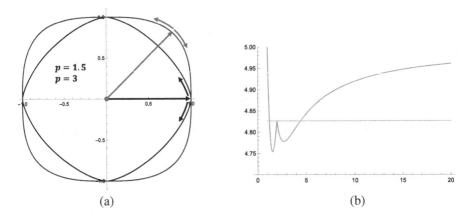

Fig. 4. (a) Figure depicts robots' trajectories for algorithms Wireless-Search$_{1.5}$(0) and Wireless-Search$_3$($\pi/4$). The inner unit circle corresponds to $p = 1.5$ and the outer to $p = 3$. (b) Blue curve depicts the worst case evacuation cost of Algorithm Wireless-Search$_p$(ϕ), where $\phi = 0$, if $p \in [1, 2)$, as a function of p. Yellow line (constant function) is the optimal evacuation cost in the Euclidean metric space.

Lemma 6. *For every $p \in [1, \infty)$, the optimal evacuation cost of* WE$_p$ *is at least* $1 + \pi p$.

Proof. The circumference of $\mathscr{C}_p$ has length $2\pi p$. Two unit speed robots can reach the perimeter of $\mathscr{C}_p$ in time at least 1. Since they are searching in parallel, in additional time $\pi p - \epsilon$, they can only search at most $2\pi p - 2\epsilon$ measure of the circumference. Hence, there exists an unexplored point P. Placing the exit at P shows that the evacuation time is at least $1 + \pi p - 2\epsilon$, for every $\epsilon > 0$.

In particular, recall that $\pi_1 = \pi_\infty = 4$, and hence no evacuation algorithm for WE$_1$ and WE$_\infty$ has cost less than 5. As a corollary, we obtain that Algorithms Wireless-Search$_1$(0) and Wireless-Search$_\infty$($\pi/4$) are optimal, hence proving the special cases $p = 1, \infty$ of Theorem 1. The remaining cases require a highly technical treatment.

The following is a generalization of a result first proved in [21] for the Euclidean metric space (see Lemma 5 in the Appendix of the corresponding conference version). The more general proof is very similar.

Lemma 7. *For every $V \subseteq \mathscr{C}_p$, with $\mu_p(V) \in (0, \pi p]$, and for every small $\epsilon > 0$, there exist $A, B \in V$ with $\widehat{d_p}(A, B) \geq \mu_p(V) - \epsilon$.*

Proof. For the sake of contradiction, consider some $V \subseteq \mathscr{C}_p$, with $\mu_p(V) \in (0, \pi p]$, and some small $\epsilon > 0$, such no two points both in V have arc distance at least $\mu_p(V) - \epsilon$. Below we denote the latter quantity by u, and note that $u \in (0, \pi p)$, as well as that $\mu_p(V) = u + \epsilon > u$. We also denote by $V^{\complement}$ the set $\mathscr{C}_p \setminus V$. The argument below is complemented by Fig. 5.

Since V is non-empty, we consider some arbitrary $A \in V$. We define the set of *antipodal* points of V

$$N := \{B \in \mathscr{C}_p : \exists C \in V, \widehat{d_p}(B, C) = \pi p\}$$

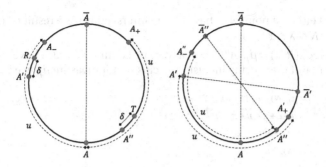

Fig. 5. An abstract ℓ_p unit circle, for some $p \geq 1$, depicted as a Euclidean unit circle for simplicity. On the left we depict points $A, \overline{A}, A_-, A_+, A', A'', T, R$. On the right we keep only the points relevant to our final argument, and add also points $A''_-, A'_+, \overline{A}', \overline{A}''$.

Note that $N \cap V = \emptyset$ as otherwise we have a contradiction, i.e. two points in V with arc distance $\pi_p > u = \mu_p(V) - \epsilon$. In particular, we conclude that $N \subseteq V^C$, and hence by Lemma 1 we have $\mu_p(N) = \mu_p(V) = u + \epsilon$.

Let $\overline{A}$ be the point antipodal to A, i.e. $\widehat{d_p}(A, \overline{A}) = \pi_p$. Next, consider points $A_-, A_+ \in \mathscr{C}_p$ at anti-clockwise and clockwise arc distance u from A, that is $\widehat{d_p}(A, A_-) = \widehat{d_p}(A_+, A) = u$. All points in $\widehat{A_+ A_-}$ are by definition at arc distance at least u from A. In particular, $\overline{A} \in \widehat{A_+ A_-}$ and $A_- \in \widehat{\overline{A}A}, A_+ \in \widehat{A\overline{A}}$. We conclude that $V \cap \widehat{A_+ A_-} = \emptyset$, as otherwise we have $A \in V$ together with some point in $V \cap \widehat{A_+ A_-}$ make two points with arc distance at least u. Note that this implies also that $\widehat{A_+ A_-} \subseteq V^C$.

Consider now the minimal, inclusion-wise, arc $\widehat{TR} \subseteq V^C$, containing $\widehat{A_+ A_-}$. Such arc exists because $A_-, A_+ \in \widehat{A_+ A_-} \subseteq V^C$. In particular, since $A \in V$, we have that $R \in \widehat{A_- A}$ and $T \in \widehat{A A_+}$.

For some arbitrarily small $\delta > 0$, with $\delta < \min\{u, \epsilon/2\}$, let $A', A'' \in V$ such that $\widehat{d}(RA') = d(A''T) = \delta$. Such points A', A'' exist, as otherwise $\widehat{TR}$ would not be minimal. Clearly, we have $A' \in \widehat{RA}$ and $A'' \in \widehat{AT}$.

Since $A' \in \widehat{RA} \subseteq \widehat{\overline{A}A}$, its antipodal point $\overline{A}'$ lies in $\widehat{A\overline{A}}$. Similarly, since $A'' \in \widehat{AT} \subseteq \widehat{A\overline{A}}$, its antipodal point $\overline{A}''$ lies in $\widehat{\overline{A}A}$. Finally, we consider point A''_- at clockwise arc distance u from A'', and point A'_+ at anti-clockwise distance u from A', that is $\widehat{d}(A''_-, A'') = \widehat{d}(A', A'_+) = u$. We observe that $A''_- \in \widehat{\overline{A}''A}$ and $A'_+ \in \widehat{A\overline{A}'}$.

Recall that $A'' \in V$, hence $\widehat{\overline{A}'' A''_-} \subseteq V^c$, as otherwise any point in $\widehat{\overline{A}'' A''_-} \cap V$ together with A', at arc distance at least u, would give a contradiction. Similarly, since $A' \in V$, hence $\widehat{A'_+ \overline{A}'} \subseteq V^c$, as otherwise any point in $\widehat{A'_+ \overline{A}'} \cap V$ together with A'', at arc distance at least u, would give a contradiction.

Lastly, abbreviate $\widehat{\overline{A}'' A}, \widehat{A'_+ \overline{A}'}$ by X, Y, respectively. Note that $\mu_p(X) = \mu_p(\widehat{\overline{A}'' A''} \setminus \widehat{A''_- A''}) = \mu_p(\widehat{\overline{A}'' A''}) - \mu_p(\widehat{A''_- A''}) = \pi_p - u$. Similarly, $\mu_p(Y) = \mu_p(\widehat{A'\overline{A}'} \setminus \widehat{A' A'_+}) = \mu_p(\widehat{A'\overline{A}'}) - \mu_p(\widehat{A' A'_+}) = \pi_p - u$. Recall that $A''_- \in \widehat{\overline{A}'' A}$ and $A'_+ \in \widehat{A\overline{A}'}$, and hence sets

X, Y intersect either at point A or have empty intersection. As a result $\mu_p(X \cap Y) = 0$, as well as $\mu_p(N \cap X \cap Y) = 0$.

Recall that $\mu_p(\widehat{RA'}) = \mu_p(\widehat{A''T}) = \delta$, and so by Lemma 1 we also have $\mu_p(X \cap N) = \mu_p(Y \cap N) = \delta$. But then, using inclusion-exclusion for measure μ_p, we have

$$\mu_p(N \cup X \cup Y) = \mu_p(N) + \mu_p(X) + \mu_p(Y) - \mu_p(N \cap X) - \mu_p(N \cap Y) - \mu_p(X \cap Y) + \mu_p(N \cap X \cap Y)$$

$$= u + \epsilon + \pi - u + \pi - u - \delta - \delta - 0 + 0$$

$$= 2\pi_p - u + \epsilon - 2\delta$$

$$> 2\pi_p - u$$

$$> 2\pi_p - \mu_p(V)$$

$$= \mu_p(V^{\complement}).$$

Hence $\mu_p(N \cup X \cup Y) > \mu_p(V^{\complement})$. On the other hand, recall that $N, X, Y \subseteq V^{\complement}$, hence $N \cup X \cup Y \subseteq V^{\complement}$, hence $\mu_p(N \cup X \cup Y) \leq \mu_p(V^{\complement})$, which is a contradiction.

We are now ready to prove a general lower bound for WE_p which we further quantify later.

Lemma 8. *For every $p \in (1, \infty)$, the optimal evacuation cost of WE_p is at least $1 + e_p/2 + \mathscr{L}_p(e_p)$.*

Proof. Consider an arbitrary evacuation algorithm $\mathscr{A}$. We show that the cost of $\mathscr{A}$ is at least $1 + e_p + \mathscr{L}_p(e_p)$. By Theorem 2, we have that $e_p \in (\pi_p, 2\pi_p]$. Let $\epsilon > 0$ be small enough, were in particular $\epsilon < e_p - \pi_p$. We let evacuation algorithm $\mathscr{A}$ run till robots have explored exactly $e_p - \epsilon$ part of $\mathscr{C}_p$.

The two unit speed robots need time 1 to reach the perimeter of $\mathscr{C}_p$. Since moreover they (can) search in parallel (possibly different parts of the unit circle), they need an additional time at least $(e_p - \epsilon)/2$ in order to explore measure $e_p - \epsilon$. The unexplored portion V of $\mathscr{C}_p$ has therefore measure $u := 2\pi_p - (e_p - \epsilon)$, where $u \in (0, \pi_p)$.

By Lemma 7, there are two points $A, B \in V$ that are at an arc distance $v \geq u - \epsilon = 2\pi_p - e_p$. By definition, both points A, B are unexplored. We let algorithm $\mathscr{A}$ run even more and till the moment any one of the points A, B is visited by some robot, and we place the exit at the other point (even if points are visited simultaneously), hence algorithm $\mathscr{A}$ needs an additional time $d_p(A, B)$ to terminate, for a total cost at least $1 + e_p/2 - \epsilon/2 + d_p(A, B)$. But then, note that $d_p(A, B) \geq \mathscr{L}_p(v) \geq \mathscr{L}_p(2\pi_p - e_p)$, where the first inequality is due Definition 1 and the second inequality due to Lemma 5, and the claim follows by recalling that $\mathscr{L}_p(2\pi_p - e_p) = \mathscr{L}_p(e_p)$.

Recall that, for every $p \in (1, \infty)$, the evacuation algorithms we have provided for WE_p have cost $1 + e_p/2 + \gamma_p$. At the same time, Lemma 8 implies that no evacuation algorithm has cost less than $1 + e_p/2 + \mathscr{L}_p(e_p)$. So, the optimality of our algorithms, that is, the proof of Theorem 1, is implied directly by the following lemma, which is verified numerically.

Lemma 9. *For every $p \in (1, \infty)$, we have $\mathscr{L}_p(e_p) = \gamma_p$.*

6   Discussion

We provided tight upper and lower bounds for the evacuation problem of two searchers in the wireless model from the unit circle in ℓ_p metric spaces, $p \geq 1$. This is just a starting point of revisiting well studied search and evacuation problems in general metric spaces that do not enjoy the symmetry of the Euclidean space. In light of the technicalities involved in the current manuscript, we anticipate that the pursuit of the aforementioned open problems will also give rise to new insights in convex geometry and computational geometry.

References

1. Acharjee, S., Georgiou, K., Kundu, S., Srinivasan, A.: Lower bounds for shoreline searching with 2 or more robots. In: 23rd OPODIS, volume 153 of LIPIcs, pp. 26:1–26:11. Schloss Dagstuhl - LZI (2019)
2. Adler, C.L., Tanton, J.: π is the minimum value of Pi. CMJ: Coll. Math. J. **31**, 102-106 (2000)
3. Ahlswede, R., Wegener, I.: Search Problems. Wiley-Interscience, Hoboken (1987)
4. Albers, S., Kursawe, K., Schuierer, S.: Exploring unknown environments with obstacles. Algorithmica **32**(1), 123–143 (2002). https://doi.org/10.1007/s00453-001-0067-x
5. Alpern, S., Gal, S.: The Theory of Search Games and Rendezvous, vol. 55. Kluwer Academic Publishers, Heidelberg (2002)
6. Alpern, S.: Ten open problems in rendezvous search. In: Alpern, S., Fokkink, R., Gąsieniec, L., Lindelauf, R., Subrahmanian, V. (eds.) Search Theory, pp. 223–230. Springer, New York (2013). https://doi.org/10.1007/978-1-4614-6825-7_14
7. Angelopoulos, S., Dürr, C., Lidbetter, T.: The expanding search ratio of a graph. Discret. Appl. Math. **260**, 51–65 (2019)
8. Baeza Yates, R., Culberson, J., Rawlins, G.: Searching in the plane. Inf. Comput. **106**(2), 234–252 (1993)
9. Baston, V.: Some Cinderella Ruckle type games. In: Alpern, S., Fokkink, R., Gąsieniec, L., Lindelauf, R., Subrahmanian, V. (eds.) Search Theory, pp. 85–103. Springer, New York (2013). https://doi.org/10.1007/978-1-4614-6825-7_6
10. Baumann, N., Skutella, M.: Earliest arrival flows with multiple sources. Math. Oper. Res. **34**(2), 499–512 (2009)
11. Beck, A.: On the linear search problem. Israel J. Math. **2**(4), 221–228 (1964). https://doi.org/10.1007/BF02759737
12. Bellman, R.: An optimal search. SIAM Rev. **5**(3), 274–274 (1963)
13. Bonato, A., Georgiou, K., MacRury, C., Pralat, P.: Probabilistically faulty searching on a half-line. In: 14th LATIN (2020, to appear)
14. Borowiecki, P., Das, S., Dereniowski, D., Kuszner, Ł.: Distributed evacuation in graphs with multiple exits. In: Suomela, J. (ed.) SIROCCO 2016. LNCS, vol. 9988, pp. 228–241. Springer, Cham (2016). https://doi.org/10.1007/978-3-319-48314-6_15
15. Brandt, S., Laufenberg, F., Lv, Y., Stolz, D., Wattenhofer, R.: Collaboration without communication: evacuating two robots from a disk. In: Fotakis, D., Pagourtzis, A., Paschos, V.T. (eds.) CIAC 2017. LNCS, vol. 10236, pp. 104–115. Springer, Cham (2017). https://doi.org/10.1007/978-3-319-57586-5_10
16. Brandt, S., Foerster, K.-T., Richner, B., Wattenhofer, R.: Wireless evacuation on m rays with k searchers. Theoret. Comput. Sci. **811**, 56–69 (2020)
17. Chávez, E., Navarro, G., Baeza-Yates, R., Marroquín, J.L.: Searching in metric spaces. ACM Comput. Surv. (CSUR) **33**(3), 273–321 (2001)

18. Chrobak, M., Gąsieniec, L., Gorry, T., Martin, R.: Group search on the line. In: Italiano, G.F., Margaria-Steffen, T., Pokorný, J., Quisquater, J.-J., Wattenhofer, R. (eds.) SOFSEM 2015. LNCS, vol. 8939, pp. 164–176. Springer, Heidelberg (2015). https://doi.org/10.1007/978-3-662-46078-8_14

19. Chuangpishit, H., Georgiou, K., Sharma, P.: Average case - worst case tradeoffs for evacuating 2 robots from the disk in the face-to-face model. In: Gilbert, S., Hughes, D., Krishnamachari, B. (eds.) ALGOSENSORS 2018. LNCS, vol. 11410, pp. 62–82. Springer, Cham (2019). https://doi.org/10.1007/978-3-030-14094-6_5

20. Chuangpishit, H., Mehrabi, S., Narayanan, L., Opatrny, J.: Evacuating equilateral triangles and squares in the face-to-face model. Comput. Geom. **89**, 101624 (2020). https://doi.org/10.1016/j.comgeo.2020.101624

21. Czyzowicz, J., Gąsieniec, L., Gorry, T., Kranakis, E., Martin, R., Pajak, D.: Evacuating robots via unknown exit in a disk. In: Kuhn, F. (ed.) DISC 2014. LNCS, vol. 8784, pp. 122–136. Springer, Heidelberg (2014). https://doi.org/10.1007/978-3-662-45174-8_9

22. Czyzowicz, J., et al.: Evacuation from a disc in the presence of a faulty robot. In: Das, S., Tixeuil, S. (eds.) SIROCCO 2017. LNCS, vol. 10641, pp. 158–173. Springer, Cham (2017). https://doi.org/10.1007/978-3-319-72050-0_10

23. Czyzowicz, J., et al.: Priority evacuation from a disk using mobile robots. In: Lotker, Z., Patt-Shamir, B. (eds.) SIROCCO 2018. LNCS, vol. 11085, pp. 392–407. Springer, Cham (2018). https://doi.org/10.1007/978-3-030-01325-7_32

24. Czyzowicz, J., Georgiou, K., Kranakis, E.: Group search and evacuation. In: Flocchini, P., Prencipe, G., Santoro, N. (eds.) Distributed Computing by Mobile Entities. Lecture Notes in Computer Science, vol. 11340, pp. 335–370. Springer, Cham (2019). https://doi.org/10.1007/978-3-030-11072-7_14

25. Czyzowicz, J., Georgiou, K., Kranakis, E., Narayanan, L., Opatrny, J., Vogtenhuber, B.: Evacuating robots from a disk using face-to-face communication. Discrete Math. Theoret. Comput. Sci. **22**(4) (2020). https://doi.org/10.23638/DMTCS-22-4-4

26. Czyzowicz, J., Kranakis, E., Krizanc, D., Narayanan, L., Opatrny, J., Shende, S.: Linear search with terrain-dependent speeds. In: Fotakis, D., Pagourtzis, A., Paschos, V.T. (eds.) CIAC 2017. LNCS, vol. 10236, pp. 430–441. Springer, Cham (2017). https://doi.org/10.1007/978-3-319-57586-5_36

27. Czyzowicz, J., Kranakis, E., Krizanc, D., Narayanan, L., Opatrny, J., Shende, S.: Wireless autonomous robot evacuation from equilateral triangles and squares. In: Papavassiliou, S., Ruehrup, S. (eds.) ADHOC-NOW 2015. LNCS, vol. 9143, pp. 181–194. Springer, Cham (2015). https://doi.org/10.1007/978-3-319-19662-6_13

28. Czyzowicz, J., Dobrev, S., Georgiou, K., Kranakis, E., MacQuarrie, F.: Evacuating two robots from multiple unknown exits in a circle. Theoret. Comput. Sci. **709**, 20–30 (2018)

29. Czyzowicz, J., et al.: Energy consumption of group search on a line. In: 46th ICALP, volume 132 of LIPIcs, Dagstuhl, Germany, pp. 137:1–137:15. Schloss Dagstuhl-LZI (2019)

30. Czyzowicz, J., et al.: Priority evacuation from a disk: the case of n =1, 2, 3, vol. 806, pp. 595–616 (2020)

31. Demaine, E.D., Fekete, S.P., Gal, S.: Online searching with turn cost. Theoret. Comput. Sci. **361**(2), 342–355 (2006)

32. Disser, Y., Schmitt, S.: Evacuating two robots from a disk: a second cut. In: Censor-Hillel, K., Flammini, M. (eds.) SIROCCO 2019. LNCS, vol. 11639, pp. 200–214. Springer, Cham (2019). https://doi.org/10.1007/978-3-030-24922-9_14

33. Dobrev, S., Královič, R., Pardubská, D.: Improved lower bounds for shoreline search. In: Richa, A.W., Scheideler, C. (eds.) SIROCCO 2020. LNCS, vol. 12156, pp. 80–90. Springer, Cham (2020). https://doi.org/10.1007/978-3-030-54921-3_5

34. Emek, Y., Langner, T., Uitto, J., Wattenhofer, R.: Solving the ANTS problem with asynchronous finite state machines. In: Esparza, J., Fraigniaud, P., Husfeldt, T., Koutsoupias, E. (eds.) ICALP 2014. LNCS, vol. 8573, pp. 471–482. Springer, Heidelberg (2014). https://doi.org/10.1007/978-3-662-43951-7_40
35. Fekete, S., Gray, C., Kröller, A.: Evacuation of rectilinear polygons. In: Wu, W., Daescu, O. (eds.) COCOA 2010. LNCS, vol. 6508, pp. 21–30. Springer, Heidelberg (2010). https://doi.org/10.1007/978-3-642-17458-2_3
36. Georgiou, K., Karakostas, G., Kranakis, E.: Search-and-fetch with one robot on a disk. In: Chrobak, M., Fernández Anta, A., Gąsieniec, L., Klasing, R. (eds.) ALGOSENSORS 2016. LNCS, vol. 10050, pp. 80–94. Springer, Cham (2017). https://doi.org/10.1007/978-3-319-53058-1_6
37. Georgiou, K., Leizerovich, S., Lucier, J., Kundu, S.: Evacuating from ℓ_p unit disks in the wireless model. CoRR, abs/2108.02367 (2021)
38. Georgiou, K., Karakostas, G., Kranakis, E.: Search-and-fetch with 2 robots on a disk: wireless and face-to-face communication models. Discrete Math. Theoret. Comput. Sci. **21**(3) (2019). https://doi.org/10.23638/DMTCS-21-3-20
39. Georgiou, K., Kranakis, E., Leonardos, N., Pagourtzis, A., Papaioannou, I.: Optimal circle search despite the presence of faulty robots. In: Dressler, F., Scheideler, C. (eds.) ALGOSENSORS 2019. LNCS, vol. 11931, pp. 192–205. Springer, Cham (2019). https://doi.org/10.1007/978-3-030-34405-4_11
40. Georgiou, K., Lucier, J.: Weighted group search on a line. In: Pinotti, C.M., Navarra, A., Bagchi, A. (eds.) ALGOSENSORS 2020. LNCS, vol. 12503, pp. 124–139. Springer, Cham (2020). https://doi.org/10.1007/978-3-030-62401-9_9
41. Georgiou, K., Kranakis, E., Steau, A.: Searching with advice: robot fence-jumping. J. Inf. Process. **25**, 559–571 (2017)
42. Kao, M.-Y., Reif, J.H., Tate, S.R.: Searching in an unknown environment: an optimal randomized algorithm for the cow-path problem. Inf. Comput. **131**(1), 63–79 (1996)
43. Keller, J.B., Vakil, R.: π_p, the value of π in ℓ_p. Amer. Math. Monthly **116**(10), 931–935 (2009)
44. Czyzowicz, J., et al.: Time-energy tradeoffs for evacuation by two robots in the wireless model. In: Censor-Hillel, K., Flammini, M. (eds.) SIROCCO 2019. LNCS, vol. 11639, pp. 185–199. Springer, Cham (2019). https://doi.org/10.1007/978-3-030-24922-9_13
45. Lamprou, I., Martin, R., Schewe, S.: Fast two-robot disk evacuation with wireless communication. In: Gavoille, C., Ilcinkas, D. (eds.) DISC 2016. LNCS, vol. 9888, pp. 1–15. Springer, Heidelberg (2016). https://doi.org/10.1007/978-3-662-53426-7_1
46. Lenzen, C., Lynch, N., Newport, C., Radeva, T.: Trade-offs between selection complexity and performance when searching the plane without communication. In: PODC, pp. 252–261. ACM (2014)
47. López-Ortiz, A., Sweet, G.: Parallel searching on a lattice. In: CCCG, pp. 125–128 (2001)
48. Mitchell, J.S.B.: Geometric shortest paths and network optimization. In: Handbook of Computational Geometry, vol. 334, pp. 633–702 (2000)
49. Nahin, P.: Chases and Escapes: The Mathematics of Pursuit and Evasion. Princeton University Press, Princeton (2012)
50. Pattanayak, D., Ramesh, H., Mandal, P.S.: Chauffeuring a crashed robot from a disk. In: Dressler, F., Scheideler, C. (eds.) ALGOSENSORS 2019. LNCS, vol. 11931, pp. 177–191. Springer, Cham (2019). https://doi.org/10.1007/978-3-030-34405-4_10
51. Pattanayak, D., Ramesh, H, Mandal, P.S., Schmid, S.: Evacuating two robots from two unknown exits on the perimeter of a disk with wireless communication. In: 19th ICDCN, pp. 20:1–20:4. ACM (2018)
52. Richter, W.-D.: Generalized spherical and simplicial coordinates. J. Math. Anal. Appl. **336**(2), 1187–1202 (2007)
53. Stone, L.: Theory of Optimal Search. Academic Press, New York (1975)

Beep-And-Sleep: Message and Energy Efficient Set Cover

Thorsten Götte[1]([✉]), Christina Kolb[2], Christian Scheideler[1],
and Julian Werthmann[1]

[1] Paderborn University, Fürstenallee 11, 33102 Paderborn, Germany
{thgoette,scheidel,jwerth}@mail.upb.de
[2] University of Twente, Drienerlolaan 5, 7522 Enschede, NB, Netherlands
c.kolb@utwente.nl

Abstract. We observe message- and energy-efficient distributed algorithms for the SETCOVER Problem in the KT_0 and BEEPING model. Given a ground set U of n elements and m subsets of U, we aim to find the minimal number of these subsets that contain all elements. In the default distributed setup of this problem, each set has a bidirected communication link with each element it contains. Our first result is a $\tilde{O}(\log^2(\Delta))$-time and $\tilde{O}(\sqrt{\Delta})(n+m))$-message algorithm with expected approximation ratio of $O(\log(\Delta))$ in the KT_0 model. The value Δ denotes the maximum of each subset's cardinality and the number of sets an element is contained in. Our algorithm is *almost* optimal concerning time and message complexity. Further, we present the first SETCOVER algorithm for general instances in the BEEPING model. It computes an $\tilde{O}(\sqrt[k]{\Delta})$-approximation in time $O(k^3)$ for any parameter $k > 3$. Thus, it can trade runtime for approximation ratio similar to the celebrated algorithm by Kuhn and Wattenhofer [PODC'03].

1 Introduction

SETCOVER is a well-understood problem in both the centralized and distributed setting. Given a collection of elements $\mathcal{U} := \{e_1, \ldots, e_n\}$ and sets $\mathcal{S} := \{s_1, \ldots, s_m\}$ with $s_i \subseteq \mathcal{U}$ the goal is to cover all elements with as few sets as possible. SETCOVER has a wide variety of applications in many areas of computer science. On the one hand, it plays an essential role in the analysis of large data sets, which is often needed in fields like operations research, machine learning, information retrieval, and data mining (see [8] and the references therein). On the other hand, it is also used in purely distributed domains like ad-hoc sensor networks. An essential task in these networks is to determine a minimum set of nodes, a so-called DOMINATINGSET, such that all nodes are sensor range of this set. This set can then fulfill particular tasks like routing, collecting sensor data from neighbors, and various other tasks. Note that DOMINATINGSET is a special case of SETCOVER where all sets are also elements.

This work is supported by the German Research Foundation (DFG) within the CRC 901 "On-The-Fly Computing" (project number 160364472-SFB901).

© Springer Nature Switzerland AG 2021
L. Gąsieniec et al. (Eds.): ALGOSENSORS 2021, LNCS 12961, pp. 94–110, 2021.
https://doi.org/10.1007/978-3-030-89240-1_7

In the centralized setting, a simple greedy algorithm that always picks the set that covers most elements has a logarithmic approximation factor, which is the best we can hope for a polynomial-time algorithm unless $P = NP$. For distributed algorithms, an instance of SETCOVER is ususally modeled as a so-called *problem graph* $G_P := \{V_\mathcal{U} \cup V_\mathcal{S}, E\}$. Each set and each element corresponds to a node in this graph and for each set $s_i \in \mathcal{S}$ there is a bidirected edge $\{e_j, s_i\} \in E$ to each element $e_j \in \mathcal{U}$ it contains. These edges model bidirected communication channels between the nodes representing the set and element in the default distributed setup. Each set and element in each round of communication can send a distinct message of size $O(\log(n + m))$ over each communication edge. There are several randomized algorithms in this model that match the optimal approximation ratio, w.h.p., and have a near-optimal runtime of $O(\log(\Delta)^2)$ where Δ is the maximum degree of G_P [9,11].

Although there are numerous results concerning the runtime of algorithms in the CONGEST model, there are only a few that consider the message complexity, i.e., how many messages are needed to compute a distributed solution to SETCOVER. To the best of our knowledge, in all popular solutions to SET COVER, all sets/elements extensively communicate with their neighborhood and send (possibly distinct) messages to all of their neighboring set and elements. This setup implies a message complexity of $O(|E|)$ per round and $\tilde{O}(|E|)$ overall. From a practical standpoint, a high message complexity makes these algorithms unsuitable for low bandwidth networks, e.g., if the sets and elements are connected via the internet. Here, the communication cost in linear in the number of messages. Therefore, our first question is:

(Q.1) *Can we find a* SETCOVER *algorithm that sends* $o(|E|)$ *messages?*

Another area of interest for communication efficient SETCOVER algorithms are ad-hoc sensor networks. Here, one needs to take special care of the limited battery life of the nodes. In particular, sending messages should be reduced to a minimum due to the high energy requirements of the radio module. However, even if we find algorithms that send few messages, they do not translate well to ad-hoc networks. In practice, it is more energy-efficient to only send a single signal, a so-called BEEP, to all neighboring nodes. Further, nodes can only distinguish if at least one or none of their neighbors beeped, i.e., they only rely on carrier sensing. This has recently been formalized in the so-called BEEPING model [2]. To the best of our knowledge there no SETCOVER or DOMINATINGSET algorithm *for general graphs* in this model. Thus, our second question is:

(Q.2) *Can we find a* SETCOVER *algorithm in the BEEPING model?*

We answer both questions affirmative and provide fast and efficient algorithms for SETCOVER in the KT_0-model (a variant of the CONGEST model for analyzing message-efficient algorithms) and the BEEPING model. Our algorithms come close to their respective lower bounds for approximation ratio, time complexity, and messages complexity. Thus, we call them *almost* optimal.

First, our KT_0 algorithm has time complexity $O(\log^2(\Delta))$ and approximation ratio $O(\log(\Delta))$ while sending only $\tilde{O}(\sqrt{\Delta}(n+m))$[1] messages, with high probability (w.h.p[2]). Thus, the approximation ratio and time complexity are on par with the best known algorithms in the CONGEST model (cf. [9,11]) and it comes close to the optimal runtime of $\Theta(\frac{\log(\Delta)}{\log(\log(\Delta))})$ [10]. Although we cannot prove that the message complexity is optimal for this particular approximation ratio, our algorithm's approximation ratio is slightly better than other algorithms in comparable models[3]. Further, it runs significantly faster than a naive simulation (which would require broadcasts). Furthermore, there is strong evidence that one cannot hope for far better results as there are instances that require $O(\sqrt{\Delta}(n+m))$ messages for a constant approximation.

Second, our BEEPING algorithm runs in $O(k^3)$ rounds and has an approximation ratio of $O(\log(\Delta)^2 \sqrt[k/3]{\Delta})$ for any parameter $k > 3$. Thus, it can trade runtime for approximation ratio similar to [11] and [10]. This implies that our algorithm achieves a non-trivial approximation ratio even for a constant runtime, which is close to the optimal one as Kuhn et al. showed than any distributed algorithm with only local communication needs $O(k)$ rounds for an approximation ratio of $O(\sqrt[k]{\Delta})$ [11]. Further, this trade-off makes it useful for practical applications: As the topology of ad-hoc networks is often rapidly changing, our algorithm can quickly react to these changes by computing a new solution faster than previous algorithms (while sacrificing quality). Note that existing solutions ([14,15]) for DOMINATINGSET have a better approximation ratio as they are designed for instances where sets and elements are points in the euclidean plane. Moreover, they have a runtime of $O(\log(n))$. Thus, for problem graphs of low degree Δ and $k \in O(\log(\Delta))$, our algorithm is massively faster while the approximation ration is still polylogarithmic in Δ. Note that the focus of this work is to prove feasibility and not optimize logarithmic factors in message complexity and approximation ratios, i.e., we explicitly do not claim our factors/analysis to be optimal.

Our main technical contribution is the BEEP-AND-SLEEP algorithm, an adapted version of Jia et al.'s. LOCALRANDOMIZEDGREEDY algorithm (LRG) for DOMINATINGSET from [9] that will be the basis for both our contributions. We adapt LRG in two *major* ways to massively reduce the number of (distinct) messages that need to be exchanged: First, we replace all instances where elements are counted through randomized approximation that only use a fraction of the messages. Second (and more importantly), we exchange the mechanism that lets sets decide to join the solution entirely. In a nutshell, the approach works as follows: Each set draws a geometrically distributed wake-up time and remains idle until that round (i.e., it sleeps). When the time has come, a set wakes up and joins the solution, given it has a certain threshold of uncovered elements (i.e., it beeps). This approach does not require *any* additional messages and coordination between sets. Note that the independent work of Grunau et al.

---

[1] $\tilde{O}(\cdot)$ hides polylogarithmic factors.

[2] An event holds w.h.p., if it holds with prob. $1 - o(n'^c)$ for some $c > 1$ and $n' = n+m$.

[3] See [8] for the algorithm and Sect. 3.2 for the relation between the models.

[6] uses a very similar technique[4], but their analysis technique does not provide all the properties that we need for our problems.

1.1 Related Work

To the best of our knowledge, there are only a few works that directly consider the message complexity of SET COVER. Most notably, in [3] Demaine et al. showed that randomization is crucially needed for a message complexity of $o(mn)$ (as it is impossible for a deterministic algorithm). However, they do consider two-party communication models where one party stores the sets and the other stores the elements, making their algorithms not directly applicable in our models. They also consider the space complexity of SET COVER in streaming models. In the streaming model, the edges of the problem graph, i.e., the information on which element belongs to which set, arrive sequentially. An algorithm can store each edge for later use and iterate over the whole input several times. The goal is to solve SETCOVER using as few passes and space as possible. Note that a trivial algorithm can iterate over the input once, store all edges, and then solve the problem using an *offline* algorithm. Later, Indyk et al. successfully used the ideas and primitives from streaming algorithms in the area of Sublinear Algorithms in [8]. Here, any connection between an element and a set must be explicitly revealed via a query. Their goal was to find an algorithm that makes *few* queries, .i.e. sublinear in the number of connections, and still computes a good approximate solution. Indyk et al. present a polynomial-time algorithm that makes $\tilde{O}(m + \sqrt{m}n)$ queries and computes a $O(\log^2(n))$-approximate solution. With exponential runtime, the approximation ratio even reduces to $O(\log(n + m))$, but the algorithm still needs to make $\tilde{O}(m + \sqrt{m}n)$ queries. Furthermore, Indyk et al. gave strong evidence that $\Omega(nm^\epsilon)$ queries are indeed necessary to achieve non-trivial approximation ratios. As we will see in Sect. 3, this model has a lot in common with our distributed model as any query can be simulated by a message and vice versa.

Next, we review some fully distributed approaches. As mentioned in the introduction, Jia et al. [9] as well as Kuhn and Wattenhofer [11] have presented fast distributed algorithms to solve the DOMINATINGSET problem in time in $O(\log(n)^2)$. In [10], Kuhn et al. presented an algorithm to to compute a $O(\sqrt[k]{\Delta})$-approximation for SETCOVER (and any covering and packing LP) in $O(k^2)$ rounds in the CONGEST model. This is close to the optimal runtime of $O(k)$, which is also proven in [10]. Recently, Ben-Basat et al. even developed a deterministic algorithm that solves SETCOVER in optimal time [1]. Finally, many works consider the DOMINATINGSET-problem in models tailored to ad-hoc networks. Both compute a $O(1)$-approximation in $O(log(n))$ rounds. First, there is a paper by Scheideler et al. [14] that observes the SINR model where the nodes are modeled as points in the euclidean plane. Second, there already is

---

[4] Instead of using geometric starting times they continuously increase a set's probability to join until it joins or does cover enough elements. From a probabilistic point of view, this is (almost) equivalent to picking geometric starting times.

a solution to the DOMINATINGSET-problem in the BEEPING-model for unit-disk graphs [15]. The latter algorithm bears some similarities with ours but does not apply to general graphs as it exploits specific properties of the unit-disc graph.

1.2 Structure of This Paper

This paper is structured as follows: In Sect. 2, we present the algorithm for the BEEPING model. Finally, Sect. 3 contains the KT_0 algorithm and an almost matching lower bound. We provide more details on the models in the respective sections. For all proofs that are either omitted or only sketched due to the space restrictions, we refer to the full version on arXiv [7].

2 An Efficient SETCOVER-Algorithm for the BEEPING-Model

We will now describe our first algorithm, which we dub the BEEP-AND-SLEEP algorithm, as most sets and elements will be idle during the execution. Before we go into the details of our result and the algorithm, let us first present the model. In this section, we use the following (standard) variant of the BEEPING model [2,4]:

1. We observe a fixed communication graph $G := (V_S \cup V_U, E)$ with $V_S = m$ and $V_U = n$. Each set $s \in V_S$ has a bidirected edge $\{s, e\} \in E$ to each element $e \in V_U$ it contains. Each node can only communicate with its neighbors in G. Further, all nodes know Δ, the maximal degree of G. This assumption can be replaced by a polynomial upper bound, which would slow the algorithm down by a constant factor. Note that the nodes do not know their exact degree, and nodes have *no* identifiers.
2. Time proceeds in so-called *slots*. In each slot, a node can either *beep* or *listen*. If a node *listens* and any subsets of its neighbors *beeps*, the *listening* node receives a BEEP. It can neither distinguish which neighbors beeped nor how many neighbors beeped, i.e., it only relies on carrier sensing. Further, a node *cannot* simultaneously beep and listen but must choose one of the two options.
3. All nodes wake up in the same slot, i.e., we observe the BEEPING model with simultaneous wake-up. We believe that our algorithm can also be extended for arbitrary wake-up as each node only needs to be in sync with neighboring nodes. If nodes do not wake up in the same round, their internal counters only differ by 1 as each node wakes up one slot after its earliest neighbor. In this case, there are some standard tricks to simulate a single slot of a simultaneous wake-up algorithm within 3 slots [2,4].

Given this model, we show the following:

Theorem 1. *There is an algorithm in the* BEEPING *model that solves* SET-COVER *in time* $O(k^3)$ *with approximation ratio* $O(\log^2(\Delta) \cdot \sqrt[k]{\Delta}^3)$ *where* $k > 3$ *is parameter known to all nodes.*

We will now describe the algorithm promised by the theorem: The core idea is that all nodes that cover the *most* neighbors add themselves to the set similar to the sequential greedy algorithm. The main difficulty stems from the fact that we need to estimate the number of uncovered neighbors correctly and avoid too many sets that cover the same elements concurrently add themselves to the solution. The algorithm runs in k phases, where in phase i all sets that cover *approximately* $\Delta_i = \frac{\Delta}{\sqrt[k]{\Delta}^i}$ elements try to add themselves to the solution. Each phase is structured in $4k$ *rounds*. Further, each round again consists of $4k + 1$ slots, which brings the total runtime to $O(k^3)$. The pseudocode for the algorithm is given in Figure 1, on a high level, it works as follows:

1. At the beginning of *phase j*, i.e., before the first round of that phase, the sets and elements do the following: Each *set s* draws a geometric random variable X_s with parameter $1 - 1/\sqrt[k]{\Delta}$. Values bigger than $4k$ are rounded down to $4k$, so $X \in [0, 4k]$ always. Then, the set waits for $4k - X_s$ *rounds* and neither beeps or listens, it just stays idle. Each uncovered *element* marks itself as *active* with probability $\frac{4k}{\Delta_j} := \frac{4k \sqrt[k]{\Delta}^j}{\Delta}$.

   Thus, each set with Δ_j (or more) uncovered elements has at least $4k$ active elements in expectation. Each active element further picks a slot number $a_u \in [0, 4k]$ uniformly at random.

2. In each *round i* of phase j, the sets and elements do the following: Each *set s* that wakes up in this round listens to BEEPS for the first $4k$ slots of this round. Further, it counts all slots in which it received a BEEP. Otherwise, it remains idle for this round. Each active *element* that has not yet been covered, beeps *only* in the slot a_u is has drawn in the beginning and remains idle otherwise. Note that, by our choice of active elements, this implies that all sets that have at least Δ_j uncovered elements, therefore, hear one BEEP per slot *in expectation.*

3. In the *last* slot of a round, i.e., in slot $4k + 1$, the sets and elements do the following: Each *set* that received a BEEP in at least $3k$ slots adds itself to the solution and beeps. Each uncovered *element* (active or not) listens and considers itself covered if a neighbor joined the solution, i.e., if it hears a BEEP. If an element is covered, it does not need to send or receive messages for the remainder of the algorithm.

Note that the last step of each round where the sets add themselves is the main difference to the classical algorithm by Jia et al. [9]. In their work, each candidate locally computed a probability to join the solution. This used information from its 2-neighborhood. This approach seems not to be trivially doable with only BEEPS. Finally, note that this algorithm can also be used to compute a DOMINATINGSET, we provide the details at the end of this section.

2.1   Proof of Theorem 1

We will now prove Theorem 1 and show that our algorithm indeed fulfills the promised bounds. Since the runtime is deterministic, we will only prove the expected approximation ratio.

Algorithm 1. BEEP-AND-SLEEP (BASED ON [9])

---

procedure SETS(s, N_s, k, Δ) ▷ Executed by the sets $s \in V_{\mathcal{S}}$
    for $i := \Delta, \Delta/\sqrt[k]{\Delta}, \ldots, 0$ **do**   ▷ k phases.
        Pick $X_s \sim Geo(1 - \frac{1}{\sqrt[k]{\Delta}})$. ▷ $Geo(p)$ is the geometric distribution with success
prob. p.
        Round X_s down to $\Phi := 4k$ if necessary.
        Wait $\Phi - X_s$ **rounds**.
        for $\ell = 1, \ldots, 4k$ **do**   ▷ $4k$ slots.
            Listen for BEEPS
        end for
        if s receives more than $3k$ BEEPS **then**
            Add s to S.   ▷ Last slot of the round
            Announce to neighbors via BEEP.   ▷ Each round takes $4k + 1$ slots.
        end if
        Wait X_s **rounds** until end of phase.   ▷ Note that $\Phi = (\Phi - X_s) + X_s$.
    end for   ▷ Each phase takes k rounds.
end procedure

procedure ELEMENTS(e, N_e, k, Δ) ▷ Executed by the elements $e \in V_{\mathcal{U}}$
    for $i := \Delta, \Delta/\sqrt[k]{\Delta}, \ldots, 0$ **do**   ▷ k phases.
        $Y_e \sim B(\frac{4k}{\Delta_i})$ ▷ $B(p)$ returns 1 with prob. p
        $a_e \sim Uni(1, \ldots, 4k)$ ▷ $Uni(a, \ldots, b)$ picks an integer in $[a, b]$ uniformly at
random
        for $j := 0, \ldots, 4k$ **do**   ▷ $4k$ rounds.
            for $\ell = 1, \ldots, 4k$ **do**   ▷ $4k$ slots.
                if $(Y_e = 1)$ *and* $(a_e = \ell)$ *and* $(e$ *is uncovered)* **then**
                    Send BEEP to all neighboring sets.
                end if
            end for
            Listen if a neighbor added itself.   ▷ Last slot of the round
            Set e as covered, if it received a BEEP   ▷ Each round takes $4k + 1$ slots.
        end for
    end for   ▷ Each phase takes $4k$ rounds.
end procedure

Lemma 1. *The algorithm outputs a* $O\left(\log^2(\Delta) \cdot \left(\sqrt[k]{\Delta}\right)^3\right)$*-approximate solution in expectation.*

As the algorithm follows the LRG algorithm by Jia et al. [9], a generalized version of their core lemma also holds in this case. However, we need to "parameterize" it further to account that we cannot count the uncovered elements precisely. For each element covered by our algorithm, we define the random variables $\eta(u)$ and $\mu(u)$. We define $\eta(u)$ to be the ratio between the *best* set in u's neighbor and the worst set picked by the algorithm, i.e., the ratio by which the choice of our algorithm differs from the greedy solution. Further, let $\mu(u)$ be the random variable that denotes the number of candidates covering $u \in V$ in the round where it is first covered. Finally, we define η and μ the corresponding variables of the elements that maximize their expected values, i.e.,

$$E[\mu] = \max_{u \in U} E[\mu(u)] \quad and \quad E[\eta] = \max_{u \in U} E[\eta(u)] \tag{1}$$

Given these definitions, the following modified version of Jia et al.'s algorithm [9] holds:

Lemma 2. *Let S be the size of the set output by our algorithm and S_{OPT} be optimal solution. Then, it holds.*

$$E[|S|] \leq 2 \cdot E[\eta] \cdot E[\mu] \cdot \log(\Delta) \cdot |S_{OPT}| \tag{2}$$

Proof. Before we go into the details of the proof, we define the functions $c_{min}(u)$ and $c_{max}(u)$ for each covered element $u \in V_{\mathcal{U}}$. Suppose u is covered by sets $s_1, \ldots, s_m$, i.e., these sets add themselves simultaneously. Further, let $d(s_1), \ldots, d(s_m)$ be *spans* of $s_1, \ldots, s_m$, i.e., the number of uncovered elements neighboring $s_1, \ldots, s_m$. Based on this, we define c_{max} based on the set with *fewest* uncovered elements,i.e., the set that devaites the most from whatever set the greedy solution would have picked. The value c_{min} on the other hand is determined by the set in u's neighborhood with biggest possible span, i.e., the set that the greedy solution would have picked. Note that this set may not be part of $s_1, \ldots, s_m$. Formally, we have:

$$c_{max}(u) = \max_{v_i \in \{s_1, \ldots, s_m\}} \frac{1}{d(s_i)} \quad and \quad c_{min}(u) = \min_{s \in N_u} \frac{1}{d(s)} \tag{3}$$

Further, by Lemma 3.5 in [9], it holds that:

$$\sum_{u \in V_{\mathcal{U}}} c_{min}(u) \leq H_\Delta |S_{OPT}| \leq 2\log(\Delta)|S_{OPT}| \tag{4}$$

where H_Δ is the Δth harmonic number. On the other hand, by the definition of $\eta(u)$, it holds:

$$c_{max}(u) = \eta(u) \cdot c_{min}(u) \tag{5}$$

Given these definitions, we now consider a single round i. In the following, let S_i be set of candidates that add themselves to S in round i. Let V_i denote the set of elements that are uncovered at the start of round i. We have:

$$|S_i| \leq \sum_{v \in S_i} \frac{d(v)}{d(v)} \leq \sum_{v \in S} |C(v)| \frac{1}{d(v)} \leq \sum_{v \in S} \sum_{u \in C(v)} c_{max}(u) \tag{6}$$

$$= \sum_{u \in V_i} c_{max}(u)\mu(u) \leq \sum_{u \in V_i} c_{min}(u) \cdot \eta(u) \cdot \mu(u) \tag{7}$$

For the expected value of S_i, this implies:

$$E[|S_i|] \leq \sum_{u \in V_i} c_{min}(u) \cdot E[\eta(u)] \cdot E[\mu(u) \mid \mu(u) > 0] \tag{8}$$

This follows from the fact that the random events that determine $\eta(u)$ and $\mu(u)$ are independent. Finally, we can use the linearity of expectation to sum over all k^2 rounds and get:

$$E\left[|S|\right] = \sum_{i=1}^{k^2} E[|S_i|] \leq \sum_{u \in V} E[\eta(u)] \cdot E[\mu(u) \mid t(u) > 0]c_{min}(u) \qquad (9)$$

$$\leq E[\eta] \cdot E[\mu] \cdot 2 \cdot \log(\Delta) \cdot |S_{OPT}| \qquad (10)$$

This proves the lemma.

Given this lemma, it remains to bound $E[\eta]$ and $E[\mu]$. We begin with the latter. Our goal is to use a result by Miller et al. [12] (which needs to be adapted for geometric values). They showed that the number of candidates that pick the earliest possible wake-up time is $\sqrt[k]{\Delta}$ in expectation. Similarly, we can show the following result[5].

Lemma 3. *For any value $t > 1$ and node $u \in V$, it holds* $\mathbf{Pr}\left[\mu_u > t\right] \leq (1 - 1/\sqrt[k]{\Delta})^t$

Proof. For each node $u \in V$ we define the random variable $\mathcal{P}$ that denotes the *phase* in which u is covered. Recall that every element is *always* covered because in the last round of the last phase, all remaining sets that cover at least one element add themselves to the solution. Thus, the variable $\mathcal{P}$ takes values in $0, \ldots, 4k$. In the remainder, we will focus only on a single phase. Throughout this proof, we divide the sets into two subsets. First, let N_u be the set of sets in u's neighborhood, i.e., the sets that can cover u. We call these the *neighboring candidates*. Second, let $NN := V_S \setminus N_u$ be all other sets. We call these the *non-neighboring candidates*. Further, we define the wakeup time Φ_s of each $s \in V_S$ as $\Phi_s := 4k - X_s$. Now we observe the round in which u is covered and see:

Lemma 4. *Suppose gets u gets covered in the first round of phase j, then*

$$\mathbf{Pr}[\mu_j \geq t \mid u \text{ is coverd in round } 0] \leq \left(1 - \frac{1}{\sqrt[k]{\Delta}}\right)^t \qquad (11)$$

The exciting stuff happens if u gets covered in any other round of phase i. This part is more complex than the previous one as it requires a more careful analysis of the starting times. First, we will fix all of the random decisions made by the algorithm **except** the decision of the neighboring sets. In particular, we condition on the following three variables:

---

[5] Note that that the analysis in [6] only bounds this term in expectation (and not exact probability) and does not parameterize it on the number of phases as we do. **We need both these aspects for our problem.** Adding these two aspects to their analysis is not straightforward as they use a rather complex term to bound the expectation. In contrast, we exploit the fundamental properties of the geometric distribution.

1. **The wakeup times of the non-neighboring sets** Z_{NN}.
   It holds $Z_{NN} := (\phi_1, \ldots, \phi'_m)$. For each $l \in [0, m']$, the non-neighboring set s_l wakes up in round ϕ_l.

2. **The BEEPS by all uncovered elements** Z_U.
   This random variable contains all random choices made by the uncovered elements, i.e., $Z_U := \{(Y_e, a_e) \mid e \in V_{\mathcal{U}}\}$. Here, the variable Y_e denotes whether e is active and beeps and a_e denotes the slot in which e beeps. Based on this, we can define the *number* of slots in which a set s receives a BEEP from an element in subset $U \subseteq V_{\mathcal{U}}$ as follows:

$$\text{SLOTS}(s, U) := |\{i \in [0, 4k] \mid \exists e \in U \cap N_s : Y_e = 1 \wedge a_e = i\}| \qquad (12)$$

3. **The initial set of uncovered elements** $\mathcal{U}_0$.
   This is the set of uncovered elements in round 0 of phase j.

If we fix all these choices, the decision if a neighboring candidate of u adds itself to the solution that depends on *solely* its wake-up time. More precisely, the random choices of the other nodes define the last possible round in which a candidate may add itself to the solution. If it wakes up before this round, the concrete round is *only* determined by the geometric distribution. If it wakes up after this round, it will not add itself.

Now we claim the following

Claim. Given $(Z_{NN}, Z_U, \mathcal{U}_0)$ for each neighboring set $s \in N_u$ there is a well-defined value $\rho_s \in [0, 4k]$ that denotes the last round in which s can cover u, i.e.,

$$\mathbf{Pr}[s \text{ covers } u \text{ first } \mid \Phi_s \geq \rho_s] = 0$$

The idea behind the construction is that the *fixed* values $\mathcal{U}_0$, Z_{NCC}, and Z_U can clearly define the sets $\mathcal{A}_0 \subset V_S$ that add themselves to the solution in round 0. Given Z_{NN}, we see which sets wake up and count the BEEPS of their uncovered elements. These BEEPS are based on $\mathcal{U}_0$ and Z_U, so we see if enough elements beep in distinct slots. In particular, the set must receive a BEEP in at least $3k$ slots, so it must hold that

$$\mathcal{A}_0 := \{s \notin N_u \mid \phi_i = 0 \wedge (|\text{SLOTS}(s, \mathcal{U}_0)| \geq 3k)\} \qquad (13)$$

Given $\mathcal{A}_0$, i.e., the sets that add themselves in round 0, we can then compute $\mathcal{U}_1 \subseteq \mathcal{U}_0$, i.e., all uncovered elements in round 1. Then, by repeating the construction, we can use $\mathcal{U}_1$, Z_{NCC}, and Z_U to determine $\mathcal{A}_1$ and therefore $\mathcal{U}_2$ and so on. This can be continued until round τ by the following recursive formulas:

$$\mathcal{A}_t = \{s \notin N_u \mid \phi_i = 0 \wedge (|\text{SLOTS}(s, \mathcal{U}_t)| \geq 3k)\} \qquad (14)$$

and

$$U_t = \left\{ e \in \mathcal{U} \setminus \{u\} \mid \exists s \in \bigcup_{i=0}^{t-1} \mathcal{A}_i \right\} \quad (15)$$

This yields the uncovered elements $\mathcal{U}_0, \ldots, \mathcal{U}_\tau$. For each candidate $s \in N_u$, we can then clearly identify the first round ρ_s where s does not receive enough Beeps to add itself:

$$\rho_s := arg \max_{0 \le \tau \le 4k} \text{SLOTS}(s, \mathcal{U}_\tau) \ge 3k \quad (16)$$

Given this observation, we can map each outcome of Z_{NCC}, Z_U, and $\mathcal{U}_0$ to a collection of thresholds $\overline{\rho} := (\rho_1, \ldots, \rho_{\Delta_u})$ with the properties above. If we now condition on $\overline{\rho}$ and $\mathcal{P} = j$, we get—similar to Miller et al. in [12]—that:

Lemma 5. *For any possible realization of thresholds $\overline{\rho}$ it holds:*

$$\mathbf{Pr}[\mu_j \le t \mid \overline{\rho}] \le \left(1 - 1/\sqrt[k]{\Delta}\right)^t \quad (17)$$

The proof only relies on the fact that the geometric distribution is memoryless. Given that there are t sets whose wake-up time is at most some round x, the probability that none of them has an even earlier wake-up time $x' < x$ is bounded by $\left(1 - 1/\sqrt[k]{\Delta}\right)^t$.

Finally, as the concrete value of the ρ_i's and the phase is immaterial, Lemma 2 follows by the law of total probability.

Thus, the geometric series implies $E[\mu] \le \sum_{t=1}^{\infty}(1 - 1/2)^t = \frac{1}{1 - 1/\sqrt[k]{\Delta}} = \sqrt[k]{\Delta}$. Further, we show that:

Lemma 6. *For $k \ge 3$ it holds $E[\eta] \le 25 \cdot \log(\Delta) \cdot \left(\sqrt[k]{\Delta}\right)^2$*

For the proof, we fix an element $u \in \mathcal{U}$. Next, we observe the event $\mathcal{B}$ that occurs if there is any set with span bigger than $h \in \tilde{O}(\sqrt[k]{\Delta} \cdot \Delta_i)$ or any set smaller than $\ell \in O(\Delta_i/\sqrt[k]{\Delta})$ joins the solution. To compute $\mathbf{Pr}[\mathcal{B}]$, let $H_u^i \subseteq N_u$ denote all neighbors that span more than h uncovered elements at any point in phase i. Likewise, let $L_u^i \subseteq N_u$ denote all neighbors that span less than ℓ elements at any point in the phase. Then, it holds via union bound that:

$$\mathbf{Pr}[\mathcal{B}] \le \mathbf{Pr}[\exists s \in H_u] + \mathbf{Pr}[\exists s \in L_u : s \text{ adds itself to the solution}] \quad (18)$$

In the full version, we show through elementary combinatorics and calculations that both summands are smaller than $1/\Delta$. Finally, if $\mathcal{B}$ occurs, it holds $\eta \le \Delta$ and $\eta \in \tilde{O}(\sqrt[k]{\Delta})$ otherwise. Given that $\mathbf{Pr}[\mathcal{B}] \in O(1/\Delta)$, the law of total expectation implies the lemma.

Thus, combining Lemmas 2, 3, and 6 yields Theorem 1.

2.2   Extension to DominatingSet

Note that the algorithm can also be extended to the DominatingSet problem, where each set is also an element. At first glance, all elements could simply also execute the code for the sets. Note, however, that a node cannot simultaneously beep and listen, which causes some problems with a direct simulation. In particular, an *active* uncovered elements cannot also listen for Beeps in all slots. To solve this, we add all active elements to the solution. In phase i, each set that is added to the solution covers $\Omega(\Delta_{i-1}\log(n))$ elements, w.h.p. This follows from an application of the Chernoff bound. Suppose there are U_i uncovered elements, then optimal solution must at least be of size $\Theta(U_i/\Delta_{i-1}\log(n))$ As in phase i there are—by Chernoff—only $O(U_i/\Delta_i\log(n))$ active elements, w.h.p. we can just add to the solution without (asymtotically) affecting the approximation ratio. Note that this also implies that for $k = \log(\Delta)$ the total number of Beeps is $\tilde{O}(|S_{OPT}|)$.

3   A Low-Message KT_0 Algorithm

We now move away from the Beeping model and present our low-message KT_0-Congest algorithm. In this section, we make the following less restrictive assumptions about the model:

1. Again, we observe a fixed communication graph $G := (V_S \cup V_{\mathcal{U}}, E)$ with $V_S = m$ and $V_{\mathcal{U}} = n$ with bidirected communication edges $\{s, e\} \in E$ between a set an its elements. Sets and elements can locally distinguish between their edges through port numbers, but no global identifiers uniquely identify a node. To simplify the presentation, all nodes know Δ and $\log(n + m)$.
2. Time proceeds in synchronous *rounds*. Each round, an element or set can send a distinct message of size $O(\log(n + m))$ to any subset of its neighbors. Messages are received in the next round.
3. All nodes wake up in the same round.

In other literature, this model is sometimes referred to as the *clean network model* [13]. Note that this model does not intend to represent ad-hoc networks faithfully but instead is used to analyze the message efficiency of distributed algorithms (see .e.g., [5] for an overview). Similar to the Beeping model, it starts with limited knowledge of its neighborhood and must *learn* everything it needs to solve the given problem. Given this model, we will show the following theorem:

Theorem 2. *There is an algorithm in the KT_0-Congest model that solves* SetCover *in time* $O(\log^2(\Delta))$, *an expected approximation ratio of* $O(\log(\Delta))$, *and sends only* $\tilde{O}(\sqrt{\Delta}(n + m))$ *messages, w.h.p., given that all nodes know Δ and an approximation of* $\log(n + m)$.

3.1 Proof of Theorem 2

We will only need a few changes to our already established algorithm to prove Theorem 2. Every BEEPING-Algorithm also works in the KT_0-CONGEST-Model mentioned above, as the model is less restricted. To obtain a message efficient algorithm, we only need to make a few minor changes to our algorithm: First, to simplify the presentation, we do not parameterize the algorithm with k. Instead, we fix $k = \log(\Delta)$ and only consider this case. Second, we do not require the notion of slots anymore as a node can count how many of its neighbors beeped in a single round as the messages arrive via distinct channels. Each *round* now only consists of precisely one slot. In particular, an active element does *not* pick a slot number anymore, but directly sends its BEEP. Further, instead of beeping *all* neighbors with probability $\frac{2^i}{\Delta}$, each element picks $\frac{\log(n+m)2^i}{\Delta}$ neighbors uniformly at random and sends a BEEP. Finally, the most significant change to the algorithm is the following: Instead of executing all phases of the algorithm, we only execute it until phase $\frac{\log(\Delta)}{2}$, i.e., until the active degree of all sets is around $O(\sqrt{\Delta})$. We call this the first *stage* of the algorithm. Then, all uncovered elements notify their respective set that they are uncovered. Denote these elements as $\mathcal{U}'$. Finally, the algorithm continues (almost) as usual for the remaining $\frac{\log(\Delta)}{2}$ phases. However, each set that joins the solution notifies *only* the elements in $\mathcal{U}'$ that they are covered. We call this the second *stage* of the algorithm.

We will now sketch the analysis. One can easily verify that most lemmas from our previous analysis are still correct. The first stage does not differ from our previous algorithm at all. Further, all nodes that do not receive any message in the second stage of the algorithm (but would have in the original algorithm) are already covered. Thus, they would be idle regardless. Thus, we only need to show that $E[\eta]$ is still small to prove the approximation ratio.

Before we start, we need the following auxiliary lemma that tightly bound the sets that add themselves to the solution in a phase i.

Lemma 7. *Suppose each elements picks $c \cdot 8 \cdot \log(n+m)\frac{2^i}{\Delta}$ active edges uniformly and independently at random. Further, each set with at least $c \cdot 4 \log(n+m)$ active edges adds itself on wake-up. Then the following two statements hold w.h.p:*

1. *At the end of phase i there is no set with $\frac{\Delta}{2^i}$ uncovered elements.*
2. *Any set that adds itself in round i covers at least $\frac{\Delta}{8 \cdot 2^i}$ elements.*

Both statements follow via an elementary application of the Chernoff Bound. Note that this lemma directly implies that $E[\eta] \in O(1)$ as it bounds the *worst* and *best* set in each rounds, w.h.p. Therefore expected approximation ratio is $O(\log(\Delta))$, which is as good as the sequential greedy solution.

Thus, it only remains to analyze the message complexity. We prove the message bound for each stage of the algorithm. We begin with the first stage and show that for it holds:

Lemma 8. *Until phase $\frac{\log(\Delta)}{2}$, the nodes send at most $\tilde{O}(n\sqrt{\Delta})$ messages.*

Proof. As each element picks (up to) $\tilde{O}(2^i)$ edges in phase i, the lemma follows immediately. The corresponding bound for the sets is less trivial as it does not directly follow from the algorithm. Here, we need to consider that only sets that add themselves to the solution send messages. In particular, each set that adds itself sends at most Δ messages and remains silent otherwise. Thus, we show that at most $\tilde{O}(n/\sqrt{\Delta})$ sets add themselves w.h.p. Note that every set that adds itself covers (at least) $\sqrt{\Delta}/8$ uncovered elements, w.h.p, otherwise it would *not* have added itself. This follows from the second statement in Lemma 7. On the other hand, each uncovered element is covered by *at most* $O(\log(n+m))$ sets, w.h.p. This follows from choosing $t \geq c\log(n+m)$ for some $c > 0$ in Lemma 3. Let $S_i \subset V_S$ be the solution in phase i and C_i be the covered elements, then it must hold:

$$|S_i| \cdot \sqrt{\Delta}/8 \leq c\log(n+m)|C_i| \Leftrightarrow |S_i| \leq \frac{8c\log(n+m)|C_i|}{\sqrt{\Delta}} \tag{19}$$

$$\Leftrightarrow |S_i| \leq \frac{8c\log(n+m)n}{\sqrt{\Delta}} \in \tilde{O}\left(\frac{n}{\sqrt{\Delta}}\right) \tag{20}$$

In other words, if there are more $\tilde{O}(\frac{n}{\sqrt{\Delta}})$ sets that added themselves, then there must exist an element covered by more than $c\log(n+m)$ sets. This is a contradiction, which implies the lemma.

This lemma concludes the analysis of the algorithm's first stage. Finally, we need to observe the second stage. In this stage, the algorithm only uses communication edges adjacent to the set of uncovered elements in phase $\log(\Delta)/2$. Thus, to determine the message complexity, we only need to count these edges. Formally, we show:

Lemma 9. *In phase $\frac{\log(\Delta)}{2}$, each set has at most $O(\sqrt{\Delta})$ uncovered elements.*

Proof. The lemma follows directly from the first statement of Lemma 7 as all sets that have more than $O(\sqrt{\Delta})$ uncovered elements must have added themselves in an earlier round w.h.p.

Thus, in the remaining $O(\log^2(\Delta))$ rounds of the algorithm, all communication will only take place via these $O(m\sqrt{\Delta})$ edges. Since at most one message passes each edge in every round, this implies that at most $O(m\sqrt{\Delta}\log^2(\Delta))$ messages are sent, which proves Theorem 2.

3.2   Lower Bound

This section proves a lower bound on the number of messages needed to approximate a solution. The proof works via a reduction to the sequential case. Here, it is well known that a large portion of the input, i.e., the connections between the nodes, must be revealed to the algorithm. In particular, it is known that the following holds:

Lemma 10 (Lower bound from [8]**).** *Consider a sequential computation model that allows the following two queries*

- ***EltOf(i,j)** - Returns the jth element of Set S_i or $\perp$ if there is no such element.*
- ***SetOf(i,j)** - Returns the jth set which contrains e_i or $\perp$ if there is no such set.*

Then, every algorithm that yields an $O(1)$-approximation for SETCOVER *needs at least $\tilde{\Omega}(m\sqrt{n})$ queries on certain graphs.*

In particular, the lower bound graph in [8] has maximal degree n and it holds $m = n$. Therefore, the bound can be rewritten as $\tilde{\Omega}((m + n)\sqrt{\Delta})$, which is exactly the message complexity of our algorithm. Now we show that if there is a distributed algorithm with less than $\tilde{\Omega}(m\sqrt{n})$ messages, it can be turned into a sequential algorithm with less than $\tilde{\Omega}(m\sqrt{n})$ queries. This is, of course, a contradiction to the lemma above. The proof's main ingredient is the observation that every message that is sent from v along its jth channel can be emulated as looking up $SetOf(v, j)$. Other than that, the proof is quite technical. The main result is as follows:

Lemma 11. *Any algorithm that yields an $O(1)$-approximation for* SETCOVER *needs at least $\tilde{\Omega}(m\sqrt{n})$ messages on certain graphs in KT_0 model.*

4   Conclusion and Future Work

In this work, we presented two different message and energy-efficient distributed algorithms for SETCOVER in the BEEPING model and the KT_0 model. Both our algorithms offer exciting avenues for future research.

Our BEEPING algorithm is tailored to find the optimal trade-off between runtime and approximation ratio in general graphs. As the lower bound for our approximation ratio of $\tilde{O}(\sqrt[k]{\Delta})$ is $O(k)$, it would be interesting to find a BEEPING algorithm that takes $o(k^3)$ rounds for the same approximation and comes closer to that lower bound. However, such an algorithm would mainly be of theoretical interest. Thus, improving our algorithm's approximation ratio on practical graphs while keeping the sublogarithmic runtime (in n) would also be worthwhile.

For the KT_0 model, a tighter lower bound would be of great interest as the current bound only works for constant factor approximations, which are not achievable on many instances of the problem unless P=NP. Finally, it would be interesting to see whether the existence of unique identifiers known to all neighbors (i.e., the $KT1$-model) can improve the message complexity or if similar lower bounds hold.

References

1. Ben-Basat, R., Even, G., Kawarabayashi, K.I., Schwartzman, G.: Optimal distributed covering algorithms. In: Robinson, P., Ellen, F. (eds.) Proceedings of the 2019 ACM Symposium on Principles of Distributed Computing, PODC 2019, Toronto, ON, Canada, 29 July – 2 August 2019, pp. 104–106. ACM (2019)
2. Cornejo, A., Kuhn, F.: Deploying wireless networks with beeps. In: Lynch, N.A., Shvartsman, A.A. (eds.) DISC 2010. LNCS, vol. 6343, pp. 148–162. Springer, Heidelberg (2010). https://doi.org/10.1007/978-3-642-15763-9_15
3. Demaine, E.D., Indyk, P., Mahabadi, S., Vakilian, A.: On streaming and communication complexity of the set cover problem. In: Kuhn, F. (ed.) DISC 2014. LNCS, vol. 8784, pp. 484–498. Springer, Heidelberg (2014). https://doi.org/10.1007/978-3-662-45174-8_33
4. Dufoulon, F., Burman, J., Beauquier, J.: Beeping a deterministic time-optimal leader election. In: Proceedings of the 32nd International Symposium on Distributed Computing (DISC 2018), volume 121 of Leibniz International Proceedings in Informatics (LIPIcs), pp. 20:1–20:17, Dagstuhl, Germany, 2018. Schloss Dagstuhl-Leibniz-Zentrum fuer Informatik (2018)
5. Gmyr, R., Pandurangan, G.: Time-message trade-offs in distributed algorithms. In: Schmid, U., Widder, J. (eds.) 32nd International Symposium on Distributed Computing, DISC 2018, New Orleans, LA, USA, 15–19 October 2018, volume 121 of LIPIcs, pp. 32:1–32:18. Schloss Dagstuhl - Leibniz-Zentrum für Informatik (2018)
6. Grunau, C., Mitrovic, S., Rubinfeld, R., Vakilian, A.: Improved local computation algorithm for set cover via sparsification. In: Proceedings of the 2020 ACM-SIAM Symposium on Discrete Algorithms, SODA 2020, Salt Lake City, UT, USA, 5–8 January 2020, pp. 2993–3011. SIAM (2020)
7. Götte, T., Kolb, C., Scheideler, C., Werthmann, J.: Beep-and-sleep: Message and energy efficient set cover (2021). http://arxiv.org/abs/2107.14570arXiv:2107.14570
8. Indyk, P., Mahabadi, S., Rubinfeld, R., Vakilian, A., Yodpinyanee, A.: Set cover in sub-linear time. In: Proceedings of the Twenty-Ninth Annual ACM-SIAM Symposium on Discrete Algorithms, SODA 2018, New Orleans, LA, USA, 7–10 January 2018, pp. 2467–2486. SIAM (2018)
9. Jia, L., Rajaraman, R., Suel, T.: An efficient distributed algorithm for constructing small dominating sets. Distrib. Comput. 15(4), 193–205 (2002)
10. Kuhn, F., Moscibroda, T., Wattenhofer, R.: The price of being near-sighted. In: Proceedings of the Seventeenth Annual ACM-SIAM Symposium on Discrete Algorithms, SODA 2006, Miami, Florida, USA, 22–26 January 2006, pp. 980–989. ACM Press (2006). http://dl.acm.org/citation.cfm?id=1109557.1109666
11. Kuhn, F., Wattenhofer, R.: Constant-time distributed dominating set approximation. In: Proceedings of the Twenty-Second ACM Symposium on Principles of Distributed Computing, PODC 2003, Boston, Massachusetts, USA, 13–16 July 2003, pp. 25–32. ACM (2003)
12. Miller, G.L., Peng, R., Vladu, A., Xu, S.C.: Improved parallel algorithms for spanners and hopsets. In: Proceedings of the 27th ACM on Symposium on Parallelism in Algorithms and Architectures, SPAA 2015, Portland, OR, USA, 13–15 June 2015, pp. 192–201. ACM (2015)
13. Peleg, D.: Distributed Computing: A Locality-Sensitive Approach. Society for Industrial and Applied Mathematics, USA (2000)

14. Scheideler, C., Richa, A., Santi, P.: An o(log n) dominating set protocol for wireless ad-hoc networks under the physical interference model. In: Proceedings of the 9th ACM Interational Symposium on Mobile Ad Hoc Networking and Computing, MobiHoc 2008, Hong Kong, China, 26–30 May 2008, pp. 91–100. ACM (2008)
15. Yu, J., Jia, L., Yu, D., Li, G., Cheng, X.: Minimum connected dominating set construction in wireless networks under the beeping model. In: 2015 IEEE Conference on Computer Communications, INFOCOM 2015, Kowloon, Hong Kong, 26 April – 1 May 2015, pp. 972–980. IEEE (2015)

Byzantine Fault Tolerant
Symmetric-Persistent Circle Evacuation

Nikos Leonardos[1], Aris Pagourtzis[2], and Ioannis Papaioannou[2(✉)]

[1] Department of Informatics and Telecommunications,
National and Kapodistrian University of Athens, Ilissia, Greece
[2] School of Electrical and Computer Engineering,
National Technical University of Athens, Zografou, Greece
pagour@cs.ntua.gr, ipapaioannou@corelab.ntua.gr

Abstract. We consider (n, f)-evacuation on a circle, an evacuation problem of a hidden exit on the perimeter of a unit radius circle for $n > 1$ robots, f of which are faulty. All the robots start at the center of the circle and move with maximum speed 1. Robots must first find the exit and then move there to evacuate in minimum time. The problem is considered complete when all the honest robots know the correct position of the exit and the last honest robot has evacuated through the exit. During the search, robots can communicate wirelessly.

We focus on symmetric-persistent algorithms, that is, algorithms in which all robots move directly to the circumference, start searching the circle moving in the same direction (cw or ccw), and do not stop moving around the circle before receiving information about the exit. We study the case of $(n, 1)$ and $(n, 2)$ evacuation. We first prove a lower bound of $1 + \frac{4\pi}{n} + 2\sin(\frac{\pi}{2} - \frac{\pi}{n})$ for one faulty robot, even a crash-faulty one. We also observe an almost matching upper bound obtained by means of an earlier search algorithm. We finally study the case with two Byzantine robots and we provide an algorithm that achieves evacuation in time at most $3 + \frac{6\pi}{n}$, for $n \geq 9$, or at most $3 + \frac{6\pi}{n} + \delta(n)$, for $n < 9$, where $\delta(n) \leq 2\sin(\frac{3\pi}{2n}) + \sqrt{2 - 4\sin(\frac{3\pi}{2n}) + 4\sin^2(\frac{3\pi}{2n})} - 2$.

1 Introduction

An important, extensively studied family of problems in mobile agent computing concerns situations where a group of robots need to find one or more targets that are located in unknown points of a territory. In a particular case of interest, the target(s) are *exit(s)* and the goal of the robots is either to locate the exit(s) (*Search* problem) or to leave the territory (*Evacuation* problem), as fast as possible. In this paper we focus on the latter problem.

1.1 Model and Preliminaries

We detail below the particular setting that we are going to study in this work.

© Springer Nature Switzerland AG 2021
L. Gąsieniec et al. (Eds.): ALGOSENSORS 2021, LNCS 12961, pp. 111–123, 2021.
https://doi.org/10.1007/978-3-030-89240-1_8

Location and Movement

The starting position of the robots is the center of a unit radius disk. The exit is located at the perimeter of the disk. All robots move with the same speed 1. During their movement, they can recognize and move along the perimeter of the disk, and they can find the exit if they are at its location. Robots are allowed to take shortcuts moving through chords in the interior of the disk.

Communication

The robots can communicate wirelessly and with no delay at any time and distance. The messages may contain information about their location, whether or not they found the exit, how far they have moved from their starting position etc. Messages are tagged with the sender's unique identifier that cannot be modified in any way. All robots can deduce their relative position from each other messages. They are also equipped with a pedometer in order to measure distances.

Fault Types

Some robots may display faulty behaviour. A crash-faulty robot may stop functioning at any time, meaning that they fail to communicate any messages, and remains idle. A Byzantine robot behaves maliciously, it can alter its trajectory and provide or hide information in order to confuse the rest of the honest robots on the location of the exit. A Byzantine robot can also behave as a crash-faulty one.

Adversary

For the worst case analysis of our algorithms, we consider an adversary who controls the location of the exit and the behaviour of the malicious robots (its trajectories as well as the messages they will broadcast) so as to maximize the resulting search and evacuation completion time. An evacuation is complete if the exit is found (has been visited by a non-faulty robot and the rest of them, if any, can be convinced (provably) of the (correct) location of the exit) and all the non-faulty robots reach the exit.

1.2   Related Work

Evacuation is closely related to Search, in fact the two problems coincide in the case of a single robot. A long line of research focused on the line search (aka Cow Path) problem (see [1–3] and references therein); more recent works include Kao et al. [4], in the randomized setting, and Demaine et al. [5] who takes into account the turn cost.

The problem was studied under the fault-tolerance perspective by Czyzowicz et al. [6,7] who considered the problem under the presence of either crash or Byzantine failures.

In circular topologies, evacuation was the first problem to be studied, in [8], who dealt with both the wireless and face-to-face communication models.

Additional work on circle evacuation followed shortly afterwards, e.g. in [9] for the face-to-face model, and in [10] for equilateral triangles (for a comprehensive survey we refer the reader to [11]).

Regarding fault-tolerant evacuation in circles, a work closely related to this paper is [12], where they study the problem with 3 robots, one of which is faulty, and provide upper and lower bounds for both cases of crash-faulty and Byzantine-faulty robot. They also introduce the notion of symmetric-persistent algorithms that we make use of in the present paper.

For the search problem in circles, under crash or Byzantine failures, a recent study [13] has shown a tight bound of $1 + \frac{4\pi}{n}$ to find the exit where n is the number of robots, one of which is Byzantine.

1.3   Results of the Paper

In Sect. 2 we consider the Evacuation problem for n robots one of which is Byzantine and we prove a lower bound for the symmetric persistent algorithms of $1 + \frac{4\pi}{n} + 2\sin(\frac{\pi}{2} - \frac{\pi}{n})$. The lower bound is almost matching to our upper bound. In Sect. 3 we present our symmetric persistent algorithm for the case of Evacuation of n robots with 2 Byzantine faults and we provide an upper bound of $3 + \frac{6\pi}{n}$, for $n \geq 9$ and $3 + \frac{6\pi}{n} + \delta(n)$ for $n < 9$, where $\delta(n) \leq 2\sin(\frac{3\pi}{2n}) + \sqrt{2 - 4\sin(\frac{3\pi}{2n}) + 4\sin^2\left(\frac{3\pi}{2n}\right)} - 2$.

2   Evacuation with One Byzantine Fault

We define (n, f) - Evacuation, to mean evacuation for $n > 1$ robots, of which f are faulty. In this work, we consider only Byzantine faults.

2.1   Lower Bound for Symmetric-Persistent Algorithms

As defined in [12], symmetric-persistent algorithms are family of natural algorithms that force all robots to immediately go to the disk perimeter and only allow a robot to stop its exploration of the assigned sector if it receives information about the exit. Symmetric-persistent algorithms force all the robots to move in the same direction (either clockwise or counter-clockwise).

Theorem 1. *Any symmetric-persistent algorithm requires time at least*

$$1 + \frac{4\pi}{n} + 2\sin\left(\frac{\pi}{2} - \frac{\pi}{n}\right) \geq 3 + \frac{4\pi}{n} - \frac{\pi^2}{2n^2}$$

for evacuation of n robots, one of which is crash-faulty, from a circle of radius 1.

Proof. Note that if $n = 2$ the result is trivial, so we assume $n \geq 3$. Let us denote by $f(n)$ the quantity displayed in the statement.

Fix a 0 on the unit circle and denote by x_i the length of the arc between robot α_i and 0 in the ccw direction. Let ψ_i denote the length of the arc between robots α_i and α_{i+2}. Since $\sum \psi_i = 4\pi$, there exists i such that $\psi_i \geq 4\pi/n = 2\theta$. Without loss of generality, let $x_2 = \psi_0 \geq 2\theta$ and denote it by ψ. For any $\epsilon > 0$, if the adversary places the exit at distance $\psi - \epsilon$ from 0 and robot α_1 is faulty, then the exit will be discovered by robot α_0 in time $1 + \psi - \epsilon$.

We now consider two cases on ψ.

First, suppose $2\theta \leq \psi < \pi$. By the maximality of ψ, there is at least one robot at distance x from 0 such that $x \in [\pi - \psi/2, \pi + \psi/2]$. The total time this robot will require to reach the exit is at least

$$1 + \psi - \epsilon + 2\sin\left(\frac{\pi - \psi/2}{2}\right) \geq 1 + 2\theta + 2\sin\left(\frac{\pi - \theta}{2}\right) - \epsilon = f(n) - \epsilon,$$

where the inequality follows because $\psi \geq 2\theta$ and the left-hand side is increasing in ψ.

Next, we consider the case $\pi \leq \psi$. In this case we will bound the time robot α_2 will need, which is at least

$$1 + \psi - \epsilon + 2\sin(\psi/2)$$

time units. Note that this is increasing in ψ. It follows that it is at least $1 + \pi - \epsilon + 2$, which for $n \geq 4$ is greater than $f(n)$. If $n = 3$, then this is at least $1 + 2\theta - \epsilon + 2\sin\theta = f(n) - \epsilon$. The equality holds since $\sin\theta = \sin(2\pi/3) = \sin(\frac{\pi}{2} - \frac{\pi}{6}) \geq \sin(\frac{\pi}{2} - \frac{\pi}{3})$.

Since the above hold for any ϵ, the first bound in the statement follows. The second bound follows from the inequality $\cos(x) \geq 1 - x^2/2$.

Theorem 2. *There exists a symmetric-persistent algorithm that requires time at most*

$$3 + \frac{4\pi}{n}$$

for evacuation of n robots, one of which is Byzantine, from a circle of radius 1.

Proof. We employ the optimal Search algorithm proposed in [13], which has a time bound of $1 + \frac{4\pi}{n}$ to find the exit, and add the length of the diameter for the furthest robot to evacuate.

Remark 1. Note that above upper bound is within $O(1/n^2)$ from the lower bound of Theorem 1.

3   Evacuation with Two Byzantine Faults

3.1   Algorithm for $(n, 2)$ - Evacuation

We will now present an algorithm for Evacuation of n robots, 2 of which are faulty, both Byzantine, and then analyze its time requirements.

Consider n robots $a_0, a_1, \ldots, a_{n-1}$ and set $\theta := 2\pi/n$. Each robot a_k moves along a radius to the point $k\theta$ of the perimeter of the unit circle. We call the arc $[k\theta, (k + 1)\theta)$ sector S_k; that is, after 1 time unit, robot a_k will be located at the beginning of sector S_k. Robots make announcements if they find the exit and confirm/disprove the announcements of other robots accordingly. Every robot searches one sector in each round, moving counter clockwise (ccw). At any moment, if an announcement is confirmed by two other robots, that announcement is correct. Also, an announcement disproved by three other robots is invalidated (announcing a different exit also counts as a disproof). When three robots make different announcements, we can deduce that two of them are Byzantine and as a result the silent ones are honest. All honest robots move through a chord to the exit to evacuate the circle and the algorithm terminates in time $E(n,2)$. Details of the main algorithm are as follows.

Algorithm 1 $(n, 2)$-Evacuation

1: Robot a_k moves along a radius of the circle to the point $k\theta$ of the unit circle.
2: Robot a_k searches ccw and makes an announcement if it finds the exit. It also disproves faulty announcements concerning sectors it has visited.
3: At time $1 + 3\theta$:
4: **if** there is no consensus regarding the position of the exit **then**
      the robot next to the contested announcements in clock wise order (called inspector robot and is uniquely determined as shown in the analysis), moves through a chord to the nearest announcement. If it is not the exit, it moves through a chord to the other announcement(s) to evacuate. A second inspector (the robot next to first inspector clockwise) may be utilized simultaneously, if it is known that the findings of the first inspector are still not enough for a consensus in the worst case.
5: All other honest robots moves through a chord to the farthest announcement to evacuate, and may change trajectory according to inspector's findings.

We define as t the time beyond the $1 + 3\theta$ needed to learn the position of the exit. If $t \leq 1$, evacuation time is unaffected and equals to $3 + 3\theta$. If $t > 1$, the evacuation time is increased by a function $\delta(n)$. For the geometric proof and the calculation of $\delta(n)$ please refer to the appendix.

Theorem 3 $((5, 2)$ **- Evacuation**)**.** *The worst-case time for $(n, 2)$ - Evacuation for $n \geq 9$ by Algorithm 1 satisfies*

$$E(n, 2) \leq 3 + \frac{6\pi}{n}$$

and $E(n, 2) \leq 1 + \frac{6\pi}{n} + 2\sin(\frac{3\pi}{2n}) + \sqrt{2 - 4\sin(\frac{3\pi}{2n}) + 4\sin^2(\frac{3\pi}{2n})}$ for $n < 9$.

Proof. If after 3 rounds only one announcement is made, that announcement is correct because in these 3 rounds every point in the circle has been searched by at least one honest robot. All robots will move through a chord towards the exit, and evacuation will be completed in time $3 + 3\theta$. For any other outcome, we consider the following cases depending on the number of announcements made during the execution of the algorithm.

Case 1: No announcement at the end of round 1.

Subcase 1-a: No announcement at the end of round 2.

- *1-a-i:* Two announcements at the end of round 3.
  Assume that they are made by robots a_0 and a_{n-1}. Robots a_1 and a_2 searched the sector with the announcement of a_0 in the previous rounds and made no announcements. Also a_0 disagrees with a_{n-1} as he made an announcement elsewhere. Three robots disagree with a_0 so that is the Byzantine one. As a result the correct exit is the one a_{n-1} announced. The exit will be known in time $1 + 3\theta$. Similar argument can be used for announcements not in consecutive sectors.

- *1-a-ii:* Three announcements at the end of round 3.
  Announcements must be in consecutive sectors (in any other case, we would have earlier announcements). Lets say announcements made by robots a_0, a_{n-1} and a_{n-2}. Then we know that the rest of the robots are honest. Robot a_1 visited the sectors with the announcements of a_0 and a_{n-1} in the previous rounds. As a result a_{n-2} is honest and the exit is on his announcement. The exit will be known in time $1 + 3\theta$.

Subcase 1-b: One announcement at the end of round 2.
  Then at round 3 there will be one or two new announcements.

- *1-b-i.* One new announcement at the end of round 3.
  If the new announcement is in a different sector than the previous one, refer to case (1-a-i). Else (two announcements in the same sector), suppose that the first announcement was made by a_0 and the second by a_{n-1}. Then we can deduce that a_1 is the one Byzantine robot (as he disagrees with both announcements, and at the end of round 3, no new announcement is made) and as a result a_{n-2} is an honest one. a_{n-2} as an inspector robot will travel through a chord to the nearest announcement. We will know the exit in time $1 + 3\theta + 2\sin(\pi/n)$. See Figs. 1–4.

- *1-b-ii:* Two new announcements at the end of round 3.

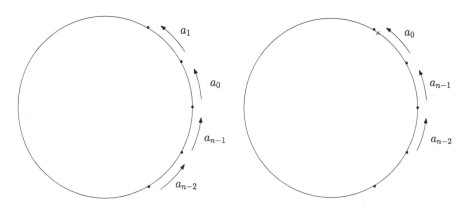

Fig. 1. time $1 + \theta$ **Fig. 2.** time $1 + 2\theta$

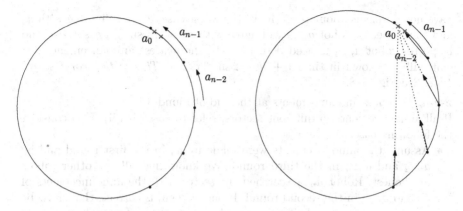

Fig. 3. time $1 + 3\theta$ **Fig. 4.** Inspection and Evacuation

If the three announcements made until the end of round 3 are in different sector, refer to case (1-a-ii). If one of the new announcements is in the same sector with the previous one, consider the following cases:

- Assume that a_0 made the announcement in the second round and a_{n-1}, a_1 made an announcement in the third round.
  We can deduce that a_1 is the Byzantine robot as he disagrees with the other two announcements and also with robots a_2 and a_3 that searched that sector in previous rounds. As a result a_{n-2} is honest. Inspector robot a_{n-2} will travel through a chord to the nearest announcement. We will know the exit in time $1 + 3\theta + 2\sin(\pi/n)$.
- Assume that a_0 made the announcement in the second round and a_{n-1}, a_{n-2} made an announcement in the third round. In that case we can deduce that all other robots are honest. Robot a_1 visited the sector with the announcements of a_{n-1} and a_{n-2}. The exit is the announcement of a_{n-2} and will be known in time $1 + 3\theta$.

Subcase 1-c: Two announcements at the end of round 2.

If there is no new announcement at round 3, refer to case (1-a-i). If there is one new announcement at the end of round 3 in a different sector, refer to case (1-a-ii). Else, if there there is one new announcement at the end of round 3 in the same sector with a previous announcement refer to case (1-b-ii).

Subcase 1-d: Three announcements at the end of round 2.

Refer to case (1-a-ii).

Case 2: One announcement at the end of round 1.

Subcase 2-a: No new announcement at the end of round 2.

- *2-a-i:* One new announcement at the end of round 3.
  If announcements in different sector, refer to case (1-a-i). If two announcements are in the same sector, say by a_0, a_{n-2}, then after 3 rounds we will

have no consensus about the exit. In the worst case, a_{n-1} will agree with a_0 and the inspector robot a_{n-3} will agree with a_{n-2}. In such a case, a second inspector robot a_{n-4} is needed to move to the nearest announcement. The exit will be known in time $1 + 3\theta + 2\sin(3\pi/2n)$. *This is the worst search time.* See Figs. 5–8.

– *2-a-ii:* Two new announcements at the end of round 3.
  If all announcements in different sectors, refer to case (1-a-ii). Else consider the following cases:

  • Assume the announcements were made by a_0 in the first round and by a_{n-2} and a_{n-4} in the third round. We know that all the other robots are honest. Robot a_{n-1} searched the sector with the announcements of a_0 and a_{n-2} in the second round. If one of them is correct, that must be the one a_0 announced (if a_{n-2} would be correct, a_{n-1} would announced it in the second round). If a_{n-1} disagrees with both of them, the exit is announced correctly by a_{n-4} and will be known in time $1 + 3\theta$.

  • Assume the announcements were made by a_0 in the first round and by a_{n-1} and a_{n-2} in the third round. We know that all the other robots are honest. Inspector robot a_{n-3} will visit the nearest announcement and the exit will be known in time $1 + 3\theta + 2\sin(\pi/n)$.

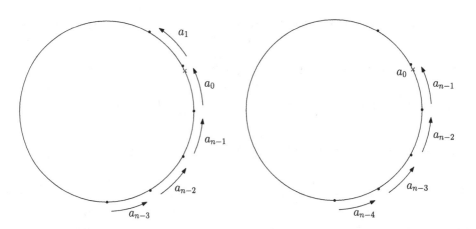

Fig. 5. time $1 + \theta$ **Fig. 6.** time $1 + 2\theta$

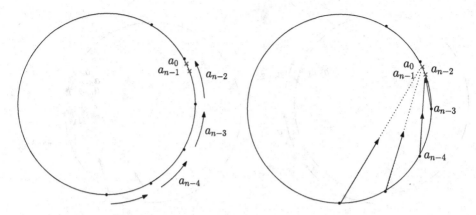

Fig. 7. time $1 + 3\theta$ **Fig. 8.** Inspection and Evacuation

Subcase 2-b: One new announcement at the end of round 2.

- *2-b-i:* No new announcement at the end of round 3.
  If we can't already differentiate the announcements, inspector robot will find us the exit at time $1 + 3\theta + 2\sin(\pi/n)$. Refer to case (2-a-i).
- *2-b-ii:* One new announcement at the end of round 3.
  If all three announcements are in different sectors, refer to case (1-a-ii). If two of the three announcements are in the same sector refer to case (2-a-ii). If all three announcements are in the same sector made by, say, a_0, a_{n-1} and a_{n-2} then after the third round, honest inspector robot a_{n-3} must visit 2 of these announcements, The exit will be known in time $1 + 3\theta + 4\sin(\pi/3n)$. See Figs. 9–12.

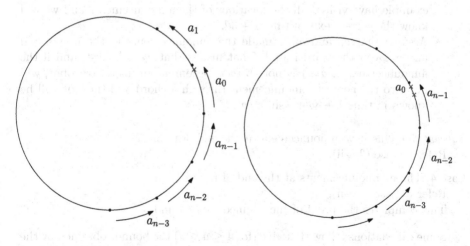

Fig. 9. time $1 + \theta$ **Fig. 10.** time $1 + 2\theta$

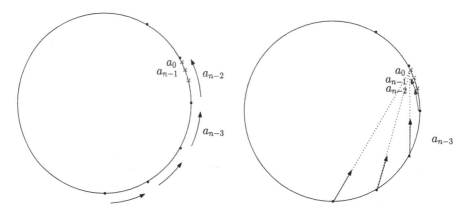

Fig. 11. time $1 + 3\theta$ **Fig. 12.** Inspection and Evacuation

Subcase 2-c: Two new announcements at the end of round 2.
    Refer to case (2-a-ii).

Case 3: Two announcements at the end of round 1.

Subcase 3-a: No new announcement at the end of round 2.

– *3-a-i.* No new announcement at the end of round 3.
    Refer to case (1-a-i).
– *3-a-ii.* One announcement at the end of round 3.
    If all three announcements are in different sectors, refer to case (1-a-ii). If two announcements are in the same sector, consider the following cases:
    • Assume that a_0 and a_{n-4} made the announcements in the first round and a_{n-2} in the third round. All other robots are honest. Robot a_{n-1} for example have visited all the locations of the announcements and we will know the correct exit in time $1 + 3\theta$.
    • Assume that a_0 and a_{n-1} made the announcements in the first round and a_{n-2} in the third round. That means that a_3 is honest, and if the announcement of a_{n-1} is not correct, becoming an inspector robot, will move to the nearest announcement through a chord and the exit will be known in time $1 + 3\theta + 2\sin(\pi/n)$.

Subcase 3-b: One new announcement at the end of round 2.
    Refer to case (3-a-ii).

Case 4: Three announcements at the end of round 1.
    Refer to case (1-a-ii).
    This completes the proof of the claimed time bound.   □

Some calculations follow that give (for $4 \le n \le 9$) the bounds obtained by the above algorithm for the $(n, 2)$ case in comparison with the lower bound obtained for the $(n, 1)$ case (which holds of course for 2 Byzantine robots as well):

n	$(n,1)$: LB	$(n,2)$: $3+3\theta$	$(n,2):\delta(n)$	$(n,2)$: UB
4	5.5558	7.7124	0.5687	8.2811
5	5.1313	6.7699	0.2361	7.0060
6	4.8264	6.1415	0.0881	6.2297
7	4.5971	5.6927	0.0318	5.7246
8	4.4186	5.3561	0.0095	5.3657
9	4.2756	5.0944	0	5.0944

4   Conclusion

We studied the evacuation problem of n robots with one or two Byzantine faults in the wireless model and provided a lower bound for the $(n,1)$-evacuation case and an upper bound for the $(n,2)$-evacuation case. An interesting possible direction after that would be to tighten our bounds, consider other communication models (like the face-to-face model) or generalize for f Byzantine robots. In particular, we conjecture that $3+3\theta$ is a lower bound for the $(n,2)$ evacuation problem for infinitely many n.

A   Appendix - $\delta(n)$ Calculation

As shown in Fig. 13, suppose at the end of round 3 the exit is not yet known, and possible exits are in D and E. Robot a_k placed at A, moves to evacuate to its farthest announcement D, at distance 2 (diameter, r=1). After $t \le r$ the inspector robot moving from F will determine the correct exit and robot a_k may need to change direction to E, but the new path that will travel is not larger than the diameter of the circle.

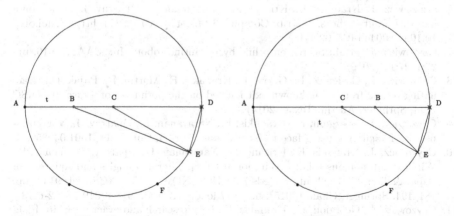

Fig. 13. $t \le 1$ Fig. 14. $t > 1$

We must show that $BE \leq BD$. Triangle CED is equilateral ($CE = CD = r = 1$) and angle $C\hat{E}D = C\hat{D}E$. As a result angle $B\hat{E}D \geq C\hat{E}D$. In triangle BED, $B\hat{E}D \geq B\hat{D}E$ meaning that $BD \geq BE$.

If $t > 1$, evacuation time is increased by $\delta(n)$.

As we can see in Fig. 14, we must calculate the distance of path ABE. We know that $AB = t$ so we continue to determine BE.

In triangle CBE, $CE = 1$, $CB = 1 - BD = 1 - (2 - t) = t - 1$. In the worst case regarding evacuation, angle $E\hat{C}D = \theta/2$. Now we can calculate BE:

$$BE^2 = CB^2 + CE^2 - 2 \cdot CB \cdot CE \cdot \cos(\pi/n)$$
$$BE^2 = t^2 - 2(t - 1)(\cos(\pi/n) + 1).$$

The total distance the robot will travel to evacuate is $AB + BE = t + BE$ and that surpasses the diameter by $\delta(n)$ defined below:

$$\delta(n) = \begin{cases} 0 & \text{if } t \leq 1 \\ t + \sqrt{t^2 - 2(t-1)(\cos(\pi/n) + 1)} - 2, & \text{if } t > 1 \end{cases}$$

References

1. Ahlswede, R., Wegener, I.: Search Problems. Wiley-Interscience, Hoboken (1987)
2. Alpern, S., Gal, S.: The Theory of Search Games and Rendezvous, vol. 55. Springer, Heidelberg (2003)
3. Stone, L.: Theory of Optimal Search. Academic Press, New York (1975)
4. Kao, M.-Y., Reif, J.H., Tate, S.R.: Searching in an unknown environment: an optimal randomized algorithm for the cow-path problem. Inf. Comput. **131**(1), 63–79 (1996)
5. Demaine, E.D., Fekete, S.P., Gal, S.: Online searching with turn cost. Theor. Comput. Sci. **361**(2), 342–355 (2006)
6. Czyzowicz, J., Kranakis, E., Krizanc, D., Narayanan, L., Opatrny, J.: Search on a line with faulty robots. Distrib. Comput. **32**(6), 493–504 (2017). https://doi.org/10.1007/s00446-017-0296-0
7. Czyzowicz, J., et al.: Search on a line by byzantine robots. In: ISAAC, 2016, pp. 27:1–27:12 (2016)
8. Czyzowicz, J., Gasieniec, L., Gorry, T., Kranakis, E., Martin, R., Pajak, D.: Evacuating robots from an unknown exit located on the perimeter of a disc. In: DISC 2014, Springer, Austin, Texas (2014)
9. Czyzowicz, J., Georgiou, K., Kranakis, E., Narayanan, L., Opatrny, J., Vogtenhuber, B.: Evacuating using face-to-face communication, CoRR abs/1501.04985
10. Czyzowicz, J., Kranakis, E., Krizanc, D., Narayanan, L., Opatrny, J., Shende, S.: Wireless autonomous robot evacuation from equilateral triangles and squares. In: Papavassiliou, S., Ruehrup, S. (eds.) ADHOC-NOW 2015. LNCS, vol. 9143, pp. 181–194. Springer, Cham (2015). https://doi.org/10.1007/978-3-319-19662-6_13
11. Czyzowicz, J., Georgiou, K., Kranakis, E.: Group search and evacuation. In: Flocchini, P., Prencipe, G., Santoro, N. (eds.) Distributed Computing by Mobile Entities. LNCS, vol. 11340, pp. 335–370. Springer, Cham (2019). https://doi.org/10.1007/978-3-030-11072-7_14

12. Czyzowicz, J., et al.: Evacuation from a disc in the presence of a faulty robot. In: Das, S., Tixeuil, S. (eds.) SIROCCO 2017. LNCS, vol. 10641, pp. 158–173. Springer, Cham (2017). https://doi.org/10.1007/978-3-319-72050-0_10
13. Georgiou, K., Kranakis, E., Leonardos, N., Pagourtzis, A., Papaioannou, I.: Optimal circle search despite the presence of faulty robots. In: Dressler, F., Scheideler, C. (eds.) ALGOSENSORS 2019. LNCS, vol. 11931, pp. 192–205. Springer, Cham (2019). https://doi.org/10.1007/978-3-030-34405-4_11

Overflow Management
with Self-eliminations

Assaf Rabinowitz and Dror Rawitz$^{(\boxtimes)}$

Faculty of Engineering, Bar Ilan University, Ramat Gan 52900, Israel
assafrabin@gmail.com, dror.rawitz@biu.ac.il

Abstract. We study admission control with packet redundancy, where
large data items, called *superpackets*, exceed some Maximum Transmission Unit (MTU) and therefore are broken into several smaller packets.
It is assumed that each superpacket is comprised of k packets, and that a
superpacket is considered useful if at least $(1-\beta)k$ of its packets arrive at
the receiving end, for some *redundancy* parameter $\beta \in [0,1)$. Our goal is
to maximize the total profit of useful superpackets, under an overloaded
network, where we are forced to drop packets.

Our starting point is an algorithm, called PRIORITY, which is based
on assigning a random priority to each superpacket. This algorithm was
shown to perform well when $\beta = 0$, with and without a buffer. However,
the performance of PRIORITY deteriorates with the increase of β, since it
delivers too many packets for high priority superpackets. To tackle this
issue, we propose an online algorithm which introduces randomized *self-
elimination* of packets, called PSE. When there is no buffer, we show that
the competitive ratio of PSE is better than the competitive ratio of PRI-
ORITY, for the case where $(1-\beta)^3 \cdot \rho_{\max} \geq 1$, where $\rho_{\max}$ is the maximal
burst size-router capacity ratio. For real-world values ($\rho_{\max} \leq 1.5$), PSE
outperforms PRIORITY for $\beta \geq 0.14$. We also present simulation results,
with a buffer, that demonstrate the behavior of PSE in comparison with
PRIORITY and TAIL-DROP. It is shown that PSE performs much better
than PRIORITY when β is large. In fact, it is shown that PSE behaves at
least as good as both algorithms.

1 Introduction

We focus on the following basic setting that is common in communication networks. Large data units are supposed to be transmitted over a network that uses
smaller transfer units. Thus data units are broken into a number of packets that
are small enough and are transmitted separately. If the network is overloaded,
packets may be dropped, and one lost packet may make the reconstruction of its
data unit impossible. One way to deal with such a problem is to use *automatic
repeat request* (ARQ) protocols. We consider the case where the application is
both loss-tolerant and time-sensitive, and thus retransmissions are not a good
solution. Another way to cope with this issue is to add *forward error correction*
(FEC) in order to mitigate the effects of packet loss. However, FEC increases

© Springer Nature Switzerland AG 2021
L. Gąsieniec et al. (Eds.): ALGOSENSORS 2021, LNCS 12961, pp. 124–139, 2021.
https://doi.org/10.1007/978-3-030-89240-1_9

the number of packets per data unit and this in turn increases traffic. In wireless sensors networks, FEC is better than ARQ protocols, since FEC decreases the use of energy inefficient wireless transmissions [23].

We consider the following setting (see Sect. 2 for a formal definition). Large data units called *superpackets* are comprised of k packets, where $k \geq 2$ is an integer. The capacity of the link at time t is denoted by $c(t)$. The number of packets arriving at time t is denoted by $\sigma(t)$. Define the maximum burst size as $\sigma_{\max} \triangleq \max_t \sigma(t)$ and the maximum ratio between the burst size to the link capacity as $\rho_{\max} \triangleq \max_t \sigma(t)/c(t)$. Note that the assumption that traffic is *burst-bounded* is not unreasonable, since it is common for traffic with QoS requirements to be regulated by a token-bucket envelope [15]. Congestion control in wireless sensor networks using leaky-bucket is studied in [24]. We assume that the system has a limited size buffer, where packets which were not transmitted may be saved to be transmitted later. To model FEC, we assume that a superpacket is *useful* if $(1-\beta)k$ packets are delivered, for some *redundancy parameter* $\beta \in [0,1)$. Also, each superpacket has a non-negative weight that may represent its importance. Consider the arrival of a stream of packets to an overloaded link, which may have a (small) buffer. What should be done when the arrival rate is larger than the link capacity? More specifically, which packets should be dropped by an admission control protocol, so as to maximize the weight of useful superpackets?

Emek et al. [4] focused on the case where $\beta = 0$ and there is no buffer. They presented an algorithm, called PRIORITY, which assigns to each super-packet a random priority that depends solely on its weight, and in case of overflows, drops packets that belong to lower priority superpackets. They showed that its competitive ratio is $O(k\sqrt{\rho_{\max}})$. In [4] it was assumed that each burst contains at most one packet per superpacket. Fraigniaud et al. [5] presented a $2k\sqrt{\rho_{\max}}$-competitive variant of PRIORITY, we refer to as PRIORITY-B, that did not rely on the above assumption. Intuitively, the main difference between both variants of the algorithm is that PRIORITY simply prefers high-priority packets, while PRIORITY-B performs a reduction to a unit capacity system, and only then prefers high-priority packets. Mansour, Patt-Shamir, and Rawitz [17] introduced the threshold redundancy setting. For unit weights and uniform capacities they showed that PRIORITY is $4k\sqrt{(1-\beta)\rho_{\max}}$-competitive. They also presented simulations showing that PRIORITY performs better than the TAIL-DROP policy, which simply discards packets in a FCFS manner.

Our Results. As demonstrated in [17], with the increase of β, the performance of PRIORITY deteriorates. This happens because the increase in traffic affects performance more than the improvement in the competitive ratio. Moreover, as β grows, PRIORITY insists on transmitting more packets than needed for high-priority superpackets. We cope with $\beta > 0$ by introducing the idea of packet *self-elimination*. This is done by a process in which each superpacket *self-eliminates* βk out of it k packets. This limits the "greediness" of PRIORITY by making sure that redundant packets (more than $1 - \beta$ packets) are not transmitted.

We study both versions of PRIORITY with self-elimination - PRIORITY WITH SELF-ELIMINATIONS (PSE) which is a modified version of PRIORITY [4] and PSE-B which is a modified version of PRIORITY-B [5]. We limit the analysis of PSE to the case where (i) the router capacity is constant and (ii) a burst does not contain more than one packet from a given superpacket. We study both versions from a competitive analysis point of view. More specifically, for the setting without a buffer, i.e., in the case where an arriving packet is either served or dropped, we show that PSE is $4 \max\{*\}(1 - \beta)^2 \rho_{\max} k, 1$-competitive and that PSE-B's ratio is better by a factor of 2. We show that in a practical setting, both algorithms improve the ratio of PRIORITY for the case where $\rho_{\max} \leq (1-\beta)^{-3}$ (see discussion at the end of Sect. 3).

We perform a simulation study to demonstrate the improvement in performance obtained by self-elimination. We observe that PSE outperforms PSE-B. Then, we present simulations showing that PSE outperforms PRIORITY, especially for high values of β, where TAIL-DROP has better performance than PRIORITY. This is demonstrated with a buffer. In fact, it is shown that PSE dominates both PRIORITY and TAIL-DROP.

Related Work. In the case of unit capacity, $\beta = 0$, and no buffer, the offline problem is the SET PACKING problem, where superpackets correspond to sets and bursts correspond to elements. Even when each element is contained in at most two sets, SET PACKING is as hard as INDEPENDENT SET, and thus cannot be approximated to within $O(n^{1-\epsilon})$-factor, for any $\epsilon > 0$ [9]. In terms of the number of elements T (time steps), SET PACKING is $O(T^{1/2})$-approximable, and hard to approximate within $T^{1/2-\epsilon}$ [7]. If the maximum set size is k, it is approximable to within $(k + 1)/3 + \epsilon$, for any $\epsilon > 0$ [3], and within $(k + 1)/2$ in the weighted case [1], but it is known to be hard to approximate to within an $O(k/\log k)$-factor [10].

Overflow management was studied quite extensively in the past from the competitive analysis viewpoint [13,16] (see also a survey [6]). The superpacket model was first introduced by Kesselman, Patt-Shamir, and Scalosub [14] who did not consider redundancy or weights. They showed that in general, no finite upper bound on the competitive ratio exists. They gave an upper bound of $O(k^2)$ and a lower bound of $\Omega(k)$ on the competitive ratio of a deterministic online algorithm under the assumption that the input sequence is *order preserving*. [1] Scalosub, Marbach, and Liebeherr [22] studied a different, possibly more realistic, order restriction.[2] They gave an exponential (in k) upper bound on the deterministic competitive ratio and a linear lower bound. They also gave simulation results in which they compared their algorithm to various versions of TAIL-DROP. This work was improved by Scalosub [21] who gave both randomized and deterministic algorithms with polynomial competitive ratio in all system parameters. Papers [14,21,22] assumed a push-out FIFO buffer architecture, since it is simple, avoids packet reordering and causes relatively small delays.

A different approach was taken by Emek et al. [4], where instead of restricting the packet order in the input, the results are expressed in terms of the maximal

---

[1] The condition is that for any $1 \leq j, j' \leq k$, packet j of superpacket i arrives before packet j of superpacket i' iff packet j' of i arrives before packet j' of i'.

[2] There are several sources, each generating a stream of packets, one superpacket after another. An arbitrary interleaving of these streams arrives at the link.

burst size. A simplifying assumption was that no buffers are available (also no redundancy). Superpackets are weighted and the link capacity may change over time. They presented Algorithm PRIORITY whose competitive ratio is $O(k\sqrt{\rho_{\max}})$, and gave a lower bound that shows that the above ratio is the best possible up to a polylogarithmic factor. Fraigniaud et al. [5] gave a modified version of PRIORITY, we refer to as PRIORITY-B, which can cope with several packets from the same superpacket arriving at the same time. They showed that the algorithm is $2k\sqrt{\rho_{\max}}$-competitive. For the special case of unit capacity in which a burst contains only a consecutive set of superpackets a deterministic $O(\log \sigma_{\max})$-competitive algorithm was given in [8] with a matching lower bound.

Mansour, Patt-Shamir, and Rawitz [17] studied the threshold redundancy setting. For unit weights they showed that PRIORITY is $k\sqrt{(1-\beta)\sigma_{\max}}$-competitive in the uncapacitated case and $4k\sqrt{(1-\beta)\rho_{\max}}$-competitive in the capacitated case. They also presented simulation results comparing PRIORITY and the TAIL-DROP policy, showing that priority performs better in many scenarios. Their simulation included the case where a buffer is used. Mansour, Patt-Shamir, and Rawitz [18] studied the model where multiple output links are available to the router. In addition, they introduced a more general model of redundancy. They presented an algorithm based on PRIORITY whose competitive ratio is $16k\sqrt{\sigma_{\max}/C}$, where C is the total capacity of the output links.

Another research direction is managing packet dependencies where each packet or superpacket has an expiration time, namely, each packet has a deadline and it must be transmitted up to its deadline. Markovitch and Scalosub [19] and Jez, Mansour, and Patt-Shamir [12] provided competitive algorithms and lower bounds for such settings.

Paper Organization. The superpacket model is defined in Sect. 2. Algorithms PSE and PSE-B are described and analyzed in Sect. 3. Our simulation results are given in Sect. 4. Finally, the conclusion is given in Sect. 5.

2   Model Definition

This section contains a formal definition of the problem. The base unit is a superpacket, which is comprised of k packets. The set of superpackets is denoted by S. Each superpacket i is associated with a non-negative weight $w(i)$. Given a packet p, we denote its comprising superpacket by $\mathrm{sp}(p)$, and its index within $\mathrm{sp}(p)$ by $\mathrm{ind}(p)$. We assume that each packet is represented by a tuple $(\mathrm{sp}(p), \mathrm{ind}(p))$.

Our time model is discrete, and the time horizon is denoted by T. The capacity of the link at time step t is denoted by $c(t)$. Denote $c_{\max} = \max_t c(t)$. Also, assume that there is a buffer of size b. A burst of $\sigma(t)$ packets arrives at each time step t. The arrival of packets is described using a matrix $A \in \mathbb{N}^{T \times |S|}$, where $a_{ti} \in \{0, \ldots, k\}$ determines how many packets from superpacket i arrive at time step t. The set of packets that arrive at time step t that belong to superpacket i is denoted by $P(t, i)$. More specifically, we assume that each packet p is represented in $P(t, i)$ by a tuple $(i, \mathrm{ind}(p))$. Observe that $|P(t, i)| = a_{ti}$. Also, observe that $\sum_t a_{ti} = k$, for every $i \in S$, and $\sum_i a_{ti} = \sigma(t)$, for every t. In addition, we assume that $a_{ti} \leq c(t)$, for every $i \in S$ and time step t, namely that all packets of a superpacket could be delivered if they were the only arriving packets in time step t. For every $S' \subseteq S$, let $S'(t)$ be the subset of superpackets from S' that participate at time-step t, i.e., $S'(t) = \{i \in S' : a_{ti} \geq 1\}$.

We define the *burst size*, $\sigma(t)$, as the number of packets participating in time t. Namely, $\sigma(t) \triangleq \sum_{i \in S} a_{ti}$. Let $\sigma_{\max}$ denote the maximum burst size, i.e., $\sigma_{\max} \triangleq \max_t \sigma(t)$. Also, define the *burst load*, $\rho(t)$, as the burst size to the capacity at time t, i.e., $\rho(t) \triangleq \sigma(t)/c(t)$. Let $\rho_{\max}$ denote the maximum burst load, i.e., $\rho_{\max} \triangleq \max_t \rho(t)$. Notice that if $c(t) = c$, for some constant c, then $\rho_{\max} = \frac{\sigma_{\max}}{c}$. In addition, we assume $\rho_{\max} > 1$. Otherwise all packets can be delivered successfully.

An execution of an online algorithm is described as follows. Initially, the buffer is empty. Each time step is composed of three sub-steps:

Arrival: A set of $\sigma(t)$ packets arrive at the link.
Drop: The buffer management algorithm drops packets that arrived earlier and are currently in the buffer or packets that arrived in this step.
Delivery: At most $c(t)$ packets are transmitted on the link.

A feasible system satisfies the following buffer constraint: no more than b packets are kept in the buffer between consecutive time steps. In the special case where there is no buffer (i.e., when $b = 0$), the algorithm serves as an admission control algorithm: it transmits at most $c(t)$ packets and the rest are dropped.

The output of the algorithm can be described as a *transmission matrix* $X \in \mathbb{N}^{T \times |S|}$, where x_{ti} represents the number of packets that belong to superpacket i that were transmitted at time step t. An assignment is feasible if it satisfies $x_{ti} \leq a_{ti}$, for every i and t, and $\sum_i x_{ti} + b \leq c(t)$, for every t.

In addition, the input contains a *redundancy parameter* $\beta \in [0, 1)$. A superpacket is considered *useful* if at least $(1 - \beta)k$ out of its k packets are not dropped. Henceforth, we assume that $(1 - \beta)k$ is integral. Note that this redundancy model is used by Reed-Solomon codes for transmission over erasure channels (see, e.g., [20]). Moreover, the zfec Python package [25] uses the same redundancy model.

Given an algorithm ALG, denote the set of useful superpackets by ALG(S) (or simply by ALG), i.e., $i \in$ ALG means that i was successfully delivered by ALG. The weight of this set is $w(\text{ALG}) = \sum_{i \in \text{ALG}} w(i)$. We measure the performance of the algorithm using competitive analysis. The *competitive ratio* of an online algorithm for a maximization problem is the supremum, over all instances S, of $\frac{w(\text{OPT}(S))}{w(\text{ALG}(S))}$, where OPT($S$) denotes a solution with maximum weight. In the case of a randomized algorithm ALG, the weight obtained by ALG for a given instance is a random variable, and we use its expected value, $\mathbb{E}[w(\text{ALG})]$. See [2] for more details about competitive analysis.

We end the section with an example of an instance which is given in Fig. 1. In this example $k = 3$. We give an optimal solution for several cases (this may not be the only optimal solution). First assume that $\beta = 0$ and unit weights:

- $b = 0$ and $c(t) = 1$, for all t: If superpacket 1 is delivered, then all other superpackets are not. Hence, OPT $= \{2, 5\}$

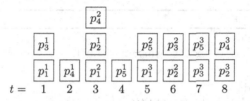

Fig. 1. An instance with $k = 3$. p_i^j stands for the jth packet of superpacket i.

- $b = 0$ and $c(t) = 2$, for all t: We need to drop one of the packets arriving at $t = 3$. Hence, OPT $= \{1, 3, 4, 5\}$.
- $b = 1$ and $c(t) = 1$, for all t: OPT $= \{1, 2, 3\}$.

Next assume that $\beta = 1/3$ and unit weights:

- $b = 0$ and $c(t) = 1$ for all t: In this case, we prefer superpacket 4 over 2. OPT $= \{1, 3, 4, 5\}$.
- $b = 0$ and $c(t) = 2$ for all t: OPT $= \{1, 2, 3, 4, 5\}$.
- $b = 1$ and $c(t) = 1$, for all t: To deliver all superpackets we need 10 packets, but we can only transmit 9. Hence OPT $= \{1, 3, 4, 5\}$.

Finally, assume that $\beta = 0$ and that superpacket 1 weighs 10, while the weight of the others is 1.

- $b = 0$ and $c(t) = 1$, for all t: We prefer superpacket 1 due to its high weight, thus OPT $= \{1\}$.

3 Algorithms and Competitive Analysis

We present two algorithms, algorithm PSE, which is based on PRIORITY [4] and algorithm PSE-B, which is based on PRIORITY-B [5]. Then, we bound their competitive ratios for the case where $b = 0$. Our addition to the algorithms is that each superpacket self-eliminates a random subset of size βk of its packets, before running PRIORITY. This process of self elimination has two effects. First, each superpacket keeps only $(1 - \beta)k$ packets. Also, on average, each burst shrinks by a factor of $(1 - \beta)$.

We present PSE and PSE-B, and describe the differences between them. Then, we analyze the competitive ratio of PSE. The analysis of algorithm PSE-B is omitted for lack of space.

The Algorithms. The common idea that both algorithms share is as follows. Superpacket i chooses a random priority $r(i)$ and a subset SE(i) of βk indices that represent the packets of superpacket i that are to be self-eliminated. For the latter, $\chi(n, m)$ denotes a random set of m indices (chosen uniformly, without repetition) from $\{1, \ldots, n\}$. The priority of superpacket i is determined as follows: $r(i) = x^{1/w(i)}$, where $x \sim U[0, 1]$. As shown in the sequel, if $w(i)$ is integral,

---

Algorithm 1: PSE

---

1 **foreach** $i \in S$ **do**
2   Pick priority $r(i) \leftarrow x^{1/w(i)}$ where $x \sim U[0,1]$
3     $\mathrm{SE}(i) \leftarrow \chi(k, \beta \cdot k)$
4 **for** $t = 1$ *to* T **do**
5   Drop all packets in $S(t) \cap \cup_i \mathrm{SE}(i)$
6   Drop all packets in $S(t) \setminus \cup_i \mathrm{SE}(i)$ apart from the $c(t)$ packets whose superpacket have the highest priorities

---

Algorithm 2: PSE-B

---

1 **foreach** $i \in S$ **do**
2   Pick priority: $r(i) \leftarrow x^{1/w(i)}$ where $x \sim U[0,1]$
3     $\mathrm{SE}(i) \leftarrow \chi(k, \beta \cdot k)$
4 **for** $t = 1$ *to* T **do**
5   **for** $\ell = 1$ *to* $c(t)$ **do** $B(t,\ell) \leftarrow \emptyset$
6   **foreach** $i \in S(t)$ **do**
7   Assign the packets in $P(t,i)$ to $B(t,1), \ldots, B(t,c(t))$ using $\chi(c(t), a_{ti})$
8   **for** $\ell = 1$ *to* $c(t)$ **do**
9        $B(t,\ell) \leftarrow B(t,\ell) \setminus \cup_i(\{i\} \times \mathrm{SE}(i))$
10   Drop all packets in $B(t,\ell)$ apart from p s.t. $\mathrm{sp}(p)$ has max priority

---

the priority $r(i) \in [0,1]$ of a superpacket i is distributed as the maximum of $w(i)$ independent $U[0,1]$ random variables.

The difference between the algorithms is in the arrival-step. Upon arrival of a burst at time-step t, PSE transmits the $c(t)$ packets that belong to the superpackets with the highest priority and the others are dropped. On the other hand, PSE-B constructs $c(t)$ bins $B(t,1), \ldots, B(t,c(t))$. Each superpacket i places its packets that arrived at t, i.e., the packets in $P(t,i)$, into a_{ti} bins that are chosen at random using $\chi(c(t), a_{ti})$. Finally, for each $\ell \in \{1, \ldots, c(t)\}$, PSE-B drops all packets that are represented by tuples in $\cup_i(\{i\} \times \mathrm{SE}(i))$ from $B(t,\ell)$. Then, the packet that belongs to the superpacket with the highest priority in each bin is transmitted and the others are dropped.

The algorithms are described without using a buffer. If there is a buffer, then at each time step, the stored packets join the arriving burst. In addition, some of the packets that are dropped are actually stored in the buffer instead, according to the priorities of their superpackets. Both algorithms are simple and easy to implement. Moreover, it is straightforward to implement them in a distributed system. A pseudo-random hash function can be used to map superpacket identification numbers to priorities and to the random self-elimination choices.

Definitions and Notation. Let se_{ij} be an indicator variable that indicates whether packet j of superpacket i is marked as self-eliminated, namely whether

$j \in SE(i)$. Notice that $SE(i)$ is selected uniformly out of $\binom{k}{\beta k}$ possible combinations. Thus $\Pr[se_{ij} = 1] = \beta$.

Define the self-eliminations arrival matrix $A^* \in \mathbb{N}^{T \times |S|}$, where a_{ti}^* is the number of packets from superpacket i that participate in time-step t and are not self-eliminated, namely $a_{ti}^* = |P(t,i) \setminus (\{i\} \times SE(i))|$. Since each packet is self-eliminated with probability β, we have that $\mathbb{E}[a_{ti}^*] = (1 - \beta)a_{ti}$.

In addition, for every superpacket $i \in S$, let $N(i)$ denote the set of superpackets that are in conflict with i, namely superpackets that have a packet arriving at the same time as some packet in i. That is, $N(i) \triangleq \{i' \in S \setminus \{i\} : \exists t \text{ s.t. } a_{ti}, a_{ti'} \geq 1\}$. $N(i)$ is called the *neighborhood* of i. In the sequel, we define the *effective neighborhood* of i, which contains superpackets that have a surviving packet that conflicts with superpacket i. This definition depends on the algorithm behavior, and is defined differently according to the analyzed algorithm.

Competitive Analysis of PSE. We analyze PSE for the case where the capacity of the router does not change over time, i.e., $c(t) = c$, for all t, where $c \in \mathbb{N}$. In addition, we assume that no more than one packet from a given superpacket arrive at time t, namely $a_{ti} \in \{0, 1\}$, for every time t and superpacket i.

The *effective neighborhood* of superpacket i contains superpackets that have a surviving packet arriving in the same time step as some surviving packet of i. Formally, we define the *effective neighborhood* of i by $\tilde{N}(i) \triangleq \{i' \in S \setminus \{i\} : \exists t \text{ s.t. } a_{ti}^*, a_{ti'}^* = 1\}$ and $\tilde{N}[i] \triangleq \tilde{N}(i) \cup \{i\}$.

First, we bound the probability that a single superpacket is useful. We use the following lemma that was proven in [4] (a proof is given for completeness).

Lemma 1 ([4]). *Let $i \in Q \subseteq S$. Then $\Pr[r(i) = \max_{i' \in Q} r(i')] = \frac{w(i)}{w(Q)}$.*

Proof. Let $r_{\max} = \max_{i' \in Q \setminus \{i\}} r(i')$. By the independence of $r(i')$ for superpackets in Q we have, for $x \in [0, 1]$, that

$$\Pr[r_{\max} < x] = \prod_{i' \in Q \setminus \{i\}} \Pr[r(i') < x] = \prod_{i' \in Q \setminus \{i\}} x^{w(i')} = x^{\sum_{i' \in Q \setminus \{i\}} w(i')} = x^{w(Q \setminus \{i\})},$$

namely $r_{\max}$ has distribution $D_{w(Q \setminus \{i\})})$, where the distribution D_z has density $f_z(x) = zx^{z-1}$ and therefore $\Pr_{y \sim D_z}[y < x] = x^z$, for $x \in [0, 1]$. Hence,

$$\Pr[r(i) > r_{\max}] = \int_0^1 \Pr[r_{\max} < x] f_{r(i)}(x) dx = \int_0^1 x^{w(Q \setminus \{i\})} w(Q) x^{w(i)-1} dx = \frac{w(i)}{w(Q)}$$

as required. $\qquad\square$

Lemmas 2 and 5 are based on Lemma 1 and 2 from [18].

Lemma 2. *Let $i \in S$. If $c = 1$ then, $\Pr[i \in \text{PSE}] \geq \mathbb{E}\left[\frac{w(i)}{w(\tilde{N}[i])}\right]$.*

Proof. A superpacket i is successfully delivered if it has the top priority among its effective neighborhood, i.e., $r(i) > \max_{i' \in \tilde{N}(i)} r(i')$. Hence, due to Lemma 1

$$\Pr\left[i \in \text{PSE}\right] \geq \Pr\left[r(i) > \max_{i' \in \tilde{N}(i)} r(i')\right]$$

$$= \sum_Q \Pr\left[\tilde{N}(i) = Q\right] \Pr\left[r(i) > \max_{i' \in Q} r(i') | \tilde{N}(i) = Q\right]$$

$$= \sum_Q \Pr\left[\tilde{N}(i) = Q\right] \frac{w(i)}{w(Q)+w(i)} = \mathbb{E}\left[\frac{w(i)}{w(\tilde{N}(i))+w(i))}\right] ,$$

as required. □

We use the two known inequalities.

Lemma 3 (Titu's Lemma). *Let* $\alpha, \gamma \in (\mathbb{R}_+)^n$*. Then,* $\sum_i \frac{\alpha_i^2}{\gamma_i} \geq \frac{(\sum_i \alpha_i)^2}{\sum_i \gamma_i}$.

Lemma 4 (Jensen). *If* $X \geq 0$ *is a random variable, then* $\mathbb{E}\left[\frac{1}{X}\right] \geq \frac{1}{\mathbb{E}[X]}$.

Lemma 5. *Let* $i \in S$*. If* $c > 1$ *then,* $\Pr\left[i \in \text{PSE}\right] \geq \frac{c}{2} \cdot \mathbb{E}\left[\frac{w(i)}{w(\tilde{N}(i))+c \cdot w(i)}\right]$.

Proof. A superpacket i is successfully delivered if it has one of the top c priorities among its neighborhood. The probability that a superpacket satisfies this condition is equivalent to the probability that this superpacket is selected as the top priority superpacket in one of c times without repetition. This probability decreases if we allow repetitions. Hence, due to Lemma 2 we have that

$$\Pr\left[i \in \text{PSE}\right] \geq 1 - \left(1 - \Pr\left[r(i) > \max_{i' \in \tilde{N}(i)} r(i')\right]\right)^c = 1 - \left(1 - \mathbb{E}\left[\frac{w(i)}{w(\tilde{N}[i])}\right]\right)^c .$$

We consider two cases. If $\mathbb{E}\left[\frac{w(i)}{w(\tilde{N}[i])}\right] \geq \frac{1}{c}$, then $\Pr\left[i \in \text{PSE}\right] \geq 1 - \left(1 - \frac{1}{c}\right)^c \geq 1 - \frac{1}{e} > \frac{1}{2}$. If $\mathbb{E}\left[\frac{w(i)}{w(\tilde{N}[i])}\right] < \frac{1}{c}$, then using the binomial expansion we get

$$\Pr\left[i \in \text{PSE}\right] \geq c \cdot \mathbb{E}\left[\frac{w(i)}{w(\tilde{N}[i])}\right] - \frac{c \cdot (c-1)}{2}\left(\mathbb{E}\left[\frac{w(i)}{w(\tilde{N}[i])}\right]\right)^2$$

$$\geq c \cdot \mathbb{E}\left[\frac{w(i)}{w(\tilde{N}[i])}\right] - \frac{1}{2}\left(c \cdot \mathbb{E}\left[\frac{w(i)}{w(\tilde{N}[i])}\right]\right)^2 \geq \frac{c}{2} \cdot \mathbb{E}\left[\frac{w(i)}{w(\tilde{N}[i])}\right] .$$

By taking both cases into account we have that

$$\Pr\left[i \in \text{PSE}\right] \geq \min\{*\}\frac{c}{2}\mathbb{E}\left[\frac{w(i)}{w(\tilde{N}[i])}\right], \frac{1}{2} = \frac{1}{2}\min\{*\}\mathbb{E}\left[\frac{c \cdot w(i)}{w(\tilde{N}(i))+w(i)}\right], 1$$

$$\geq \frac{1}{2}\min\{*\}\mathbb{E}\left[\frac{c \cdot w(i)}{w(\tilde{N}(i))+c \cdot w(i)}\right], 1 = \frac{c}{2}\mathbb{E}\left[\frac{w(i)}{w(\tilde{N}(i))+c \cdot w(i)}\right] .$$

□

Similar to Lemma 4 from [18], we provide a lower bound on the expected performance of the algorithm.

Lemma 6. $\mathbb{E}\left[w(\text{PSE})\right] \geq \frac{c}{2} \cdot \frac{w(S)^2}{\mathbb{E}\left[\sum_{i \in S} w(\tilde{N}(i))\right] + c \cdot w(S)}$.

Proof. From the definition of expectation, we have that $\mathbb{E}\left[w(\text{PSE})\right] = \sum_{i \in S} w(i) \cdot \Pr\left[i \in \text{PSE}\right]$. Hence, according to Lemma 5,

$$\mathbb{E}\left[w(\text{PSE})\right] \geq \frac{c}{2} \cdot \sum_{i \in S} w(i) \cdot \mathbb{E}\left[\frac{w(i)}{w(\tilde{N}(i)) + c \cdot w(i)}\right] = \frac{c}{2} \cdot \mathbb{E}\left[\sum_{i \in S} \frac{w(i)^2}{w(\tilde{N}(i)) + c \cdot w(i)}\right] .$$

It follows that

$$\mathbb{E}\left[w(\text{PSE})\right] \geq \frac{c}{2} \cdot \mathbb{E}\left[\frac{(\sum_{i \in S} w(i))^2}{\sum_{i \in S}(w(\tilde{N}(i)) + c \cdot w(i))}\right] \geq \frac{w(S)^2 c/2}{\mathbb{E}\left[\sum_{i \in S}(w(\tilde{N}(i)) + c \cdot w(i))\right]}$$

$$= \frac{w(S)^2 c/2}{\mathbb{E}\left[\sum_{i \in S} w(\tilde{N}(i))\right] + c \cdot w(S)} ,$$

where the last two inequalities are due to Titu's Lemma and Jensen's Ineq.   □

Next, we give an upper bound on $\mathbb{E}\left[\sum_{i \in S} w(\tilde{N}[i])\right]$.

Lemma 7. $\mathbb{E}\left[\sum_{i \in S} w(\tilde{N}[i])\right] \leq (1 - \beta)^2 \cdot \sigma_{\max} k \cdot w(S)$.

Proof. By definition of effective neighborhood and linearity of expectation, we get that

$$\mathbb{E}\left[\sum_{i \in S} w(\tilde{N}[i])\right] = \mathbb{E}\left[\sum_{i \in S} \sum_{t=1}^{T} \sum_{i' \in S, i' \neq i} a_{ti}^* a_{ti'}^* w(i')\right] = \sum_{i \in S} \sum_{t=1}^{T} \sum_{i' \in S, i' \neq i} \mathbb{E}\left[a_{ti}^* a_{ti'}^* w(i')\right]$$

Since a_{ti}^* and $a_{ti'}^*$ are chosen independently, the expectation of the product equals to the product of the expectations. Hence,

$$\mathbb{E}\left[\sum_{i \in S} w(\tilde{N}[i])\right] = \sum_{i \in S} \sum_{t=1}^{T} \sum_{\substack{i' \in S \\ i' \neq i}} \mathbb{E}\left[a_{ti}^*\right] \mathbb{E}\left[a_{ti'}^*\right] w(i') = \sum_{i \in S} \sum_{t=1}^{T} \sum_{\substack{i' \in S \\ i' \neq i}} (1 - \beta)^2 a_{ti} a_{ti'} w(i')$$

$$\leq (1 - \beta)^2 \sum_{t=1}^{T} \sum_{i \in S} a_{ti} \sum_{i' \in S} a_{ti'} w(i') \leq (1 - \beta)^2 \sum_{t=1}^{T} \sigma(t) \sum_{i' \in S} a_{ti'} w(i')$$

$$\leq (1 - \beta)^2 \cdot \sigma_{\max} \sum_{i' \in S} w(i') \sum_{t=1}^{T} a_{ti'} \leq (1 - \beta)^2 \cdot \sigma_{\max} k \cdot w(S)$$

□

We now combine the above lemmas.

Lemma 8. $\mathbb{E}\left[\text{PSE}\right] \geq \frac{w(S)}{2 \cdot (1 + (1-\beta)^2 \cdot k \rho_{\max})}$.

Proof. Combining Lemma 6 and Lemma 7 yields

$$\mathbb{E}\left[w(\text{PSE})\right] \geq \frac{c}{2} \cdot \frac{w(S)^2}{(1-\beta)^2 \sigma_{\max} k w(S) + c w(S)} = \frac{c \cdot w(S)}{2(c + (1-\beta)^2 \sigma_{\max} k)} = \frac{w(S)}{2(1 + (1-\beta)^2 k \rho_{\max})}$$
□

It remains to bound the competitive ratio of PSE.

Theorem 1. PSE *is at most* $4\max\{*\}(1-\beta)^2\rho_{\max}k, 1$-*competitive.*

Proof. Lemma 8 and $w(S) \geq w(\text{OPT})$ imply that $\mathbb{E}\left[w(\text{PSE})\right] \geq \frac{w(\text{OPT})}{2\cdot(1+(1-\beta)^2\cdot k\rho_{\max})}$.
There are two cases. If $(1-\beta)^2 \cdot k\rho_{\max} \geq 1$, then $\frac{w(\text{OPT})}{\mathbb{E}[w(\text{PSE})]} \leq 2\cdot 2(1-\beta)^2 \cdot k\rho_{\max}$.
If $(1-\beta)^2 \cdot k\rho_{\max} < 1$, then $\frac{w(\text{OPT})}{\mathbb{E}[w(\text{PSE})]} \leq 2\cdot 2 = 4$.   □

Competitive Analysis of PSE-B. We bound the competitive ratio of PSE-B in the full version of the paper.

Theorem 2. PSE-B *is* $2\max\{*\}(1-\beta)^2\rho_{\max}k, 1$-*competitive.*

Discussion. PSE is a variant of PRIORITY which was shown to be $4k\sqrt{(1-\beta)\rho_{\max}}$-competitive [17]. Theorem 1 imply the following. If $k\rho_{\max}(1-\beta)^2 \geq 1$, then the ratio between PRIORITY competitive-ratio and PSE competitive-ratio is $1/\sqrt{(1-\beta)^3\rho_{\max}}$. If $k\rho_{\max}(1-\beta)^2 < 1$, then the above ratio is $k\sqrt{(1-\beta)\rho_{\max}}$. By Theorem 2, PSE-B improves PSE by a factor of 2. Recall that self elimination has two effects: each superpacket remains with only $(1-\beta)k$ packets, and on average, each burst shrinks by a factor of $(1-\beta)$. This explains the improvement in the ratio in the above ranges.

We now examine our results in a practical setting. Assume that $\beta \leq 0.5, k \geq 4$. Thus, $k\rho_{\max}(1-\beta)^2 \geq 1$. In that case, the ratio between PSE-B competitive-ratio and PRIORITY competitive-ratio is $2/\sqrt{(1-\beta)^3\rho_{\max}}$. In addition, we may focus in the case where the network is overloaded to a reasonable extent. For that matter we assume $\rho_{\max} \leq 4$. Under such settings, PSE-B competitive-ratio improves PRIORITY competitive-ratio by at least a factor of $(1-\beta)^{-\frac{3}{2}}$.

4   Simulation Results

In Sect. 3 we considered the problem from a worst-case point of view. However, it is also interesting to examine the performance of our approach on stochastic input. We performed simulations that enable us to test the behavior of self-elimination under various conditions and compared to PRIORITY and TAIL-DROP.

Parameters and Measurement. The stochastic process used to generate traffic is similar to the one used in [17]. We run several independent Markov Poisson processes with two states, ON and OFF, with parameters λ_{ON} and λ_{OFF}, resp. We aggregate the processes in order to create a traffic profile and assign packets to superpackets randomly. Note that in our simulations we allow several packets that belong to the same superpacket to participate in the same burst. In order to create more congested traffic, we increase $\lambda_{\text{ON}}/\lambda_{\text{OFF}}$ and vice versa. We note that when β is increased, the load increases by a factor of $(1-\beta)^{-1}$, to maintain the same level of *effective load*, denoted by $\tilde{\sigma}$. That is, $\tilde{\sigma} = (1-\beta)\bar{\sigma}$, where $\bar{\sigma}$ is the average burst size.

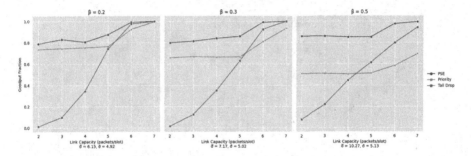

Fig. 2. The effect of varying capacity for various values of β. Here $k = 10$ and $b = 10$.

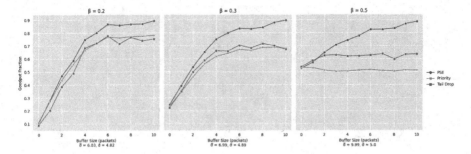

Fig. 3. The effect of varying buffer size for various values of β. Here $k = 10$ and $c = 4$.

We examine the effect of the following parameters on the goodput fraction: (i) the capacity of the link c (assumed to be constant), (ii) the buffer size b, (iii) the average burst size $\bar{\sigma}$, (iv) the number of packets in superpacket k, and (v) the portion β of redundant packets. Since even approximating OPT within a factor of $O(k/\log k)$ is NP-hard [11], we compare our results to easily computed upper bounds. In most simulations we consider unit weights, and in this case we measure the performance in comparison to the maximum number of superpacket that fit in the given capacity, i.e., to the total capacity of the system Tc divided by the number of packets required to complete a superpacket $(1 - \beta)k$. In the weighted case, we use the total weight of superpackets, i.e., $w(S)$.

We compare our self-elimination approach to two algorithms: PRIORITY and TAIL-DROP, which discards the last packets to arrive. Note that self-eliminated packets are not immediately dropped in our simulations. After serving non-eliminated packets, TAIL-DROP is used to serve eliminated packets with the residual capacity.

Simulation Results. Recall that there are two variants of PRIORITY. In the full version we compare PSE-B with PSE and show that PSE outperforms PSE-B. Hence, we prefer using PSE for any practical use. The rest of our simulations focus on measuring PSE with respect to PRIORITY and tail-drop.

In Fig. 2 we can see the effect of varying the link capacity, while holding the *effective load* (i.e., $(1 - \beta)\bar{\sigma}$) fixed. For low capacity values, tail-drop performs

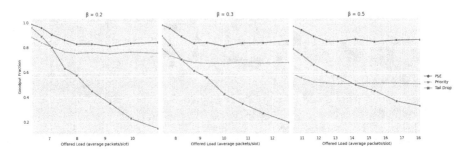

Fig. 4. The effect of varying $\bar{\sigma}$ for various values of β. Here $k = 10$, $c = 6$ and $b = 10$.

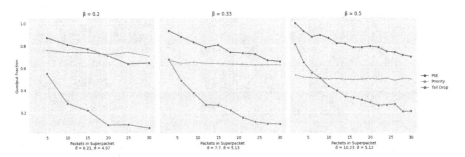

Fig. 5. The effect of varying k for various values of β. Here $c = 4$ and $b = 10$.

very poorly in comparison to PSE and PRIORITY. For high capacity values, tail-drop exceeds PRIORITY performance, but still PSE dominates them both. As β grows, the gap between PSE and PRIORITY increases. Overall, PSE has the best performance in all scenarios.

In Fig. 3 we study the effect of varying the buffer size. The performance of PRIORITY deteriorates as β increases due to its insistence to transmit packets belonging to high priority superpackets. Again, PSE outperforms both PRIORITY and tail-drop.

Figure 4 demonstrates the effect of varying the offered-load around a constant effective-load. It can be seen that tail-drop performance decreases almost linearly with $\bar{\sigma}$, for any β. PRIORITY and PSE suffer a minor decrease until the effective load reaches the link capacity, and then they stabilize. The gap between them is the starting point, which is high for PSE, for any value of β. This gap is increasing with the increase of β. While PRIORITY performs poorly for high β, PSE maintains good performance when the load and the effective load are much larger than the capacity, for any β.

We examine the effect of increasing k in Fig. 5, where it can be seen that for various values of β, the performance deteriorates with the increase of k. However, the effect on tail-drop is much more pronounced than on PSE. On the contrary, PRIORITY is almost not being affected by the increase of k, but it can be seen that, as β grows, its performance is getting worse. Notice that when β is low and

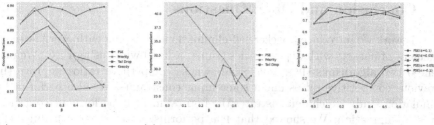

(a) The effect of β for the weighted case. Here $k = 10$, $b = 10$, $\tilde{\sigma} = 5.08$ and $c = 4$.

(b) The effect of β on completed superpackets. Here $b = 10$, $\tilde{\sigma} = 5.14$ and $c = 4$.

(c) The effect of α on the completed superpackets. Here $b = 10$, $\tilde{\sigma} = 4.54$ and $c = 4$.

Fig. 6. Additional figures.

k is high, PSE falls behind PRIORITY. A possible reason is that the insistence to deliver all packets of a superpacket of PRIORITY outperforms the commitment of PSE to specific $(1 - \beta)k$ bursts.

Next, we examine PSE under a weighted setting. We used a weight function that gives 20% of the superpackets a weight of 5, while the rest have unit weights. In this case we added another algorithm that chooses which packets to transmit in a greedy manner. It simply transmits the $c(t)$ packets with the highest weights. In case of equality, it chooses randomly which packets to drop, similarly to tail-drop. In Fig. 6a we can see that for $\beta = 0$, the greedy algorithm succeeds to transmit almost exclusively the superpackets with high weights. As β grows, PRIORITY, tail-drop and the greedy algorithm performance deteriorates, while PSE is the only algorithm that maintains its high performance. For $0.2 \leq \beta \leq 0.4$, the greedy algorithm performance is almost as good as PRIORITY. For $\beta \geq 0.4$, it outperforms PRIORITY.

In Fig. 6b we examine the effect of changing β. We change β, while keeping the effective load fixed. Both PRIORITY and tail-drop struggle with the increase of β, while PSE is indifferent. In the figure we vary the redundancy by adding redundant packets to a 10-packet superpacket. Adding 1 redundant packet means $\beta = \frac{1}{11}$, etc.

Another interesting question is whether self-eliminating exactly βk packets is the best strategy. Maybe $\beta k + 1$ or $\beta k - 1$ self-eliminations would yield better performance? We added a tunable parameter $\alpha \in (\beta - 1, \beta)$ which sets the fraction of packets that is self-eliminated, that is $(\beta - \alpha)k$ packets self-eliminate (instead of βk packets). In Fig. 6c we can see that for low values of β, setting $\alpha = 0.05$ (eliminating $(\beta - 0.05)k$ packets) yields the best results - better than eliminating βk or $(\beta - 0.1)k$. For high values of β setting $\alpha = 0$ gives the best performance. On the other hand, eliminating even slightly more than βk packets cause a significant performance drop.

5   Conclusion and Open Questions

In this work we introduced packet self-elimination for coping with overflow management of packets with dependencies (superpackets) when using FEC. We presented two algorithms (PSE and PSE-B) whose competitive ratios improve the previous competitive ratios under some input constraints. We also performed a simulation study which demonstrates the improvement in performance obtained by self-elimination. We showed that PSE performs better that both PRIORITY and the tail-drop policy in most scenarios.

At first glance the self-elimination approach may seem counter-intuitive and even folly, since redundancy is inserted just to be eliminated later. However, notice that redundancy is not totally eliminated, since the self-eliminated packets are chosen at random. This random choice is unknown to an oblivious adversary.

While PSE performs better than PSE-B in practice, the latter is easier to analyze, thus yielding a slightly better competitive-ratio. Moreover, analysis is easier for the case where several packets from the same superpacket may arrive at the same time step. A natural open question is to extend the analysis of PSE to the above setting. Another direction is to extend the results to a more general settings where the redundancy model is more general and there are multiple links as was done with PRIORITY in [18]. Finally, it would be interesting to find out whether randomized self-elimination could be used in other applications.

References

1. Berman, P.: A $d/2$ approximation for maximum weight independent set in d-claw free graphs. Nord. J. Comput. **7**(3), 178–184 (2000)
2. Borodin, A., El-Yaniv, R.: Online Computation and Competitive Analysis. Cambridge University Press, Cambridge (1998)
3. Cygan, M.: Improved approximation for 3-dimensional matching via bounded pathwidth local search. In: 54th FOCS, pp. 509–518 (2013)
4. Emek, Y., Halldórsson, M.M., Mansour, Y., Patt-Shamir, B., Radhakrishnan, J., Rawitz, D.: Online set packing. SIAM J. Comput. **41**(4), 728–746 (2012)
5. Fraigniaud, P., Halldórsson, M.M., Patt-Shamir, B., Rawitz, D., Rosén, A.: Shrinking maxima, decreasing costs: new online packing and covering problems. Algorithmica **74**(4), 1205–1223 (2016)
6. Goldwasser, M.H.: A survey of buffer management policies for packet switches. SIGACT News **41**(1), 100–128 (2010)
7. Halldórsson, M.M., Kratochvíl, J., Telle, J.A.: Independent sets with domination constraints. Discrete Appl. Math. **99**(1–3), 39–54 (2000)
8. Halldórsson, M.M., Patt-Shamir, B., Rawitz, D.: Online scheduling with interval conflicts. Theory Comput. Syst. **53**(2), 300–317 (2013). https://doi.org/10.1007/s00224-012-9408-1
9. Håstad, J.: Clique is hard to approximate within $n^{1-\epsilon}$. Acta Math. **182**(1), 105–142 (1999)
10. Hazan, E., Safra, S., Schwartz, O.: On the complexity of approximating k-dimensional matching. In: Arora, S., Jansen, K., Rolim, J.D.P., Sahai, A. (eds.) APPROX/RANDOM -2003. LNCS, vol. 2764, pp. 83–97. Springer, Heidelberg (2003). https://doi.org/10.1007/978-3-540-45198-3_8

11. Hazan, E., Safra, S., Schwartz, O.: On the complexity of approximating k-set packing. Comput. Complex. **15**(1), 20–39 (2006). https://doi.org/10.1007/s00037-006-0205-6
12. Jeż, Ł, Mansour, Y., Patt-Shamir, B.: Scheduling multipacket frames with frame deadlines. J. Sched. **20**(6), 623–634 (2017). https://doi.org/10.1007/s10951-017-0522-4
13. Kesselman, A., Lotker, Z., Mansour, Y., Patt-Shamir, B., Schieber, B., Sviridenko, M.: Buffer overflow management in QoS switches. SIAM J. Comput. **33**(3), 563–583 (2004)
14. Kesselman, A., Patt-Shamir, B., Scalosub, G.: Competitive buffer management with packet dependencies. In: 23rd IPDPS, pp. 1–12 (2009)
15. Kurose, J.F., Ross, K.W.: Computer Networking - A Top-Down Approach Featuring the Internet. Addison-Wesley-Longman, Boston (2001)
16. Mansour, Y., Patt-Shamir, B., Lapid, O.: Optimal smoothing schedules for real-time streams. Distrib. Comput. **17**(1), 77–89 (2004). https://doi.org/10.1007/s00446-003-0101-0
17. Mansour, Y., Patt-Shamir, B., Rawitz, D.: Overflow management with multipart packets. Comput. Netw. **56**(15), 3456–3467 (2012)
18. Mansour, Y., Patt-Shamir, B., Rawitz, D.: Competitive router scheduling with structured data. Theoret. Comput. Sci. **530**, 12–22 (2014)
19. Markovitch, M., Scalosub, G.: Bounded delay scheduling with packet dependencies. In: IEEE INFOCOM, pp. 257–262 (2014)
20. Roth, R.M.: Introduction to Coding Theory. Cambridge University Press, Cambridge (2006)
21. Scalosub, G.: Towards optimal buffer management for streams with packet dependencies. Comput. Netw. **129**, 207–214 (2017)
22. Scalosub, G., Marbach, P., Liebeherr, J.: Buffer management for aggregated streaming data with packet dependencies. IEEE Trans. Parallel Distrib. Syst. **24**(3), 439–449 (2013)
23. Singh, M.P., Kumar, P.: An efficient forward error correction scheme for wireless sensor network. Procedia Technol. **4**, 737–742 (2012)
24. Srinivas, J., Gowtham, Y., Amith, S.S., Chaitanya, K., Archana, R., Gunasekaran, R.: Leaky bucket based congestion control in wireless sensor networks. In: 10th IEEE ICoAC, pp. 172–174 (2018)
25. zfec python package (2020). https://pypi.org/project/zfec/

Population Protocols with Unreliable Communication

Mikhail Raskin[✉][iD]

Technical University of Munich, Munich, Germany
raskin@mccme.ru, raskin@in.tum.de

Abstract. Population protocols are a model of distributed computation intended for the study of networks of independent computing agents with dynamic communication structure. Each agent has a finite number of states, and communication occurs nondeterministically, allowing the involved agents to change their states based on each other's states.

In the present paper we study unreliable models based on population protocols and their variations from the point of view of expressive power. We model the effects of message loss. We show that for a general definition of protocols with unreliable communication with constant-storage agents such protocols can only compute predicates computable by immediate observation (IO) population protocols (sometimes also called one-way protocols). Immediate observation population protocols are inherently tolerant to unreliable communication and keep their expressive power under a wide range of fairness conditions. We also prove that a large class of message-based models that are generally more expressive than IO becomes strictly less expressive than IO in the unreliable case.

Keywords: Population protocols · Message loss · Expressive power

1 Introduction

Population protocols have been introduced in [1,2] as a restricted yet useful subclass of general distributed protocols. In population protocols each agent has a constant amount of local storage, and during the protocol execution pairs of agents are selected and permitted to interact. The selection of pairs is assumed to be done by an adversary bound by a fairness condition. The fairness condition ensures that the adversary cannot trivially stall the protocol. A typical fairness condition requires that every configuration that stays reachable during an infinite execution is reached infinitely many times.

Population protocols have been studied from various points of view, such as expressive power [5], verification complexity [19], time to convergence [3,17], privacy [13], impact of different interaction scheduling [10] etc. Multiple related

The project has received funding from the European Research Council (ERC) under the European Union's Horizon 2020 research and innovation programme under grant agreement No 787367 (PaVeS).

L. Gąsieniec et al. (Eds.): ALGOSENSORS 2021, LNCS 12961, pp. 140–154, 2021.
https://doi.org/10.1007/978-3-030-89240-1_10

models have been introduced. Some of them change or restrict the communication structure: this is the case for immediate, delayed, and queued transmission and observation [5], as well as for broadcast protocols [18]. Some explore the implications of adding limited amounts of storage (below the usual linear or polynomial storage permitted in traditional distributed protocols): this is the case for community protocols [23] (which allow an agent to recognise a constant number of other agents), PALOMA [11] (permitting logarithmic amount of local storage), mediated population protocols [26] (giving some constant amount of common storage to every pair of agents), and others.

The original target application of population protocols and related models is modelling networks of restricted sensors, starting from the original paper [1] on population protocols. On the other hand, verifying distributed algorithms benefits from translating the algorithms in question or their parts into a restricted setting, as most problems are undecidable in the unrestricted case. Both applications motivate study of fault tolerance. Some papers on population protocols and related models [4,12,23,24] consider questions of fault tolerance, but in the context of expressive power the fault is typically expected to be either a total agent failure or a Byzantine failure. There are some exceptions such as a study of fine-grained notions of unreliability [14,15] in the context of step-by-step simulation of population protocols by distributed systems with binary interactions. However, these studies answer a completely different set of questions, as they are concerned with simulating a protocol as a process as opposed to designing a protocol to achieve a given result no matter in what way.

In a practical context, many distributed algorithms pay attention to a specific kind of failure: message loss. While the eventual convergence approach typical in study of population protocols escapes the question of availability *during* a temporary network partition (the problem studied, for example, in [22]), the onset of a network partition may include message loss in the middle of an interaction. In such a situation the participants do not always agree whether the interaction has succeeded or failed. In terms of population protocols, one of the agents assumes that an interaction has happened and updates the local state, while a counterparty thinks the interaction has failed and keeps the old state.

In the present paper we study the expressive power of a very wide class of models with interacting constant-storage agents when unreliability of communication is introduced. This unreliability corresponds to the loss of atomicity of interactions due to message loss. Indeed, in the distributed systems ensuring that both sides agree on whether the interaction has taken place is often the costliest part; a special case of it is "exactly-once" message arrival, known to be much more complex to ensure than "at most-once". We model such loss of atomicity by allowing some agents to update their state based on an interaction, while other agents keep their original state because they assume the interaction has failed. For a bit more generality, corresponding, for example, to request-response interactions with the response being impossible if the request is lost, we allow to require that some agents can only update their state if the others do.

We consider the expressive power in the context of computing predicates by protocols with eventual convergence of individual opinions. We show that under very general conditions the expressive power of protocols with unreliable communication coincides with the expressive power of immediate observation population protocols. Immediate observation population protocols, modelling interactions where an agent can observe the state of another one without the observe noticing, provide a model that inherently tolerates unreliability and is considered a relatively weak model in the fully reliable case. This model also has other nice properties, such as relatively low complexity (**PSPACE**-complete) of verification tasks [21]. Our results hold under any definition of fairness satisfying two general assumptions (see Definition 5), including all the usually used versions of fairness.

We prove it by observing a general structural property shared by all protocols with unreliable communication. Informally speaking, protocols with unreliable communication have some special fair executions which can be extended by adding an additional agent with the same initial and final state as a chosen existing one. This property is similar to the copycat arguments used, for example, for proving the exact expressive power of immediate observation protocols. The usual structure of the copycat arguments includes a proof that we can pick an agent in an execution and add another agent (copycat) which will repeat all the state transitions of the chosen one. In the immediate observation case the corresponding property is almost self-evident once defined. A slightly stronger but still straightforward argument is needed in the case of reconfigurable broadcast networks [8]. The latter model is equivalent to unreliable broadcast networks; a sender broadcasts a message and changes the local state, and an arbitrary set of receivers react to the message (immediately). However, unlike all the previous uses of the copycat-like arguments in the context of population protocols and similar models, proving the necessary copycat-like property for a general notion of protocols with unreliable communication (sufficient to handle assymmetry of message loss where loss for sender requires loss for receiver) requires careful analysis using different techniques.

Note that although the natural way to design population protocols for our setting involves the use of immediate observation population protocols, we still need to rule out additional opportunities arising from the fact that eventually a two-agent interaction with both agents correctly updated will happen. However, in contrast to self-stabilising protocols [6,16], the protocols cannot rely on the message loss being absent for an arbitrarily long time.

Surprisingly, asynchronous transmission and receipt of messages, which provides more expressive power than immediate observation population protocols in the reliable setting, turns out to have strictly less expressive power in the unreliable setting. Note that message reordering is allowed already in the reliable setting, while unreliability is essentially a generalisation of message loss. One could say that an unbounded delay in message delivery becomes a liability instead of an asset once there is message loss.

The rest of the present paper is organised as follows. First, in Sect. 2 we define a general protocol framework generalising many previously studied approaches. Then in Sect. 3 we summarise the results from the literature on the expressive power of various models covered by this framework. Afterwards in Sect. 4 we formally define our general notion of a protocol with unreliable communication. Then in Sect. 5 we formalise the common limitation of all the protocols with unreliable communication, and provide the proof sketches of this restriction and the main result. Afterwards in Sect. 6 we show that fully asynchronous (message-based) models become strictly less powerful than immediate observation in the unreliable setting. The paper ends with a brief conclusion and some possible future directions.

Due to the space constraints the detailed proofs are provided in the full version [27].

1.1 Main Results (Preview)

The precise statements of our results require the detailed definitions introduced later. However, we can roughly summarise them as follows.

First, we characterise the expressive power of all fixed-memory protocols given unreliable communication.

Proposition 1. *Adding unreliability of communication to population protocols restricts the predicates they can express to boolean combinations of comparisons of arguments with constants.*

This is the same expressive power as the immediate observation protocols.

Next we show that unreliability of communication changes the expressive power non-monotonically for some natural classes.

Proposition 2. *Queued transmission protocols with unreliable communication are strictly less expressive than immediate observation population protocols (with or without unreliable communication).*

Note that without unreliability queued transmission protocols are strictly more expressive than immediate observation population protocols.

2 Basic Definitions

2.1 Protocols

We consider various models of distributed computation where the number of agents is constant during protocol execution, each agent has a constant amount of local storage, and agents cannot distinguish each other except via the states. We provide a general framework for describing such protocols. Note that we omit some very natural restrictions (such as decidability of correctness of a finite execution) because they are irrelevant for the problems we study. We allow agents to be distinguished and tracked individually for the purposes of analysis, even though they cannot identify each other during the execution of the protocol.

We will use the following problem to illustrate our definitions: the agents have states q_0 and q_1 corresponding to input symbols 0 and 1 and aim to find out if all the agents have the same input. They have an additional state $q_\perp$ to represent the observation that both input symbols were present. We will define four protocols for this problem using different communication primitives.

- Two agents interact and both switch to $q_\perp$ unless they are in the same state (population protocol interaction).
- An agent observes another agent and switches to $q_\perp$ if they are in different states (immediate observation).
- An agent can send a message with its state, q_0, q_1 or $q_\perp$. An agent in a state q_0 or q_1 can receive a message (any of the pending messages, regardless of order); the agent switches to $q_\perp$ if the message contains a state different from its own (queued transmission).
- An agent broadcasts its state without changing it; each other agent receives the broadcast simultaneously and switches to $q_\perp$ if its state is different from the broadcast state (broadcast protocol interaction).

Definition 1. *A protocol is specified by a tuple $(Q, M, \Sigma, I, o, \mathrm{Tr}, \Phi)$, with components being a finite nonempty set Q of (individual agent) states, a finite (possibly empty) set M of messages, a finite nonempty input alphabet Σ, an input mapping function $I : \Sigma \to Q$, an individual output function $o : Q \to \{true, false\}$, a transition relation Tr (which is described in more details below), and a fairness condition Φ on executions.*

The protocol defines evolution of populations of agents (possibly with some message packets being present).

Definition 2. *A population is a pair of sets: A of agents and P of packets. A configuration C is a population together with two functions, $C_A : A \to Q$ provides agent states, and $C_P : P \to M$ provides packet contents.*

Note that if M is empty, then P must also be empty. As the set of agents is the domain of the function C_A, we use the notation $\mathrm{Dom}(C_A)$ for it. The same goes for the set of packets $\mathrm{Dom}(C_P)$. Without loss of generality $\mathrm{Dom}(C_P)$ is a subset of a fixed countable set of possible packets.

The message packets are only used for asynchronous communication; instant interaction between agents (such as in the classical rendezvous-based population protocols or in broadcast protocols) does not require describing the details of communication in the configurations.

Example 1. The four example protocols have the same set of states, namely $Q = \{q_0, q_1, q_\perp\}$. The first two protocols have the empty set of messages, and the last two have the set of messages $M = \{m_0, m_1, m_\perp\}$. The example protocols all have the same input alphabet $\Sigma = \{0, 1\}$, input mapping $I : i \mapsto q_i$, and output mapping $o : q_0 \mapsto true, q_1 \mapsto true, q_\perp \mapsto false$.

The definition of the transition relation uses the following notation.

Definition 3. *For a function f and $x \notin \mathrm{Dom}(f)$ let $f \cup \{x \mapsto y\}$ denote the function g defined on $\mathrm{Dom}(f) \cup \{x\}$ such that $g\mid_{\mathrm{Dom}(f)} = f$ and $g(x) = y$. For $u \in \mathrm{Dom}(f)$ let $f[u \mapsto v]$ denote the function h defined on $\mathrm{Dom}(f)$ such that $h\mid_{\mathrm{Dom}(f)\backslash\{u\}} = f\mid_{\mathrm{Dom}(f)\backslash\{u\}}$ and $h(u) = v$. For symmetry, if $w = f(u)$ let $f \backslash \{u \mapsto w\}$ denote restriction $f\mid_{\mathrm{Dom}(f)\backslash\{u\}}$.*

Use of this notation implies an assertion of correctness, i.e. $x \notin \mathrm{Dom}(f)$, $u \in \mathrm{Dom}(f)$, and $w = f(u)$. We use the same notation with a configuration C instead of a function if it is clear from context whether C_A or C_P is modified.

Now we can describe the transition relation that tells us which configurations can be obtained from a given one via a single interaction. In order to cover broadcast protocols we define the transition relation as a relation on configurations. The restrictions on the transition relation ensure that the protocol behaves like a distributed system with arbitrarily large number of anonymous agents.

Definition 4. *The* transition *relation of a protocol is a set of triples $(C, A^{\odot}, C')$, called* transitions, *where C and C' are configurations and $A^{\odot} \subset \mathrm{Dom}(C_A)$ is the set of* active *agents (of the transition); agents in $\mathrm{Dom}(C_A) \backslash A^{\odot}$, are called* passive. *We write $C \xrightarrow{A^{\odot}} C'$ for $(C, A^{\odot}, C') \in \mathrm{Tr}$, and let $C \to C'$ denote the projection of Tr: $C \to C' \Leftrightarrow \exists A^{\odot} : C \xrightarrow{A^{\odot}} C'$. The transition relation must satisfy the following conditions for every transition $C \xrightarrow{A^{\odot}} C'$:*

- **Agent conservation.** *$\mathrm{Dom}(C_A) = \mathrm{Dom}(C'_A)$.*
- **Agent and packet anonymity.** *If h_A and h_P are bijections such that $D_A = C_A \circ h_A$, $D'_A = C'_A \circ h_A$, $D_P = C_P \circ h_P$, and $D'_P = C'_P \circ h_P$, then $D \xrightarrow{h^{-1}(A^{\odot})} D'$.*
- **Possibility to ignore extra packets.** *For every $p \notin \mathrm{Dom}(C_P) \cup \mathrm{Dom}(C'_P)$ and $m \in M$: $C \cup \{p \mapsto m\} \xrightarrow{A^{\odot}} C' \cup \{p \mapsto m\}$.*
- **Possibility to add passive agents.** *For every agent $a \notin \mathrm{Dom}(C_A)$ and $q \in Q$ there exists $q' \in Q$ such that: $C \cup \{a \mapsto q\} \xrightarrow{A^{\odot}} C' \cup \{a \mapsto q'\}$.*

Informally speaking, the active agents are the agents that transmit something during the interaction. The passive agents can still observe other agents and change their state. The choice of active agents is used for the definition of protocols with unreliable communication, as a failure to transmit precludes success of reception. The formal interpretation will be provided in Definition 8.

Many models studied in the literature have the transition relation defined using pairwise interaction. In these models the transitions are always changing the states of two agents based on their previous states. When discussing such protocols, we will use the notation $(p, q) \to (p', q')$ for a transition where agents in the states p and q switch to states p' and q', correspondingly.

Example 2. The four example protocols have the following transition relations.

- In the first protocol for a configuration C and two agents $a, a' \in \text{Dom}(C_A)$ such that $C_A(a) \neq C_A(a')$ we have $C \xrightarrow{\{a,a'\}} C[a \mapsto q_\perp][a' \mapsto q_\perp]$ (in other notation, $(C, \{a, a'\}, C[a \mapsto q_\perp][a' \mapsto q_\perp]) \in \text{Tr}$).
- In the second protocol for a configuration C and two agents $a, a' \in \text{Dom}(C_A)$ such that $C_A(a) \neq C_A(a')$ we have $C \xrightarrow{\{a\}} C[a \mapsto q_\perp]$. We can say that a observes a' in a different state and switches to $q_\perp$.
- In the third protocol there are two types of transitions. Let a configuration C be fixed. For an agent $a \in \text{Dom}(C_A)$, $i \in \{0, 1, \perp\}$ such that $C_A(a) = q_i$, and a new message identity $p \notin \text{Dom}(C_P)$ we have $C \xrightarrow{\{a\}} C \cup \{p \mapsto m_i\}$ (sending a message). If $C_A(a) = q_i$ for some $i \in \{0, 1\}$, for each message $p \in \text{Dom}(C_P)$, we also have $C \xrightarrow{\{a\}} C[a \mapsto q'] \setminus \{p \mapsto C_P(p)\}$ where q' is equal to q_i if $C_P(p) = m_i$ and $q_\perp$ otherwise (receiving a message).
- In the fourth protocol, for a configuration C and an agent $a \in \text{Dom}(C_A)$ we can construct C' by replacing C_A with C'_A that maps each $a' \in \text{Dom}(C_A)$ to $C_A(a')$ if $C_A(a) = C_A(a')$ and $q_\perp$ otherwise. Then we have $C \xrightarrow{\{a\}} C'$. We can say that a broadcasts its state and all the agents in the other states switch to $q_\perp$.

2.2   Fair Executions

In this section we define the notion of fairness. This notion is traditionally used to exclude the most pathological cases without a complete probabilistic analysis of the model. For the population protocols fairness has been a part of the definition since the introduction [1,2]. However, in the general study of distributed computation there has long been some interest in comparing effects of different approaches to fairness in execution scheduling [7]. For example, the distinction between weak fairness and strong fairness and the conditions where one can be made to model the other has been studied in [25]. The difference between weak and strong scheduling is that strong fairness executes infinitely often every interaction that is enabled infinitely often, while weak fairness only guarantees anything for continuously enabled interactions. As there are multiple notion of fairness in use, we define their basic common traits. Our results hold for all notions of fairness satisfying these basic requirements, including all the notions of fairness used in the literature, as well as much stronger and much weaker fairness conditions.

Definition 5. *An execution is a sequence (finite or infinite) C_n of configurations such that at each moment i either nothing changes, i.e. $C_i = C_{i+1}$ or a single interaction occurs, i.e. $C_i \to C_{i+1}$. A configuration C' is reachable from configuration C if there exists an execution $C_0, \ldots, C_n$ with $C_0 = C$ and $C_n = C'$ (and unreachable otherwise).*

A protocol defines a fairness condition Φ which is a predicate on executions. It should satisfy the following properties.

– A *fairness condition* is eventual, *i.e.* *every finite execution can be continued to an infinite fair execution.*
– A *fairness condition* ensures activity, *i.e.* *if an execution contains only configuration C after some moment, only C itself is reachable from C.*

Definition 6. *The* default fairness condition *accepts an execution if every configuration either becomes unreachable after some moment, or occurs infinitely many times.*

It is clear that the default fairness condition ensures activity.

Lemma 1. *[adapted from [5]] Default fairness condition is eventual.*

The fairness condition is sometimes said to be an approximation of probabilistic behaviour. In our general model the default fairness condition provides executions similar to random ones for protocols without messages but not always for protocols with messages. The arguments from [20] with minimal modification prove this. The core idea in the case without messages is observing we have a finite state space reachable from any given configuration; a random walk eventually gets trapped in some strongly connected component, visiting all of its states infinitely many time. If we do have messages, the message count might behave like a biased random walk; while consuming all the messages stays possible in principle, with probability one it only happens a finite number of times.

2.3 Functions Implemented by Protocols

In this section we recall the standard notion of a function evaluated by a protocol. Here the standard definition generalises trivially.

Definition 7. *An* input configuration *is a configuration where there are no packets and all agents are in input states, i.e. $P = \varnothing$ and $\mathrm{Im}(C_A) \subseteq \mathrm{Im}(I)$ where Im denotes the image of a function. We extend I to be applicable to multisets of input symbols. For every $\overline{x} \in \mathbb{N}^\Sigma$, we define $I(\overline{x})$ to be a configuration of $|\overline{x}|$ agents with $\sum_{I(\sigma)=q_i} \overline{x}(\sigma)$ agents in input state q_i (and no packets).*
A configuration C is a consensus *if the individual output function yields the same value for the states of all agents, i.e. $\forall a, a' \in \mathrm{Dom}(C_A) : o(C_A(a)) = o(C_A(a'))$. This value is the* output value *for the configuration. C is a* stable consensus *if all configurations reachable from C are consensus configurations with the same value.*
A protocol implements *a predicate $\varphi : \mathbb{N}^\Sigma \to \{true, false\}$ if for every $\overline{x} \in \mathbb{N}^\Sigma$ every fair execution starting from $I(\overline{x})$ reaches a stable consensus with the output value $\varphi(\overline{x})$. A protocol is* well-specified *if it implements some predicate.*

Example 3. It is easy to see that each of the four example protocols implements the predicate $\varphi(\overline{x}) \Leftrightarrow (x(0) = 0) \vee (x(1) = 0)$ on $\mathbb{N}^2$. In other words, the protocol accepts the input configurations where one of the two input states has zero agents and rejects the configurations where both input states occur.

This framework is general enough to define the models studied in the literature, such as population protocols, immediate transmission protocols, immediate observation population protocols, delayed transmission protocols, delayed observation protocols, queued transmission protocols, and broadcast protocols. The details can be found in the full version.

3 Expressive Power of Population Protocols and Related Models

In this section we give an overview of previously known results on expressive power of various models related to population protocols. We only consider predicates, i.e. functions with the output values being true and false because the statements of the theorems become more straightforward in that case.

The expressive power of models related to population protocols is expressed in terms of semilinear, **coreMOD**, and counting predicates. Semilinear predicates on tuples of natural numbers can be expressed using the addition function, remainders modulo constants, and the order relation, such as $x + x \geq y + 3$ or $x \mod 7 = 3$. Roughly speaking, **coreMOD** is the class of predicates that become equivalent to modular equality for inputs with only large and zero components. An example could be $(z = 1 \land x \geq y) \lor (x + y \mod 2 = 0)$, a semilinear predicate which becomes a modular equality whenever $z = 0$ or z is large (i.e. $z \geq 2$). Counting predicates are logical combinations of inequalities including one coordinate and one constant each, for example, $x \geq 3$.

Theorem 1 (see [5] for details). *Population protocols and queued transmission protocols can implement precisely semilinear predicates.*

Immediate transmission population protocols and delayed transmission protocols can implement precisely all the semilinear predicates that are also in **coreMOD**.

Immediate observation population protocols implement counting predicates.

Delayed observation protocols implement the counting predicates where every constant is equal to 1.

Theorem 2 (see [9] for details). *Broadcast protocols implement precisely the predicates computable in nondeterministic linear space.*

4 Our Models

4.1 Proposed Models

We propose a general notion of an unreliable communication version of a protocol. Our notion models transient failures, so the set of agents is preserved. The intuition we formalise is the idea that for every possible transition some agents may fail to update their states (and keep their corresponding old states). We also require that for some passive agent to receive a transmission, the transmission has to occur (and active agents who transmit do not update their state if they fail to transmit, although a successful transmission can still fail to be received).

Definition 8. *A protocol with unreliable communication, corresponding to a protocol $\mathcal{P}$, is a protocol that differs from $\mathcal{P}$ only in the transition relation. For every allowed transition $C \xrightarrow{A^{\odot}} C'$ we also allow all the transitions $C \xrightarrow{A^{\odot}} C''$ where C'' satisfies the following conditions.*

- *$\textbf{Population preservation.}$ $\mathrm{Dom}(C''_A) = \mathrm{Dom}(C'_A)$, as well as $\mathrm{Dom}(C''_P) = \mathrm{Dom}(C'_P)$.*
- *$\textbf{State preservation.}$ For every agent $a \in \mathrm{Dom}(C''_A)$ we have $C''_A(a) \in \{C_A(a), C'_A(a)\}$.*
- *$\textbf{Message preservation.}$ For every packet $p \in \mathrm{Dom}(C''_P)$: $C''_P(p) = C'_P(p)$.*
- *$\textbf{Reliance on active agents.}$ Either for every agent $a \notin A^{\odot}$ we have $C''_A(a) = C_A(a)$, or for every agent $a \in A^{\odot}$ we have $C''_A(a) = C'_A(a)$.*

Example 4. – Population protocols with unreliable communication allow an interaction to update the state of only one of the two agents.
- Immediate transmission population protocols with unreliable communication allow the sender to update the state with no receiving agents.
- Immediate observation population protocols with unreliable communication do not differ from ordinary immediate observation population protocols, because each transition changes the state of only one agent. Failing to change the state means a no-change transition which is already allowed anyway.
- Queued transmission protocols with unreliable communication allow messages to be discarded with no effect. Note that for delayed observation protocols unreliable communication doesn't change much, as sending the messages also has no effect.
- Broadcast protocols with unreliable communication allow a broadcast to be received by an arbitrary subset of agents.

4.2   The Main Result

Our main result is that no class of protocols with unreliable communication can be more expressive than immediate observation protocols.

Definition 9. *A cube is a subset of $\mathbb{N}^k$ defined by a lower and upper (possibly infinite) bound for each coordinate. A counting set is a finite union of cubes.*

A counting predicate is a membership predicate for some counting set. Alternatively, we can say it is a predicate that can be computed using comparisons of input values with constants and logical operations.

Theorem 3. *The set of predicates that can be implemented by protocols with unreliable communication is the set of counting predicates. All counting predicates can be implemented by (unreliable) immediate observation protocols.*

5   Proof of the Main Result

Our main lemma is generalises of the copycat lemma normally applied to specific models such as immediate observation protocols. The idea is that for every initial configuration there is a fair execution that can be extended to a possibly unfair execution by adding a copy of a chosen agent. In some special cases, for example, broadcast protocols with unreliable communication, a simple proof can be given by saying that if the original agent participates in an interaction, the copy should do the same just before the original without anyone ever receiving the broadcasts from the copy. The copycat arguments are usually applied to models where a similar proof suffices. The situation is more complex for models like immediate transmission protocols with unreliable communication. As a message cannot be received without being sent, the receiver cannot update its state if the sender doesn't. We present an argument applicable in the general case.

Definition 10. *Let E be an arbitrary execution of protocol P with initial configuration C. Let $a \in \mathrm{Dom}(C_A)$ be an agent in this execution. Let $a' \notin \mathrm{Dom}(C_A)$ be an agent, and $C' = C \cup \{a' \mapsto C_A(a)\}$. A set $\mathfrak{E}_a$ of executions starting in configuration C' is a* shadow extension *of the execution E around the agent a if the following conditions hold:*

- *removing a' from each configuration in any execution in $\mathfrak{E}_a$ yields E;*
- *for each moment during the execution, there is a corresponding execution in $\mathfrak{E}_a$ such that a and a' have the same state at that moment.*

The added agent a' is a shadow agent, *and elements of $\mathfrak{E}_a$ are* shadow executions. *A protocol P is* shadow-permitting *if for every configuration C there is a fair execution starting from C that has a shadow extension around each agent $a \in \mathrm{Dom}(C_A)$.*

Note that the executions in $\mathfrak{E}_a$ might not be fair even if E is fair.

Not all population protocols are shadow-permitting. For example, consider a protocol with one input state q_0, additional states q_+ and q_-, and one transition $(q_0, q_0) \rightarrow (q_+, q_-)$. As the number of agents in the states q_+ and q_- is always the same, one can't add a single extra agent going from state q_0 to state q_+.

Lemma 2. *All protocols with unreliable communication are shadow-permitting.*

The intuition behind the proof is the following. We construct a fair execution together with the shadow executions and keep track what states can be reached by the shadow agents. The set of reachable states will not shrink, as the shadow agent can always just fail to update. If an agent a tries to move from a state q to a state q' not reachable by the corresponding shadow agent in any of the shadow executions, we "split" the shadow execution reaching q: one copy just stays in place, and in the other the shadow agent a' takes the place of a in the transition while a keeps the old state. In the main execution there is no a' so a participates in the interaction but fails to update. Afterwards we restart the process of building a fair execution.

We also use a straightforward generalisation of the truncation lemma from [5]. The lemma says that all large *amounts* of agents are equivalent for the notion of stable consensus.

Definition 11. *A protocol is* truncatable *if there exists a number K such that for every stable consensus adding an extra agent with a state q that is already represented by at least K other agents yields a stable consensus.*

Lemma 3. *[adapted from [5]] All protocols (not necessarily with unreliable communication) are truncatable.*

Lemma 4. *If a predicate φ can be implemented by a shadow-permitting truncatable protocol, then φ is a counting predicate.*

For the lower bound, we adapt the following lemma from [5].

Lemma 5. *All counting predicates can be implemented by immediate observation protocols (possibly with unreliable communication), even if the fairness condition is replaced with an arbitrary different (activity-ensuring) one.*

Theorem 3 now follows from the fact that all the protocols with unreliable communication are shadow-permitting (by Lemma 2) and truncatable (by Lemma 3), therefore they only implement counting predicates. By Lemma 5 all counting predicates can be implemented.

6 Non-monotonic Impact of Unreliability

In this section we observe that, surprisingly, while delayed transmission protocols and queued transmission protocols are more powerful than immediate observation population protocols, their unreliable versions are strictly less expressive than immediate observation population protocols (possibly with unreliable communication).

Definition 12. *A protocol is* fully asynchronous *if for each allowed transition $(C, A^\odot, C')$ the following conditions hold.*

- *There is exactly one active agent, i.e. $|A^\odot| = 1$.*
- *No passive agents change their states.*
- *Either the packets are only sent or the packets are only consumed, i.e. either $\mathrm{Dom}(C_P) \subseteq \mathrm{Dom}(C'_P)$ or $\mathrm{Dom}(C_P) \supseteq \mathrm{Dom}(C'_P)$. Packet contents do not change, i.e. $C_P \restriction_{\mathrm{Dom}(C_P) \cap \mathrm{Dom}(C'_P)} = C'_P \restriction_{\mathrm{Dom}(C_P) \cap \mathrm{Dom}(C'_P)}$.*

To prove that fully asynchronous protocols with unreliable communication cannot compute some counting predicates, we consider a simple predicate: all agents have the same input, and the protocol must determine whether there are at least two agents.

Theorem 4. *A well-specified fully asynchronous protocol with unreliable communication having a single-letter input alphabet yields the same value for the input configurations with one and two agents, correspondingly.*

Remark 1. This result doesn't mean that fundamentally asynchronous nature of communication prevents us from using any expressive models for verification of unreliable systems. It is usually possible to keep enough state to implement, for example, Immediate observation via request and response.

7   Conclusion and Future Directions

We have studied unreliability based on message loss, a practically motivated approach to fault tolerance in population protocols. We have shown that inside a general framework of defining protocols with unreliable communication we can prove a specific structural property that bounds the expressive power of protocols with unreliable communication by the expressive power of immediate observation population protocols. Immediate observation population protocols permit verification of many useful properties, up to well-specification, correctness and reachability between counting sets, in polynomial space. We think that relatively low complexity of verification together with inherent unreliability tolerance and locally optimal expressive power under atomicity violations motivate further study and use of such protocols.

It is also interesting to explore if for any class of protocols adding unreliability makes some of the verification tasks easier. Both complexity and expressive power implications of unreliability can be studied for models with larger per-agent memory, such as community protocols, PALOMA and mediated population protocols. We also believe that some models even more restricted than community protocols but still permitting a multi-interaction conversation are an interesting object of study both in the reliable and unreliable settings.

Acknowledgements. I thank Javier Esparza for useful discussions and the feedback on the drafts of the present article. I thank Chana Weil-Kennedy for useful discussions. I thank the anonymous reviewers for their valuable feedback on presentation.

References

1. Angluin, D., Aspnes, J., Diamadi, Z., Fischer, M.J., Peralta, R.: Computation in networks of passively mobile finite-state sensors. In: ACM Symposium on Principles of Distributed Computing, pp. 290–299. ACM (2004)
2. Angluin, D., Aspnes, J., Diamadi, Z., Fischer, M.J., Peralta, R.: Computation in networks of passively mobile finite-state sensors. Distrib. Comput. **18**(4), 235–253 (2006). https://doi.org/10.1007/s00446-005-0138-3
3. Angluin, D., Aspnes, J., Eisenstat, D.: Fast computation by population protocols with a leader. In: Dolev, S. (ed.) DISC 2006. LNCS, vol. 4167, pp. 61–75. Springer, Heidelberg (2006). https://doi.org/10.1007/11864219_5
4. Angluin, D., Aspnes, J., Eisenstat, D.: A simple population protocol for fast robust approximate majority. In: Pelc, A. (ed.) DISC 2007. LNCS, vol. 4731, pp. 20–32. Springer, Heidelberg (2007). https://doi.org/10.1007/978-3-540-75142-7_5
5. Angluin, D., Aspnes, J., Eisenstat, D., Ruppert, E.: The computational power of population protocols. Distrib. Comput. **20**(4), 279–304 (2007). https://doi.org/10.1007/s00446-007-0040-2
6. Angluin, D., Aspnes, J., Fischer, M.J., Jiang, H.: Self-stabilizing population protocols. ACM Trans. Auton. Adapt. Syst. **3**(4), 13:1–13:28 (2008)
7. Apt, K.R., Francez, N., Katz, S.: Appraising fairness in languages for distributed programming. Distrib. Comput. **2**(4), 226–241 (1988). https://doi.org/10.1007/BF01872848

8. Bertrand, N., Bouyer, P., Majumdar, A.: Reconfiguration and message losses in parameterized broadcast networks. In: 30th International Conference on Concurrency Theory, CONCUR 2019, August 27–30, 2019, Amsterdam, the Netherlands. LIPIcs, vol. 140, pp. 32:1–32:15. Schloss Dagstuhl - Leibniz-Zentrum für Informatik (2019)
9. Blondin, M., Esparza, J., Jaax, S.: Expressive power of oblivious consensus protocols (2019). arXiv:1902.01668
10. Chatzigiannakis, I., Dolev, S., Fekete, S.P., Michail, O., Spirakis, P.G.: Not all fair probabilistic schedulers are equivalent. In: Abdelzaher, T., Raynal, M., Santoro, N. (eds.) OPODIS 2009. LNCS, vol. 5923, pp. 33–47. Springer, Heidelberg (2009). https://doi.org/10.1007/978-3-642-10877-8_5
11. Chatzigiannakis, I., Michail, O., Nikolaou, S., Pavlogiannis, A., Spirakis, P.G.: Passively mobile communicating logarithmic space machines. Technical report (2010)
12. Delporte-Gallet, C., Fauconnier, H., Guerraoui, R., Ruppert, E.: When birds die: making population protocols fault-tolerant. In: Gibbons, P.B., Abdelzaher, T., Aspnes, J., Rao, R. (eds.) DCOSS 2006. LNCS, vol. 4026, pp. 51–66. Springer, Heidelberg (2006). https://doi.org/10.1007/11776178_4
13. Delporte-Gallet, C., Fauconnier, H., Guerraoui, R., Ruppert, E.: Secretive birds: privacy in population protocols. In: Tovar, E., Tsigas, P., Fouchal, H. (eds.) OPODIS 2007. LNCS, vol. 4878, pp. 329–342. Springer, Heidelberg (2007). https://doi.org/10.1007/978-3-540-77096-1_24
14. Di Luna, G.A., Flocchini, P., Izumi, T., Izumi, T., Santoro, N., Viglietta, G.: On the power of weaker pairwise interaction: fault-tolerant simulation of population protocols. Theoret. Comput. Sci. **754**, 35–49 (2019)
15. Di Luna, G.A., Flocchini, P., Izumi, T., Izumi, T., Santoro, N., Viglietta, G.: Population protocols with faulty interactions: the impact of a leader. Theor. Comput. Sci. **754**, 35–49 (2019)
16. Dijkstra, E.W.: Self-stabilizing systems in spite of distributed control. Commun. ACM **17**(11), 643–644 (1974)
17. Doty, D., Soloveichik, D.: Stable leader election in population protocols requires linear time. In: Moses, Y. (ed.) DISC 2015. LNCS, vol. 9363, pp. 602–616. Springer, Heidelberg (2015). https://doi.org/10.1007/978-3-662-48653-5_40
18. Emerson, E.A., Namjoshi, K.S.: On model checking for non-deterministic infinite-state systems. In: LICS, pp. 70–80. IEEE Computer Society (1998)
19. Esparza, J., Ganty, P., Majumdar, R., Weil-Kennedy, C.: Verification of immediate observation population protocols. In: 29th International Conference on Concurrency Theory (CONCUR 2018). LIPIcs, vol. 118, pp. 31:1–31:16. Schloss Dagstuhl - Leibniz-Zentrum fuer Informatik (2018)
20. Esparza, J., Jaax, S., Raskin, M., Weil-Kennedy, C.: The complexity of verifying population protocols. Distrib. Comput. **34**(2), 133–177 (2021). https://doi.org/10.1007/s00446-021-00390-x
21. Esparza, J., Raskin, M., Weil-Kennedy, C.: Parameterized analysis of immediate observation petri nets. In: Donatelli, S., Haar, S. (eds.) PETRI NETS 2019. LNCS, vol. 11522, pp. 365–385. Springer, Cham (2019). https://doi.org/10.1007/978-3-030-21571-2_20
22. Friedman, R., Birman, K.: Trading consistency for availability in distributed systems. Technical report (1996)
23. Guerraoui, R., Ruppert, E.: Even small birds are unique: population protocols with identifiers (2007)

24. Guerraoui, R., Ruppert, E.: Names trump malice: tiny mobile agents can tolerate byzantine failures. In: Albers, S., Marchetti-Spaccamela, A., Matias, Y., Nikoletseas, S., Thomas, W. (eds.) ICALP 2009. LNCS, vol. 5556, pp. 484–495. Springer, Heidelberg (2009). https://doi.org/10.1007/978-3-642-02930-1_40
25. Karaata, M.H.: Self-stabilizing strong fairness under weak fairness. IEEE Trans. Parallel Distrib. Syst. **12**(4), 337–345 (2001)
26. Michail, O., Chatzigiannakis, I., Spirakis, P.G.: Mediated population protocols. Theoret. Comput. Sci. **412**(22), 2434–2450 (2011)
27. Raskin, M.: Population protocols with unreliable communication (2021). arXiv:1902.10041

Author Index

Printed in the United States
by Baker & Taylor Publisher Services